CASINO CRAPS
Shoot to Win!

Frank Scoblete
with Dominator

TRIUMPH
B O O K S

Library of Congress Cataloging-in-Publication Data TK

This book is available in quantity at special discounts for your group or organization. For further information, contact:

Triumph Books
814 N. Franklin
Chicago, Illinois 60610
(312) 337-0747
www.triumphbooks.com

Printed in U.S.A.
ISBN: 978-1-60078-332-6
Design by Patricia Frey

For

The Captain

Who brought modern dice control to the table

and

The Arm

The greatest dice controller of all time.

They will always be remembered.

_____

For Carlo, Concetta, and Anna LoRiggio,
I miss them...Dominator

Contents

Acknowledgments

We have to give a big thanks to John "Skinny," who checked over the contents of the book several times, giving me valuable aid. Also to Jerry "Stickman" who helped us with his expertise and to Billy "the Kid" for allowing us to use his rant.

FOREWORD

The Captain Invented the Modern Dice-Control Movement

The Captain of Craps, the Atlantic City legend, was responsible for discovering how to beat the modern casino game of craps with controlled shooting—which he used to call "rhythmic rolling" as well as "controlling the dice." He applied this technique to beat the casinos from the late 1970s through 2007—almost 30 years of constant play. Yes, he won millions.

Since 1998, some writers have tried to take away the dice-control laurels from the Captain and assign them to other people who merely tried to build (sometimes incorrectly) on what the Captain had created. These pretenders to the throne are many, of course, because a good idea is always worth pilfering.

In 1993, my book *The Captain's Craps Revolution!* was published, and in it the Captain addressed the issue of controlled shooting—long before any of the pretenders came out of the woodwork to try to take credit for this brilliant technique and his brilliant ideas. Here is an excerpt from the above-referenced book:

The Captain: "I don't need to guess. I know that some people have trained themselves privately or at the tables to control the fall of the dice. The Arm has had remarkable success fixing [setting] and controlling the dice. The Arm consistently has major rolls. Recently at the Sands casino in Atlantic City, during a Sinatra weekend, with the place packed with freewheeling high rollers, and then several days later at the Claridge right across the street, the Arm had monster rolls of positively legendary proportions. This isn't coincidence or merely fluctuations in randomness. **The Arm controls the dice!** [Bold lettering mine]

"Does it mean that every time the Arm picks up those cubes, a big one is coming? Of course not. There are times when she isn't at the right spot on the table or the throw is a little off. Having played with the Arm for years, I can recognize the signs of an off night. So can she. But if the groove isn't there, just like a pitcher, the Arm leaves the game and does not roll.

"When we talk about fixing and controlling the dice, we aren't looking for perfection. Pitchers don't pitch perfect games every time out. In fact, each separate roll of the dice to a player who can control them is like a pitch in a game. The good pitchers will consistently throw strikes and have good games, not every time out, but enough that you can say this isn't just randomness or luck. Also, you have to define what you mean by a good roll. My definition is simple: a good roll is one where the seven doesn't show long enough to make me money or one where I can make a good profit because there is a rapid succession of repeating numbers. Fixing and controlling the dice has more to do with certain numbers being repeated than it does with monster rolls. You don't have to have monster rolls to win. I've seen rolls by the Arm where the four will come up four or five times in a row, followed by some other numbers, then another string of fours before sevening-out. It's a wonderful feeling to be up on only one number after the 5-Count [more on this coming up] and have that number hit repeatedly in rapid succession. People who can control the dice will tend to have certain faces of the dice appear more often than these faces would otherwise by chance."

In the book, the Captain then continued about how one should practice to actually get control over the dice, how many rolls one should do to see if such control was actually there. He mentioned that he sometimes had control but other times he didn't, but he denied he was very good at it. He thought of himself more as a rhythmic roller, which is, I guess, the equivalent to "control light." I also guess that assessment of himself was his humility talking, because in my more than a dozen years of steadily playing with him (and the Arm) in the late 1980s and 1990s, he was damn good and had the prototypical roll that works best for most controllers. He was aware that using the word "control" meant a high degree of accuracy with the dice—so he considered himself more of an influencer. This coming from a man who rolled 100 times and 147 times before sevening-out—the only player who has had two hands of 100 or more rolls!

To me the use of words such as "dice control," "rhythmic rolling," and "dice influence" all mean the same thing: the shooter has the capability to get an edge over the casinos.

Unlike today, when you can find controlled shooters in greater numbers, in the Captain's early days they were few and far between. But they were there. The greatest of them was the Arm, and the most brilliant of them was the Captain.

The Captain was the first to fully understand dice control and its ramifications, and no amount of taking his words out of context or trying to give the laurels to someone else who arrived on the scene years after him can take these achievements away from him. All the current vocabulary of dice control, all the analogies to baseball or golf or other sports, all the talk about being at the right spot on the table, all of our understanding of when to leave the table, all the knowledge that repeating numbers can also be the way to win money even without monster rolls—yes, all the modern parlance of the dice-control world—came from him.

Dominator and I could never have written this book if the Captain hadn't existed. Read this and learn from him.

The Captain was *the man* then, and he will remain *the man* forever.

Please note: *Although this book is a joint effort between Frank Scoblete and Dominator, the voice will be Frank's, and it is written in the first person.*

CHAPTER 1

Welcome to the Wonderful World of Craps

To a new player, craps looks like a most intimidating game. Just look at that layout; it resembles an ancient Egyptian tablet covered in hieroglyphs that tells some elaborate sacrificial story. Nothing could be further from the truth. Craps is a simple game, made even simpler because most of the bets are worthless to the smart player, although ploppies—the unschooled, unthinking masses of casino craps players—will fall all over themselves to wager on them.

If you have never played craps before or if you are a veteran looking to get an edge or a new craps player looking to learn the game *and* get an edge, then this book is for you. I'll explain how the game is played and the various bets of the game. Because most of the bets at the craps table are a waste of your time and, more important, a serious waste of your money, this book will be a heads up for you gamblers. I'll explain why that is true, and I will use *house-edge* percentages and also what kind of *money edges* the casinos really have on each and every bet. This book can lead you to an advantage over the casino—and that would be a great thing for you, wouldn't it?

So, here we go!

The Dice

A die has six sides, so there are 36 possible combinations of two dice in the game of craps: six sides × six sides = 36 combinations. Each side (or face) of a die will have various numbered *pips:* 1-pip, 2-pips, 3-pips, 4-pips, 5-pips, and 6-pips. Given two dice, the lowest number that can be rolled is a 2 (1-pip + 1-pip); the highest number is 12 (6-pips + 6-pips). There is only one way to make a 2 and only one way to make a 12. The following graph shows you the possible combinations that can be made with two dice.

Possible Combinations with Two Dice

Number	Ways to Make	Combinations
2	one	1:1
3	two	2:1, 1:2
4	three	3:1, 1:3, 2:2
5	four	4:1, 1:4, 3:2, 2:3
6	five	5:1, 1:5, 4:2, 2:4, 3:3
7	six	6:1, 1:6, 5:2, 2:5, 4:3, 3:4
8	five	6:2, 2:6, 5:3, 3:5, 4:4
9	four	6:3, 3:6, 5:4, 4:5
10	three	6:4, 4:6, 5:5
11	two	6:5, 5:6
12	one	6:6

As you can see the 7 is the number that comes up the most. It is the key number in the game of craps. If you look at a set of casino dice you will find that the front side and its opposite back side add up to 7. So opposite the 1-pip is the 6-pip; opposite the 2-pip is the 5-pip; opposite the 3-pip is the 4-pip.

Casino dice can come in various sizes, colors, and opacity. The usual sizes are 5/8" and 3/4". Some dice are clear; some are frosted.

The Personnel

Craps tables generally have four people working the game—three dealers and a *box person*. One dealer, called the *stickman*, stands on the side of the table with the players. He is called the stickman because he has a long stick that he uses to move the dice. He gives the dice to the shooter, takes the dice to the middle of the table between rolls, and announces the payoffs of the winning bets in the middle of the table for the dealers to pay the winning bettors.

The other two dealers stand on the opposite side of the table from the stickman, one to his left and one to his right. Each of these dealers is responsible for paying off winning bets and taking losing bets from the players on their side of the table. Dealers will move from one position to another at a table, usually in 20-minute intervals.

Between the two dealers is the *box person*, who supervises the game to make sure no bets are mishandled and that buy-ins and payouts are done correctly. The box person also resolves most of the disputes at the table. In the pit, behind the box person will be a *floor person*, in charge of supervising various craps tables in his pit, rating the players, and giving (usually) non-gourmet comps. In serious disputes, the floor person will be brought in to give his or her judgment. In charge of all the craps tables and perhaps other games as well is the *pit boss*.

The Table

There are different types of craps tables, each with minor differences in their layouts and sometimes in the payoffs of their bets. Because most craps wagers stink—and I mean they *stink*—I am going to give you a generic layout.

Both the left and right sides of the table are the same in terms of which bets are offered. Going around the outside of the layout is the *Pass Line* (a good bet); above that is the *Don't Pass Line* (a good bet) with the word *bar* and the dice showing a 12. The "bar" means that the 12 is a tie if it appears for Don't bettors (also known as *Darkside* bettors). On

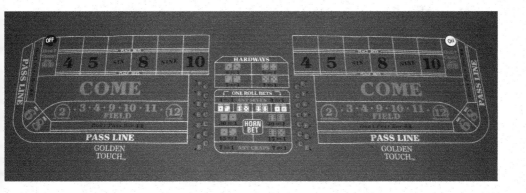

some of the older tables you will note a 6/8 bet in the corners. This is a sucker's bet.

Above the Don't Pass Line is a bet called the *Field* (a bad bet). The Field combines the numbers 2, 3, 4, 9, 10, 11, and 12. Above the Field is the *Come* area. The Come bet is a good bet. At the top of the layout are the *Point numbers*, also called the *Box numbers*—4, 5, 6, 8, 9, and 10. These Point/Box numbers can be good or bad, depending on how they are being used. More on that later, when I discuss betting methods.

In the upper corners of the layout are the *Don't Come* boxes. The Don't Come is also a good bet but one most craps players shun, which I'll explain in a later chapter.

Okay, now take a look at the center of the table. These are the worst bets in the game of craps, known as *Crazy Crapper bets*, so named by the legendary Captain. They are also called *Proposition bets*. These are awful bets. Here are the names of these bets: the *Hardways* (2:2, 3:3, 4:4, 5:5), the *2* (*Snake Eyes*), the *12* (*Boxcars*), the *11* (*Yo*), the *3* (*Triad*), and *Any Craps*. There are also combination bets called the *Whirl* or the *World*, the *Horn*, also a multitude of *Hop* bets and the dastardly *Any Seven*. Some tables will have other proposition bets such as the money-gobbling *Fire bet*. As stated, these bets are awful—they should be called "suicide bets" for your average craps player.

I'll explain fully the good, bad, and ugliness of all the various bets when I discuss betting methods. If craps bets are compared to movie genres, then the Crazy Crapper bets would be slasher films, cutting your bankroll into bloody chum to be fed to great white sharks—i.e., the casinos.

How the Game is Played

The game begins with the stickman pushing five (sometimes six) dice to the player, from which the player will choose two. The three (or four) that have been rejected will be put into a bowl that is usually on the stickman's side of the table, against the wall under him. To shoot, the player must have a bet on the Pass Line or the Don't Pass Line. Look at the photo on page 3, and you will see that the Pass Line goes all around the side of the layout.

The Pass Line bettors are called *Rightside, Lightside, Right,* or *Do* players. These players make up more than 95 percent of the craps players. So let's look at this bet first, because the flow of the game is hinged on it.

The shooter picks up the dice and rolls them to the end of the table, where they hit the back wall composed of foam rubber *pyramids.* These pyramids are supposed to make the game of craps totally random, which it is for almost all players—except for *controlled shooters,* one of which you may become after reading this book.

The shooter now has the dice, and the game begins.

This roll is called the *Come-Out* roll. If the shooter rolls a 7 or 11, the Pass Line bet wins; if he rolls a 2, 3, or 12, the Pass Line bet loses. He has eight ways to win (six ways on the 7 and two ways on the 11) and four ways to lose (one on the 2, two on the 3, and one on the 12). So on this Come-Out roll the Rightside players have a 2-to-1 edge over the casino. This edge reverses itself when the Come-Out is over and the *Point Cycle* begins.

There are 24 other dice combinations in the game. Should he roll one of these (4, 5, 6, 8, 9, 10) this number becomes his *Point.* The dealer will put a *puck* on the Point number with the white side facing up. This side will have *on* printed on it. The reverse side of the puck is black with *off* printed on it. When the Come-Out roll is taking place, the puck will be over on the side of the table on its black/off side.

The shooter must now make that Point number before the 7 appears in order to win. If the 7 appears before he makes his Point, the shooter and everyone else who bet the Pass Line loses. The dice will then be passed to the next shooter. When the 7 appears to end a roll, it is called *sevening-out.* The stickman will actually call "Seven out!" when this happens, telling everyone loudly that this shooter's hand is finished. Generally there will be moans at the table when this happens. During the Point Cycle, the edge is heavily in the casino's favor.

And that is the essential game of craps:

1. The Come-Out roll where the 7 or 11 wins for the Rightside player.
2. The 2, 3, or 12 loses for the Rightside player.
3. The Point is established, which will be one of these numbers: 4, 5, 6, 8, 9, or 10.

4. The Point must be hit again before the 7 to win.
5. If the 7 comes up before the Point, the Pass Line loses and the shooter gives up the dice.

The Pass Line is an excellent bet to make. The house edge is 1.41 percent. That means for every $10 on the Pass Line, your expectation is to lose 14 cents. For every $100 your expectation is to lose $1.41. Obviously, these dollar amounts are averages over time. On the Pass Line, the house wins 251 decisions; the player wins 244 decisions. It's close. That seven-bet difference comes to 1.41 percent in the house's favor. Any ploppies who recommend not using the Pass Line bet have little knowledge of the game of craps. Avoid their advice.

The Odds Bet: Taking the Odds

Once your Point is established, the casino will allow you to place *Odds*, sometimes called "free" Odds, behind your wager. If the casino allows 2X Odds (translation: two-times odds or *double odds*), on a $10 Pass Line bet, you can put $20 in Odds behind this. The Odds is the best bet at the craps table because the house has no edge on the bet. The Odds bet is paid off at the true odds, which makes sense given its name. The odds of all the Pass Line bets are based on the Point number's relation to the 7.

Here are the payoffs for the Odds bets:
1. The 4 or 10 pays 2-to-1 (six ways to make the 7, three ways to make a 4 or 10)
2. The 5 or 9 pays 3-to-2 (six ways to make the 7, four ways to make the 5 or 9)
3. The 6 or 8 pays 6-to-5 (six ways to make the 7, five ways to make the 6 or 8)

The Pass Line is a 1-to-1 or *even-money* wager. You bet $10, you win or lose $10. So a $10 Pass Line bet with $20 in Odds results in a win of $50 on the 4 or 10 ($10 + $40 = $50), a win of $40 on the 5 or 9 ($10 + $30 = $40), and a win of $34 on the 6 or 8 ($10 + $24 = $34).

It doesn't take an Einstein to realize that the money you place in Odds has the best return of any bet at the game. No house edge = good for the players. That is a hard and fast rule. Again, if someone tells you not to take the Odds because it is a bad bet—run!

> **Please Note:** *Here's the bad news. There is a slight catch with the Odds bet. Come on, you didn't think the casino would just create a no-house-edge bet without a catch, did you? The catch is the fact that the Odds bet can be made only after the shooter has established a Point. So the house always has an edge on you, because that Pass Line bet comes in with a 1.41 house edge.*
>
> *That $10 you bet on the Pass Line will lose you 14 cents whether you have placed Double Odds or 100X odds. Still, if you wanted to bet $30, you'd be better off doing it as $10 on the Pass Line with $20 in Odds, losing just 14 cents, than putting all $30 on the Pass Line and losing 42 cents.*
>
> *You can just play the Pass Line without knowing anything else about craps because that bet is the essential bet of the game for Rightside/Do players.*

The Come Bet

After the shooter has established his Point, you can place a *Come bet* on the layout. This bet acts just like a Pass Line bet. If the shooter rolls a 7 or 11, the bet wins; if the shooter rolls a 2, 3, or 12, the bet loses. If the shooter rolls a Box Number, the Come bet goes onto that number. It is placed in the number's box at the top of the layout. Now the shooter has to make that number before the 7 shows for the Come to win; if the 7 shows, the Come loses.

You can also place Odds on the Come bet. The Odds will actually be placed on top of the bet, somewhat skewed. The Come is a good bet with the same house edge as the Pass Line bet, 1.41 percent.

If you have a Pass Line bet up and a Come bet as well, if the shooter is on another Come-Out roll and rolls a 7, the Come bet will lose. Yes, the Pass Line bet wins on that 7, but the Come bet is a separate game between the Come bettor and the casino. The Odds are usually off for Come bets on the Pass Line's Come-Out roll, so those won't be lost on a Come-Out 7. However, you can keep those Odds working if you wish. Very few players do that.

Please note: *Once your Pass Line and/or Come bets are up on a number, they cannot be taken down. They stay up until they win or lose. Why is this the rule? Because on the Come-Out roll, the player has a mighty edge of 2-to-1, but when the bet is on a number, the edge now turns in favor of the casino. These bets are called contract bets.*

How the Odds Reduces the House Edge

I said previously that the Odds is a great bet with no house edge even though you have to make the Pass Line and/or Come bets, which do have a house edge, to be allowed to bet the Odds. The Odds will reduce the house edge on the *total amount* wagered with the one catch above. You will always lose 1.41 percent of your Pass Line and/or Come bets no matter how much you put in Odds. However, if you intend to bet $30, as I showed previously, you are always better putting the least on the Pass Line or Come and the most in Odds. In such a case, you are really smashing down the overall house edge on that $30.

House Edge Reduction Using Odds

Number of Odds	House Edge	Losses & Added Information
1X	0.85 percent	85 cents per $100 wagered
2X	0.61 percent	61 cents per $100 wagered
Full 2X Odds	0.57 percent	Allows 2.5X Odds on 6 and 8 57 cents per $100 wagered
3X	0.47 percent	47 cents per $100 wagered
3X—4X—5X	0.37 percent	3X on 4/10; 4X on 5/9; 5X on 6/8 37 cents per $100 wagered

Number of Odds	House Edge	Losses & Added Information
5X	0.33 percent	33 cents per $100 wagered
10X	0.18 percent	18 cents per $100 wagered
20X	0.10 percent	10 cents per $100 wagered
100X	0.02 percent	2 cents per $100 wagered

The Don't Pass

Now we go to the Darkside of craps, which the Don't players inhabit. The Don't Pass and all Darkside wagers are almost the exact opposite of the Lightside/Rightside way to play the game. While 95 percent of the craps players are making their Pass Line bets, the Darkside/Don't player puts up his Don't Pass bet. On the Come-Out roll this bet will lose on the 7 and 11 but win on the 2 and 3. The 12 is a push (bar/tie), except in some casinos that use the 2 as the bar/tie instead of the 12. Although the Darkside player is bucking big odds on the initial placement of the bet (he faces an 8-to-3 house advantage), once the Point is established, he has a decided edge over every number.

Still, the Don't Pass bet is only marginally better than the Pass Line bet, as the casino wins 976 decisions and the player wins 949 decisions, with ties making up 55 decisions. The house edge, if you count ties, is 1.36 percent; if you don't count ties, it is 1.40 percent. Thus, for a $10 Don't Pass wager, your expectation is to lose 13.6 cents or 14 cents. The difference between those two figures is just how you decide to do the math, whether you count the ties or not.

Interesting note: *Is a tie something that actually happened? What is the difference between a tie and nothing in a game if the tie has no impact? Or is the time the tie uses up considered more than nothing because during that time no money can be lost or won? This is a raging debate among the philosophers of craps, of which there are very few.*

One important thing to be aware of—most Lightside players have a total disdain, if not hate, for Darkside players, because these Rightside players feel the Darksiders win when they lose. During the Point Cycle of the game, when the shooter is trying to make his Point and avoid the 7, the Darkside player is rooting for the 7 to show, so that he may win.

That's correct—when everyone else loses to the 7, the Darksider wins. Many Darksiders will shoot the dice too—hoping they seven-out quickly on their own rolls. This can also infuriate Rightsiders. In a random game, Darksiders have no negative or positive influence on the game. But emotions do count when you are at a table, and craps players are quite emotional at times. The only time a Darksider and a Lightsider both win is if the Rightsider has a Come bet out on the Come layout and a 7 is rolled. The Darksider wins his Don't Pass bet and the Rightsider wins his Come bet.

Laying the Odds on the Darkside

The Darkside/Don't bettor can also take advantage of the Odds bet, only this time he *lays* the Odds, because he has the better of the game once a Point or number is established. In short, he lays the long money to the casino's short money. Again, the Odds bet can be made only once a Point is established.

Here are the Odds you can lay on the various Point numbers:
1. If you have a 4 or 10 with a $10 Don't Pass bet, you can lay $40 in odds to win $20
2. If you have a 5 or 9 with a $10 Don't Pass bet, you can lay $30 to win $20
3. If you have a 6 or 8 with a $10 Don't Pass bet, you can lay $24 to win $20

Please note: *The Odds on the Darkside is how much you want to win, which in the above case is $20, double your $10 Pass Line bet.*

The Don't Come

The *Don't Come bet*, like the Come bet, can be made only after the shooter's Point is established. It functions just like a Don't Pass bet, winning on the 2 and 3, losing on the 7 and 11, and pushing (tying) on the 12 (or 2 at some casinos). Once up on a number, a 7 will win the bet, and the hitting of the number will lose the bet. As with the Don't Pass, you can lay Odds on the Don't Come as well. The house edge on the Don't Come bet is 1.36 percent (or 1.40 percent, depending on how you count ties), which means you will lose $1.36 or $1.40 for every $100 you bet. This is a good bet.

Please note: *Don't Pass and Don't Come bets can be taken down if you desire to do so. Why? Because the house edge on the Darkside bets comes on the first placement of the bet, but the game shifts heavily in favor of the Darksider once the bet is up on a number. The casinos aren't being kind in allowing you to take down your Darkside bets; they are being clever, because some players will actually take down some of these bets once they are up on a number. And that is a foolish choice that Rightsiders can exploit for their own benefit. (See "Frequently Asked Questions" at the end of the book.)*

Now, with the knowledge of the Pass Line, Don't Pass, Come, and Don't Come bets, along with taking or laying Odds, you can play the strongest craps game against the casinos. The house edge is small; your chances of winning are far greater than just about all the other craps players who make foolish bets. The only way to play a stronger game is to learn how to control the dice.

How Odds Lower the House Edge on the Darkside

Darkside House Edge Reduction Using Odds

Number of Odds	House Edge	Losses/Added Information
1X	0.68 percent	68 cents per $100 wagered
2X	0.46 percent	46 cents per $100 wagered
Full 2X Odds	0.43 percent	43 cents per $100 wagered
3X	0.34 percent	34 cents per $100 wagered
3X—4X—5X	0.27 percent	27 cents per $100 wagered
5X	0.23 percent	23 cents per $100 wagered
10X	0.12 percent	12 cents per $100 wagered
20X	0.07 percent	7 cents per $100 wagered
100X	0.01 percent	1 cent per $100 wagered

Place Bets

Take a look at those Point/Box numbers at the top of the layout. Yes, you can use the best bets we've just discussed to establish those numbers—the Pass Line, Don't Pass, Come, or Don't Come bets. However, some players prefer to *Place bet* (also called *Placing*) these numbers, and the casino will allow you to go right up on them. Just tell the dealer you want to Place the number, and he will take your chips and place them on whichever of those numbers you want. To have that Place-bet privilege, these numbers will not pay off at the correct odds. The casino will have a bigger edge on these bets than it does on the Pass Line, Come, Don't Pass, and Don't Come. The following table will show you the difference between the *true odds* and the *Place odds*:

True Odds vs. Place Odds

Numbers	True Odds	Place Odds	Payment	House Edge
4 and 10	2-to-1	9-to-5	$9 to $5 wagered	6.67 percent
5 and 9	3-to-2	7-to-5	$7 to $5 wagered	4.0 percent
6 and 8	6-to-5	7-to-6	$7 to $6 wagered	1.52 percent

The 6 and 8 should be bet in increments of $6. The placement of the 6 and/or 8 is a good bet, not much worse than the Pass Line or Come in terms of the house edge. Your expectation is to lose nine cents for every $6 you bet, or $1.52 for every $100. With no other enhancements, placing the other numbers is a true waste of your money. For every $5 you bet on the 4 or 10, your expectation is to lose 33 cents, or $6.67 per $100 wagered. Your expectation on a $5 Place bet on the 5 or 9 is to lose 20 cents or $4 per $100 wagered.

Darkside/Don't Place Bets and Lay Bets

These bets are also the reverse of the Rightside/Lightside Place bets because you are placing them to win on a 7 and lose on the number. There are two ways to do this. You can use a strict Don't Place bet, or you can use a Lay bet. Not all casinos will allow *Darkside Place bets*, though almost all allow *Lay bets*.

With the *Don't Place bet* you put up the following wager to win the following amounts on the following numbers:

1. If you want to bet against the 6 or 8, you bet $5 to win $4. The house edge is 1.82 percent. That means for every $5 you bet, your expectation is to lose nine cents. For every $100 you bet, your expectation is to lose $1.82.
2. If you want to bet against the 5 or 9, you bet $8 to win $5. The house edge is 2.5 percent. Your expectation is to lose 20 cents for every $8 you bet. For every $100 you bet, your expectation is to lose $2.50.
3. If you want to bet against the 4 or 10, you bet $11 to win $5. The house edge is 3.03 percent. Your expectation is to lose 33 cents for every $11 you bet. Your expectation for every $100 you bet is to lose $3.03.

The second way to bet against numbers is to use a *Lay bet*. You pay a 5 percent commission on the bet, and the house will then pay you the true odds. Here is how it works:

1. If you want to Lay against the 4 or 10, you bet $40 to win $20. The 5 percent is taken out of $20. Your payment of the vig (commission) is $1. The house edge is 2.44 percent. Your expectation for every $100 you bet is to lose $2.44.
2. If you want to Lay against the 5 or 9, you bet $30 to win $20. Your payment of the vig is $1. The house edge is 3.23 percent. For every $100 you wager, your expectation is to lose $3.23.
3. If you want to Lay against the 6 or 8, you bet $24 to win $20. Your payment of the vig is $1. The house edge is 4 percent. For every $100 you wager, your expectation is to lose $4.

With these Darkside Place/Lay bets you must use the one that has the least house edge attached to it. In casinos that allow both types of wagers, you will mix and match—although we would recommend that you make only the ones with a lower than 2 percent house edge, and there is only one of those.

The Put Bets

The *Put bets* can be made right after the Point is established. This is a Pass Line or Come bet that pays even money but that can have Odds placed on it. So if the Point is 6 with double odds, you can bet $10 as the even-money portion and add $20 in Odds to the bet. The payoff will be $34 for your $30 wager. The house edge is 3.03 percent, an expected loss of $3.03 per $100 wagered. The Odds a casino allows will determine whether the Put bet is one worth making. Check this chart out. Many casinos will not allow Put bets. Although some Put bets come in with some good edges—better than the Place house edges at times—they are never as good as Pass Line or Come bets with Odds. The bets in bold are decent Put wagers to make.

Picking Your Put Wager

Odds Allowed	4 or 10 Put House Edge	5 or 9 Put House Edge	6 or 8 Put House Edge
No odds	33.33 percent	20 percent	9.09 percent
1X	16.67 percent	10 percent	4.55 percent
2X	11.11 percent	6.67 percent	3.03 percent
3X	8.33 percent	5 percent	2.27 percent
4X	6.67 percent	4 percent	**1.82 percent**
5X	5.56 percent	3.33 percent	**1.52 percent**
10X	3.03 percent	**1.82 percent**	**0.83 percent**
20X	**1.59 percent**	**0.95 percent**	**0.43 percent**
100X	**0.33 percent**	**0.20 percent**	**0.09 percent**

The Crazy Crapper/Proposition Bets

Welcome to the betting world of the ploppy—high-house-edge bets that dangle the hope of winning big right now against the almost guaranteed monster losses that ultimately occur when these bets are made, over and over again. I wish I didn't have to include these bets in the book, but they are a part of the game...so here goes.

The Crazy Crapper bets come in two varieties: one-roll bets that are decided on each and every roll of the dice and (possible) multiroll bets that are not necessarily decided with each and every roll. All of these bets gain their house edge from being paid at less than true odds. The casino acts as your partner in your wins on Crazy Crapper/Proposition bets, sharing those wins with you, but should you lose the bet, well, you are a sole proprietor. Take, for example, the dreaded Any Seven one-roll bet. The true odds are 5-to-1 or $5 to $1, but the casino pays $4 to $1. It literally takes that extra dollar from you.

The casino also plays a little game concerning the naming of the payouts of these bets. The use of the words "to" and "for" is an attempt to cloud the issue of the true return. A bet that has 10-to-1 true odds might be paid off at 9-to-1 or it might be paid off as 10 *for* 1. This different wording actually means the *same thing*. The 10 *for* 1 just means the casino counts the initial bet as a part of the payoff. Very clever, no? Makes it sound as if you are getting more when you aren't. Very, very clever.

Multiroll Crazy Crapper Bets

The Hardway 4 or Hardway 10 (also called Hard 4 or Hard 10): A Hardway bet is one where the dice show doubles. A Hard 4 is 2:2; a Hard 10 is 5:5. This bet is made for the Hardway to be rolled before the 7 or before the number is made the *soft way* (that is, 3:1 or 1:3 for the 4; 6:4 or 4:6 for the 10). For some bizarre reason these Hardway bets have attracted many players to them. The Hard 4 or Hard 10 occur only once in 36 rolls, while the 7 and the soft ways can be made eight times when combined. So the true odds are 8-to-1. The casino pays 7-to-1 (or 8 *for* 1), and the house edge is a large 11.11 percent, an expected loss of $11.11 for every $100 wagered.

The Hardway 6 or the Hardway 8 (also called Hard 6 or Hard 8): The player is looking to hit a 3:3 or a 4:4 before the 7 or a soft way appears. The true odds are 10-to-1; the casino pays off at 9-to-1 (or 10 *for* 1). House edge is 9.09 percent, which translates into an expected loss of $9.09 for every $100 wagered.

The Big 6 and the Big 8: A true ploppy delight. This bet is the same as the Place bet of the 6 or 8 but is paid at even money as opposed to $7 to $6. The house edge is 9.09 percent. You won't find this bet on all craps tables.

Fire Bet: Oh, this is a tempting bet, really seductive, like the devil promising you the riches of the world if you just sell your soul. The bet is a side bet (which will usually appear on the layout if offered) that the shooter will hit each and every Point number during his roll. Thus, he must hit the 4, 5, 6, 8, 9, and 10 on the Pass Line during the Point Cycle before sevening-out to win the big jackpot. If he hits four or five of the numbers, smaller jackpots are won. The *maximum* bet is usually $5. There are various payouts for the Fire bet, depending on the casino, but here is the bad news (oh, come on, you knew that bad news was coming): the house edge ranges from 20 percent to about 25 percent. That means the expectations are losses between $20 and $25 for every $100 wagered. That is a fiery hell and the worst bet at the craps tables that have it.

The One-Roll Crazy Crapper Bets

The 2 or 12: The ploppy throws out his chip and screams, "Give me a 2 [or 12]!" and the dealer places it on the number. These numbers hit once every 36 rolls, so the odds of hitting a 2 or 12 are 35-to-1. The casino does not pay you 35-to-1; instead it shortchanges you by paying 30-to-1 (or 31 *for* 1). The house edge is a whopping 13.89 percent. Translated: the player loses $13.89 for every $100 wagered on this crazy bet. Some casinos will change the payouts on these, but I have never heard of any casino making these bets worthwhile.

The 3 or 11: Same thing for these numbers—throw out the chip, chip goes on the number, but, hooray! the 3 or 11 comes in with a slightly smaller edge of 11.11 percent. The payout is 15-to-1 (or 16 *for* 1) when the true odds are 17-to-1. You'll hear the players and dealers use the term "yo-eleven" for the 11. This is done to distinguish it from the seven, because "eleven" and "seven" sound alike. The expectation is to lose $11.11 for every $100 you bet on these foolish wagers. Some casinos will change the payouts on these, but I have never heard of any casino making these bets worthwhile either.

Any Craps: The bettor wants any one of these numbers to hit: 2, 3, or 12. The true odds are 8-to-1, the payoff is 7-to-1 (or 8 *for* 1), and the house edge is 11.11 percent. The loss? For every $100 wagered on this nutty proposition, the house will take $11.11 from the ploppy player.

Any Seven or Big Red: There's truth in advertising here. On this bet, the player wants the next roll to be a 7. The payout is 4-to-1; the true odds are 5-to-1. The house edge is a mountainous 16.67 percent. The player's bankroll will be a *big red* if he keeps making this Crazy Crapper bet. The expectation is to lose $16.67 for every $100 wagered on this money-sucking vampire. Bet this, and you had better bring some garlic with you.

Craps/11 or C&E: The poor ploppy is betting that one of the following numbers will appear: 2, 3, 11, or 12 on the next roll. Half the bet goes on the craps numbers (2, 3, and 12); the other half on the 11. If a craps number appears, the payout is 7-to-1, but the 11 loses. If the 11 appears, the payoff is 15-to-1 and the craps numbers lose. The house edge is 11.11 percent or an expected loss of $11.11 for every $100 wagered.

Field Bet: The player wants any one of these numbers to appear on the next roll: 2, 3, 4, 9, 10, 11, or 12. There are 16 ways to make these numbers and 20 ways to make all the other numbers. In most casinos the 2 and 12 will pay 2-to-1. The house edge on this bet is 5.56 percent or an expected loss of $5.56 per $100 wagered. Some casinos will pay 3-to-1 on either the 2 or 12, and this will reduce the house edge to 2.78 percent; an expected loss of $2.78 per $100 wagered.

Hardway Hop Bets: A Hardway is doubles—so if the ploppy yells out, "Give me a Hardway six on the hop!" The odds are 35-to-1 to hit this; the payoff is 30-to-1—a house edge of 13.89 percent, an expected loss of $13.89 per $100 wagered. The Hardway hops are 1:1, 2:2, 3:3, 4:4, 5:5, and 6:6.

Hop Bets: All numbers and combinations can be done as Hop bets. You can call out that you want a 3, which would be made as 2:1 or 1:2. The payouts for all Hop bets of this type are 15-to-1; the true odds are 17-to-1. The house edge is 11.11 percent, an expected loss of $11.11 per $100 wagered.

Horn: The ploppy wants one of the following numbers to show: 2, 3, 11, or 12. The bet must be made in multiples of $4. You win on the number that shows (30-to-1 on the 2 and 12, 15-to-1 on the 3 and 11), but you lose the three other bets. The house edge on this bet is 12.5 percent; a loss of $12.50 per $100 wagered. There is an offshoot of this Horn bet, the *Horn High* variation. Here the ploppy throws out $5 and has the extra dollar put on any one of the four numbers. The house edge on this Horn High is 12.22 percent on the 3 or 11 and 12.78 percent on the 2 or 12. As you can see, these are all bad bets. Some craps tables will not have a separate box for Horn bets, so the dealers will put the chips on the line—indicating all of these numbers—or simply put the bets on the numbers directly.

Over 7 or Under 7: You will see this bet more often in church Las Vegas nights, and you will need the help of the Lord to make money on it. You are betting that the next roll will be over 7 or you are betting that the next roll will be under 7. You have 15 ways to win and 21 ways to lose. The payouts are even money. The house edge is 16.67 percent or a loss of $16.67 for every $100 wagered. God help you!

Whirl or World: If the Horn isn't bad enough, now comes the *Whirl* or *World* bet. Here the ploppy is looking to make one of the following numbers: 2, 3, 7, 11, or 12. The house edge is 13.33 percent. He throws out a multiple of $5 and yells out, "I am an idiot!" No, sorry, he yells out, "Whirl! [or World.]" Each number is paid off at house odds with the other numbers' losses being subtracted from it. Some craps tables will not have a separate box for Whirl or World bets, so the dealers will put the chips on the line, indicating all of these numbers, or simply put the bets on the numbers directly.

> **Please note:** *You can place the Pass Line and Don't Pass bets your-self. You can also put the Odds down behind them. You can place the Come and Don't Come bets, but the Odds for these bets are put on by the dealer. Just place the amount you want in Odds on the Come section and say, "Odds." All Place bets, Don't Place bets, and Lay bets are placed by the dealer, as are all Crazy Crapper/Proposition bets except for the Field, which you place yourself. Because none of you will ever make these bets again after reading this book, these bets are not something to even think about. A strong game of craps will not include them.*

As you can see, the Crazy Crapper bets are a waste of money. The Captain said, "You have to be crazy to make them." He was right. You'll note that I put in a couple of side bets that are popular either in the casinos or in church games. Many casinos usher in new side bets and usher them out again because most craps players don't go for them. The rule of thumb and brain is this: it is a rare snowball's chance in hell that a casino is going to put in a side bet that is any good or even just slightly bad. Ignore them and feel sorry for the hopeless, hapless players who make them. The casinos thrive on ploppies—and you never want to be one of them.

Total Recap

1. Put Pass Line or Don't Pass bet down. Come-Out roll will win even money for Pass Line bettors if a 7 or 11 is rolled. It will lose if a 2, 3, or 12 is rolled. Pass Line bettor has a 2-to-1 edge on the Come-Out roll, as the 7 and 11 can be made eight ways while the 2, 3, and 12 can be made four ways. The other 24 dice combinations are no-decisions but become the Point if rolled. If you are betting the Don't Pass, you win if a 2 or 3 is rolled (three ways), tie on a 12 (one way), and lose on a 7 or 11 (eight ways). The casino has an 8-to-3 edge on the Come-Out roll for Darksiders. Again, the other numbers are no-decisions but become the Point if hit.
2. Once a Point is established, you can place Odds or Lay Odds on your Pass Line or Don't Pass bets.
3. You can get on other numbers by using Come or Don't Come betting. They work the same way as the Pass Line and Don't Pass. You may also take or lay Odds on these bets by putting the Odds down and telling the dealer, "Odds."
4. The shooter continues until he sevens-out. Rightsiders will not lose as long as the 7 doesn't show; Darksiders will win if the 7 shows. Sometimes Darksiders will shoot the dice, and if they make their Point or hit Box numbers that they are betting against, they lose! If they seven-out, they win!
5. The Placing of any bet with a house edge under 2 percent is okay but not as good as the Pass, Come, Don't Pass, and Don't Come with Odds. No other bets should be considered by smart players.

CHAPTER 2

Pushing the House in Betting: How to Lower the House Edge Even More

While craps seems to have the most bets of any game, all of them spelled out on the felt or on the walls of the table, there are still variations of these bets that do not necessarily appear on the layout or on the signs posted on either side of the table right under the dealers and box person.

In fact, with these variations in the game, smart players can get still lower house edges than discussed in the first chapter. The concept we are dealing with was coined by the Captain as *pushing the house*, which means literally pushing the casino to give you a better game than advertised.

The Captain is not the first player to push the house. This was done in Las Vegas by an anonymous player who was the first to get the casinos to accept a *buy bet* of the 4 or 10 for $25 at a $1 commission—the usual buy bet had been $20 with a $1 commission. The Captain merely built on what came before him.

But let's not get ahead of ourselves here. Let's look at pushing the house in various ways.

Buy Bets

If we look at the Place bets for the 4 and 10, 5 and 9, we see rather high house edges of 6.67 percent and 4 percent respectively, while the 6 and 8 come in with a respectable 1.52 percent house edge. The 4 and 10, 5 and 9 have way too high of a house edge to bother betting them. However, with a variation called a *buy bet*, we can literally pay the house to give us a better game on four of these numbers.

Here's how buy bets work. You pay the casino a commission of 5 percent on every $20 you wager on these numbers, and then the casino will give you the true odds of the bet, should you win. That means you will win 2-to-1 on the 4 and 10 and 3-to-2 on the 5 and 9. The commission for the $20 wager is $1, with this commission often called the *vig* or *vigorish*.

Casinos have two ways to handle these buy bets—they can take the vig out of both winning and losing bets (called *pig vig*), or they can take the vig out of only winning bets (called *fig vig*). Needless to say, pig vig is not as good as fig vig.

The Pig Vig

If you have to pay the vig on both winning and losing $20 buy bets of the 4 and 10, the house edge is 4.76 percent, which is rotten but still better than its original 6.67 percent house edge. However, if you can push the house to accept a buy of $25 for that same $1 vig, then the house edge drops to 3.85 percent—still not so hot, but you can see where we are going.

That $25/$1 vig bet was accepted in Vegas more than 50 years ago. It was accepted in Atlantic City in 1978 when Atlantic City's first casino, Resorts, opened. But the Captain was able to get Atlantic City to accept a $35/$1 vig buy bet *and* a $39/$1 vig buy bet as well. Take a look at this chart and see what happens to that bloated 6.67 percent house edge on the 4 and 10 when you can push the house to give you a better buy.

Pushing the House

Bet	Payoff	Commission Always Paid	House Edge	Money
Place 4 or 10	9-to-5	0	6.67 percent	Lose $6.67 per $100 wagered
Buy the 4 or 10 for $20	2-to-1	$1	4.76 percent	Lose $4.76 per $100 wagered
Buy the 4 or 10 for $25	2-to-1	$1	3.85 percent	Lose $3.85 per $100 wagered
Buy the 4 or 10 for $30	2-to-1	$1	3.23 percent	Lose $3.23 per $100 wagered
Buy the 4 or 10 for $35	2-to-1	$1	2.78 percent	Lose $2.78 per $100 wagered
Buy the 4 or 10 for $39	2-to-1	$1	2.50 percent	Lose $2.50 per $100 wagered

The bet is made simply. Just throw out your chips with that $1 vig and say, "Buy the 4 for $35." (Alas, many casinos won't allow that $39 buy bet anymore.) The dealer will take the dollar (or get change) and put your chips on the number with a small marker on top that has *buy* printed on it.

Most casinos will charge you a $3 commission if you try to buy both the 4 and the 10 for $35 at the same time. They do this because these buy bets are supposed to be made in multiples of $20, and two $35 buys equals $70. So make these buy bets in a staggered way—make one, then if you want another one, wait a roll and make the other one.

The problem now comes in as you decide to buy up the chain of bets on the 4 and 10. The next level is a $55 buy with a $2 vig to get the house edge as low as the casino will allow it to go. This bet comes in with a 3.51 percent house edge.

Here is a chart with other possible buys, none reducing the house edge as much as that $35 or $39 $1 buy.

Bet	Payoff	Commission Always Paid	House Edge	Money
Buy the 4 or 10 for $55	2-to-1	$2	3.51 percent	Lose $3.51 per $100 wagered
Buy the 4 or 10 for $75	2-to-1	$3	3.85 percent	Lose $3.85 per $100 wagered
Buy the 4 or 10 for $95	2-to-1	$4	4.04 percent	Lose $4.04 per $100 wagered
Buy the 4 or 10 for $115	2-to-1	$5	4.17 percent	Lose $4.17 per $100 wagered

Please note: *In essence you are adding $15 to each level of the $20 buy ($20 + $15 = $35, $40 + $15 = $55, $60 + $15 = $75, and so on up the ladder). The highest the house edge can be on any buy of the 4 or 10 using these figures above will not be more than 4.76 percent if you go in multiples of $20. If the casino allows you to use $19 in addition to the $20 level, then the house edge goes down still more. All you do is add $19 to the $20 to get $39, $19 to the $40 to get $59, and so on up the ladder. I doubt you will find many casinos that allow the addition of $19. Still, no harm in trying.*

And what about buying the 5 and 9 at casinos taking the vig on both winning *and* losing bets? For a $20/$1 vig buy, the house edge is 4.76 percent—even worse than the normal house edge of 4 percent on these two numbers. I have not yet played in a casino that allows the pig vig buy bet to go to $30 or, at max, $38, which has a 2.56 percent house edge, but these casinos may be around somewhere out there in casinoland. In those cases, the house edge would fall below 4 percent and the bet, while not great, would be better than its Place-bet counterpart. The result of pig vig on the 5 and 9? Don't waste your money.

The Fig Vig

There is a much better type of buy bet that can be found in many casinos across the country. This one is called the *fig vig* buy bet because you don't pay the commission unless the bet actually wins. So why is this bet called the fig vig? In ancient days and in biblical times, the fig was a most honored fruit, and, indeed, many readers believe that the fig tree played an important role in the Genesis story in the bible. Recall that Adam and Eve, after they ate the fruit of the tree of the knowledge of good and evil, put fig leaves on themselves to hide their nakedness. In short, the fig covered up for them.

Well, paying the vig on *wins only* for buy bets remarkably reduces the casino's house edge. In fact, it covers up the rottenness of the house edges on both the 4 and 10 *and* the 5 and 9, making them betable wagers. Here are the edges possible in the fig-vig casinos:

Possible Fig-Vig Edges

Bet	Payoff	Commission on Wins Only	House Edge	Money
Place the 4 or 10 for $20	9-to-5	0	6.67 percent	Lose $6.67 per $100 wagered
Buy the 4 or 10 for $20	2-to-1	$1	1.67 percent	Lose $1.67 per $100 wagered
Buy the 4 or 10 for $25	2-to-1	$1	1.33 percent	Lose $1.33 per $100 wagered
Buy the 4 or 10 for $35	2-to-1	$1	0.95 percent	Lose 95 cents per $100 wagered
Buy the 4 or 10 for $40	2-to-1	$2	1.67 percent	Lose $1.67 per $100 wagered

Bet	Payoff	Commission on Wins Only	House Edge	Money
Buy the 4 or 10 for $50	2-to-1	$2	1.33 percent	Lose $1.33 per $100 wagered
Buy the 4 or 10 for $55	2-to-1	$2	1.21 percent	Lose $1.21 per $100 wagered
Buy the 4 or 10 for $60	2-to-1	$3	1.67 percent	Lose $1.67 per $100 wagered
Buy the 4 or 10 for $75	2-to-1	$3	1.33 percent	Lose $1.33 per $100 wagered
Buy the 4 or 10 for $80	2-to-1	$4	1.67 percent	Lose $1.67 per $100 wagered
Buy the 4 or 10 for $95	2-to-1	$4	1.40 percent	Lose $1.40 per $100 wagered
Buy the 4 or 10 for $100	2-to-1	$5	1.67 percent	Lose $1.67 per $100 wagered

You can see from this chart just how terrific the fig-vig buy bets are on the 4 and 10. Paying the commission only on wins and starting with those $20 units, the highest house edge is 1.67 percent, just slightly higher than the placing of the 6 or 8. These are all good bets in the scheme of things and can be a part of a strong attack against the casinos.

It is *Ripley's Believe It or Not* time when it comes to buying the 5 and 9 at fig-vig games. A $20 buy bet with a $1 vig has a house edge of 2 percent, which is half as much as the normal 4 percent Place-bet edge on these two numbers and right on the line for bets that are not too awful to make. But a $30 buy bet on the 5 or 9 paying that $1 vig only on wins comes in with a 1.33 percent house edge. So buying the 5 and 9 in fig-vig games is also a good thing if they let you go to $30 for a $1 vig. Check out this chart:

Bet	Payoff	Commission on Wins Only	House Edge	Money
Place the 5 or 9 for $20	7-to-5	0	4 percent	Lose $4 per $100 wagered
Buy the 5 or 9 for $20	3-to-2	$1	2 percent	Lose $2 per $100 wagered
Buy the 5 or 9 for $30	3-to-2	$1	1.33 percent	Lose $1.33 per $100 wagered
Buy the 5 or 9 for $38	3-to-2	$1	1.05 percent	Lose $1.05 per $100 wagered
Buy the 5 or 9 for $40	3-to-2	$2	2 percent	Lose $2 per $100 wagered
Buy the 5 or 9 for $50	3-to-2	$2	1.60 percent	Lose $1.60 per $100 wagered
Buy the 5 or 9 for $58	3-to-2	$2	1.38 percent	Lose $1.38 per $100 wagered
Buy the 5 or 9 for $60	3-to-2	$3	2 percent	Lose $2 per $100 wagered
Buy the 5 or 9 for $70	3-to-2	$3	1.71 percent	Lose $1.71 per $100 wagered
Buy the 5 or 9 for $78	3-to-2	$3	1.54 percent	Lose $1.54 per $100 wagered
Buy the 5 or 9 for $80	3-to-2	$4	2 percent	Lose $2 per $100 wagered
Buy the 5 or 9 for $90	3-to-2	$4	1.78 percent	Lose $1.78 per $100 wagered
Buy the 5 or 9 for $98	3-to-2	$4	1.63 percent	Lose $1.63 per $100 wagered
Buy the 5 or 9 for $100	3-to-2	$5	2 percent	Lose $2 per $100 wagered

There are some casinos that will not let you jump to the next level without charging you more in vig. For example, you want to go from $20 to $30 for $1, but the vig becomes $2 as opposed to $1 at the cheaper casinos. This is still a better game than placing either the 5 or 9, but you are well over a 2 percent house edge in such casinos on the 5 and 9, so making these bets isn't so good.

Pushing the House on Lay Bets

Although all Darksider Lay bets are buy bets because you must pay the 5 percent commission, some casinos might allow you to push them into allowing a higher bet for the same vig. This is just like the buy bets at Rightside play discussed above, although now you are rooting for the 7 to make its appearance and putting in the long end of the bet (i.e., you bet more money to win less money because the odds favor you). Instead of trying to win $40 on a Lay bet of 4 or 10, bet $78, which then will pay you $39, coming in with a house edge of 1.27 percent. Using a Lay bet at $57 for the 5 or 9 has a house edge of 1.72 percent.

No buy bets, Rightside or Darkside, are as good on the 6 or 8 as simply Placing those numbers.

> **Please note:** *The above house edges on most of these buy bets look really good, but keep in mind that you are making these bets over and over during a session (heck, during a playing career!). When you see a loss of a dollar and change on $100 wagered, do not think to yourself, Hey, I can go nuts; look how small that house edge is! In a two-hour session at a table, betting these numbers in bunches can lose you a lot of money. So always tread cautiously even when betting decent bets. Players who make the bad bets will almost invariably lose a lot of money. But unless you are a dice controller, your expectation, even on the best bets, is to lose.*

Pushing the House on the Odds Bets

As you can see with those fig-vig buy bets, pushing the house is the only way to go if you can afford the betting levels. Now, pushing the house on the best bets in the game—Pass and Come—is an extraordinary thing to do.

This chart will show you how good pushing the house can be on Pass Line and Come bets. The asterisk shows where the house can be pushed.

> **Please note:** *We are giving minimum bets generally. You can multiply these bets to get to your betting level. So on the $6 Pass or Come bet, the odds at a 1X game are $6, $6, $10. If you wish to bet $60 on the Pass or Come, then the odds would be $60, $60, $100. Asterisks and bold lettering will show where the house can usually get pushed. Around the country you might find bets we don't have listed. Some casinos will allow even more generous pushes of the house, and some won't allow any pushing of the house.*

Pushing on the Odds Bet

Bet Size	1X on 4 and 10	1X on 5 and 9	1X on 6 and 8	2X on 4 and 10	2X on 5 and 9	2X on 6 and 8	5X on 4 and 10	5X on 5 and 9	5X on 6 and 8
$6/$60/$600	$6	$6	*$10*	$12	$12	*$20*	$30	$30	*$50*
$10	$10	$10	$10	$20	$20	*$25*	$50	$50	$50
$15	$15	*$20*	*$25*	$30	*$40*	*$50*	$75	*$100*	*$125*
$30	$30	*$40*	*$50*	$60	*$80*	*$100*	$150	*$200*	*$250*

By pushing the house, the overall edges for these Pass and Come bets will go down. Here's a look at how much:

Odds Bet	Normal House Edge	Pushing the House Edge
1X Odds	0.85 percent	0.73 percent
2X Odds	0.61 percent	0.50 percent
5X Odds	0.33 percent	0.25 percent

I can hear some ploppy reading this book saying, "Oh, come on, big deal, you go down from 0.85 percent to 0.73 percent and 0.61 percent to 0.50 percent and 0.33 percent to 0.25 percent when pushing the house. This is not at all significant. What baloney!"

On the contrary, it is significant. Let's say you put $100,000 in action over the years (and even low rollers who play a lot will hit this figure) on any one of the above Pass Line or Come bets, either using regular odds or pushing-the-house odds. Let's see what you save:

$100,000 Wagered	Normal Loss	Push the House	Loss Difference
1X	$850	$730	$120
2X	$610	$500	$110
5X	$330	$250	$80

Isn't it better to have that money in your pocket than in the casino treasury? Why not save what you can when you play? It doesn't diminish the fun, does it, when you lose less?

CHAPTER 3

Best Bets for Savvy Players

We have to make a distinction in this book among ploppy players, savvy players, and dice controllers in terms of betting and expectation. Competent dice controllers *who bet properly* will have a positive expectation over the casinos. In short, they should win over time.

If you never learn how to control the dice, you can still be a tough player for the casino to deal with if you follow the betting advice I am going to give you. Will you win if you follow this advice? Your mathematical expectation is to lose whether you are a savvy player or a ploppy player, especially if you play over long periods of time in your craps career. But the key for the savvy player is that you will lose much less money (much, *much* less money) and have just as much fun, and you'll also know that you have given the casino the ride of its life, as the casino has given you just such a ride.

You are a gambler if you play a negative-expectation game, no doubt about that. No betting system can turn that around, and anyone who says there are such winning betting systems is either a liar or a ploppy, probably both.

But you can be a smart gambler or a ploppy gambler—the choice is yours. If you get caught up in the hysteria of craps and make all sorts of suicidal bets whose edges are through the roof, don't be shocked when you find you lost the ranch because you bet the farm. A good bet is a much more exciting prospect than a bad bet because you have a better chance to be ahead making such bets—or at least be less behind! Ploppy bettors, although they may have a stunning night now and again or stunning moments that imprint themselves on other players' minds ("This guy is so hot; he hit three 12s in a row!"), will have their mushy heads handed to them big time in the long haul. Short spurts of magnificent luck will never overcome the bloody drain of time on the ploppy's bankroll.

So don't be a ploppy. That's my first piece of advice.

Now to the important stuff—what bets should you make, and which bets should you avoid? In short, how should you play a savvy game of craps? How do you become a tough out for the casinos?

Here's how:
1. Use the 5-Count on all shooters (See Chapter 6).
2. Make only bets that come in with house edges less than 2 percent.
3. Understand the mathematics of the game in terms of what the house edge actually means in terms of dollars and cents.
4. Use little tricks to get more in comps than you deserve.
5. Play within your bankroll limitations.
6. Create a 401G account (see Chapter 20).

The Best Bets

The top-of-the-line bets are not hard to figure out—on the Rightside/Lightside are the Pass Line and Come bets with full Odds—pushing the house if you can afford to do so; on the Darkside/Don't are the Don't Pass and Don't Come bets with full Odds.

Just check out the charts to see what to bet and what Odds to take. I mentioned this before, but it bears repeating. If I bet $10 on the Pass line or Come with no Odds, and you bet $10 on the Pass Line or Come with 2X (or more) Odds, we both will lose 14 cents for those $10 bets. However, if you bet $10 with $20 in Odds on the Pass Line or Come, and I bet $30 on the Pass Line or Come, your expectation is to lose 14 cents, but my expectation is to lose 42 cents—three times more. So the rule is less on the Pass Line and Come and more on the Odds.

For Darksiders, the rules are the same—Don't Pass and Don't Come, as low on those as you need to go to be able to afford full Odds. If you must put yourself in opposition to those Lightside players, at least get the most bang for your bucks and ignore all those hateful stares you are doomed to receive. (Yes, yes, some Lightside players don't care what Darkside players bet, but the Lightside versus Darkside is a real part of the emotional underpinnings of craps.)

How Many Bets to Make?

Every bet you make that has a house edge loses you money over time. That is an indisputable fact. One bet on the Pass Line with full Odds would be the way to go. There is no difference between two $10 Come bets (or one Pass Line and one Come) on the table or one $10 Come bet in terms of expectation per bet, but *in terms of time*, there's a big difference. Both will be decided as 14 cents for that $10 over time. However, with two $10 bets on the table, you lose 28 cents. The difference is the fact that with one bet it will take twice the time to lose 28 cents. The end result is the same—you lose; but the time to get there is much different because you lose more slowly. You have more playing time with one bet than you do with two bets. Your time has been doubled.

Okay, let's be realistic now. Most craps players can't see themselves making just one "stinking" bet when the game is in full blossom. If you are like such players, then make two Come (or a Come and Pass Line) bets or, if you can't resist, make three bets and hold them there. Three bets will give you plenty of action. More than three at the get-go can cost you a lot of money with a quick seven-out.

The Best of the Best Bets

Without question, the best bets at the game of craps are the Pass Line with full Odds and the Come with full Odds and also the Don't Pass with full Odds and the Don't Come with full Odds. No matter what *combobulations* critics of these bets attempt to proselytize to dismiss them and advocate other "less-good" bets, these sad ploppies are actually the flat-worlders of craps, denying that earth is a sphere and that math dictates proper betting.

Please note: *When we say "full Odds" it is possible that you can't afford to take those odds. No problem; just take what you can afford. You must always gamble within your comfort zone.*

Some hopeless, hapless critics of these best-of-the-best bets will state such inept arguments against Pass and Come betting as these:

1. "You have to hit the number twice on the Come to win; whereas with a Place bet you have to hit your number only once!"
2. "You can't take the Come bet down when it is up on a number, but you can take down your Place bets."
3. "The Odds are a trick by the casino to get you to bet more!"

No. 1 is idiotic. You don't have to hit your number twice. The first placement of both the Pass Line and Come is not looking to hit a number—it is desiring a hit on the 7 or 11, two numbers that give the Pass Line and the Come bettor a 2-to-1 edge over the casino at that moment before a Point/Box number is established, while the Place bettor is facing a 6.67 percent house edge on the 4 and 10, a 4 percent house edge on the 5 and 9, and a decent edge of 1.52 on the 6 and 8 (decent, yes, but *not better* than Pass Line or Come) at that moment. Who is better off? Do not listen to the ploppies.

No. 2 is somewhat less idiotic...*sounding*, that is. The problem comes in with the fact that you'd have to turn off or take down, say, your 4 about 80 percent of the time to make it the equivalent monetary loss of the Pass Line or Come bet over time. The house edge doesn't change, of course, but by turning off or taking down your Place bets, the house edge has less money to work on, thus reducing your overall loss. But we know of no one who takes down his Place bets 80 percent of the time on the 4 or 10 or 65 percent of the time on the 5 or 9. So although it sounds good that you can take down the Place bets and thus lose less money, you won't see many players doing it. It's a shadow argument, not a real one.

No. 3 could be true to an extent if you actually do put out more money in Odds if you are playing on a tight bankroll. But we advocate small Pass Line and Come bets with maximum Odds in direct proportion to what you would have bet otherwise. That is, $10 on Pass with $20 Odds ($30 total = 14 cent loss) rather than $30 on the Pass Line ($30 total = 42 cents loss) with maximum Odds. There's no trick involved here if you actually know how to play the game and use the Odds bet properly. Again, just bet within your bankroll.

For Darkside players the advice is exactly the same as for Lightsiders. Make Don't Pass and Don't Come wagers, keeping those bets low, and lay full Odds on them. Again, the best way to do this is to just go with one number. Interestingly enough, many Darksiders actually do prefer to go up on only one number. You can also use a money-management strategy to save you from getting hurt by one shooter. If you get up on a number and the shooter knocks you off, then you go on another number. If he knocks you off again, stop, and then wait for the next shooter. Don't ever let one shooter hit you too hard. Would this change the house edge against you? No. But like taking down bets on the Rightside, waiting out shooters will save you money over time because you are not betting while waiting for the next shooter to get the dice. It is a more comfortable way to play the Don't side of the game.

The Second-Best of the Best Bets

So you don't want to use Pass Line or Come bets with full Odds or Don't Pass or Don't Come bets with full Odds, but you still want to keep the house edge lower than 2 percent (the highest house edge you should *ever* allow yourself to buck). Then Placing the 6 and 8 at that 1.52 percent house edge is a good Place bet, as are buying the 4 and 10 at $25 for a $1 vig on wins only and buying the 5 or 9 at $30 or $38 on games with a $1 vig that also take the commissions on wins only (follow the fig-vig charts to handle the buying of the 4 or 10 and 5 or 9).

If you play in pig-vig casinos where you can't buy numbers on wins only, then Place the 6 and 8—*period*. Don't let yourself get caught up in the craps mob-mania when you see other numbers hitting—it's all luck, and those numbers are not destined to continue hitting more than probability indicates. Streaks are normal in all random events, and they are not (*NOT! NOT! NOT!*) predictable. If they were, the casinos would go broke with streak players, because many casino gamblers are streak freaks.

Darkside players can Don't Place bet against the 6 and 8, a bet that has a 1.82 percent house edge. All other Don't Place and Lay bets are just not worth it going against the high house edges.

Mix and Match

You can also mix and match bets, using a combination of Place bets, Pass Line, and Come bets. You have to follow the above advice concerning keeping the house edge under 2 percent, but mixing and matching is a very popular way to play—for savvy players and for ploppies. It all depends on what Place/Buy bets you are mixing and matching with Pass Line and Come bets.

If you are up on the 6 and 8 and you want a third number, put out a Come bet. Should the Come bet go to the 6 or 8, say to the dealer, "Full odds on the Come, down on my 8 [or 6]." You will now have a Come bet with full Odds on the number. Now Place another Come bet to try to get up on that third number. In fig-vig casinos, you can go with buys of the outside numbers if you wish.

Please note: *In a book I wrote more than two decades ago, I explained how the Captain advocated playing his "Supersystem"—a combination of simultaneously betting exact amounts on the Pass Line/Don't Pass and Come/Don't Come, and just relying on the Odds to attack the casinos. The Captain was the greatest craps player who ever lived, but in this case he was mistaken in his assumption. The house edge works on both sides of the bet, so you are getting no benefit simultaneously betting the Do and the Don't (also called the Doey-Don't). You are far better off just making either a Pass Line or Come with Odds—or a Don't Pass or Don't Come with Odds—than playing the Doey-Don't. Okay, so the Captain was wrong...once. It proves he's human.*

That's it. Look over all the other bets on the craps layout, and they are all a waste of your time and your money. Ploppy craps players will come up with all manner of reasons why they should throw their money away, but they are just excuses for poor thinking and out-of-control emotions. Don't listen to this kind of advice, be it from writers or friends. If they don't advocate the best bets, they are advocating more and bigger losses for you.

Oh, yes, I know from long experience that there is a mania at a craps table when shooters have had good rolls. You can slice the excitement with a knife—metaphorically speaking. There is a compulsion on the part of craps players to throw out money looking for a big score because the adrenaline flows fast and furious, and the cheering reaches crescendos you hear at no other casino game. You'll hear the players shouting over the din: "Give me a Yo!" "Give me a Hard everything!" "C&E, my man!" "Boxcars, baby!" "A Horn, honey!" These shouts are really the screams of people who are thinking they can jump off the Empire State Building and make a soft landing. Squish, squash, splat!

Don't fall into the casinos' real traps for unwary players. Follow the advice in this book; it's the only smart way to play.

CHAPTER 4

Dippy, Dopey, Dumb Bets

You've read the best bets to make at a craps game in Chapter 3; now you can read about some of the worst. It is unbelievable, yet true, that most craps players have no idea how to bet at the game—and I'd guess the majority have no real idea of what the house edge is or what it means on the various bets they make at the table. What follows is not an exhaustive list, just the more common dippy, dopey, dumb bets that craps players make.

Placing $44 Inside

We all know that any bet on random rollers is a losing bet in the long run even if you win it once, twice, or many times in succession. The house edge will have its way no matter what you think, wish, or "logic" out. The casinos go to the bank with the money from players following poor advice or idiot intuitions.

Only foolish ploppies think the house edge does not work in the short run because true players who play often enough will start to be in some form of the long run—regardless of what happened today or tonight. Heed the math or face bankroll extinction. If you play frequently, even once a month, ultimately you will pay the price.

Now a very popular bet, pushed by gamblers who have no idea of true gambling, has been around a long time—you Place $44 dollars on the *inside* numbers of 5, 6, 8, and 9. This bet can be any multiple of $22 as you go up and down the scale. I am using $44 because there are now so many $10 minimum tables.

The house edge on the 5 and 9 is a *large* 4 percent. The house edge on the 6 and 8 is a bearable 1.5 percent. On the $44 inside bet, you will lose 40 cents on the 5 and 40 cents on the 9 ($10 X .04 = 40 cents), and you will lose 18 cents on the $12 placement of the 6 and 18 cents on the $12 placement of the 8 ($12 X .015 = 18 cents).

Most gamblers don't realize that the proper way to look at their bets is to subtract the house edge from each and every bet.

Most gamblers think in terms of wins and losses. "Hey, I won five sessions in a row betting the inside numbers." Yes, you did, but in truth you actually lost money when you won those sessions if you understand how the house edge really works. By the way, the casinos understand this completely. That's why they are the casinos and the players are not.

A player's wins and the losses camouflage the fact that the casino will ultimately win its edge from each and every bet as these bets start to be extended in time. The idea that somehow the "short run" can make up for the math of the long run is not applicable for players who play often in the casinos.

Yes, if you play once or twice in your lifetime, then you might escape the ravages of the house edge because you really didn't put in the time to see that edge work itself out in your particular playing days. However, here is the *big* myth: if you take thousands upon thousands upon thousands of players playing just two days of inside numbers, what do you think the end result will be?

Why, it will be close to the house edge on all the money bet during those two days. That's right, on the random game of placing those inside numbers, the totality will be just about what the math says it will be whether you personally are on the winning side of the curve or on the losing side of the curve. Most players will be on the losing side of the curve.

The only way a smart gambler should see that house edge grinding away at his or her money is to figure that every time you Place those inside numbers for $44, you are giving the house its percentage as shown above. And the more you play, the closer you will be in reality to those inside numbers' edges. Most craps players in random games are gamblers without a clue. Any "expert" who recommends this way of betting is saying it is okay to lose a lot for placing those inside numbers against random rollers.

A word to the wise—short of never playing random rollers, short of not playing the 5-Count, you are still in much better shape just betting the Pass and Come with Odds. All those combination bets are a waste of time and money.

Hedges

The most common dippy, dopey, dumb bets at the craps table are the ones called *hedge* bets. Most of these are made in order to "protect" the Pass Line bet from losing on the 2, 3, or 12. Are these ploppy bets? Yes!

Hedging is using one bet to offset another bet. Let us say you bet a $5 Pass Line bet, but you want to make sure a 2, 3, or 12 can't hurt you. So you bet the 2, 3, and 12 for $1 as an Any-Craps bet. Now you can't lose on the Pass Line. If a 7 rolls or an 11, you win your $5 on the Pass Line but lose that $1 on the Any-Craps bet. So far it sounds brilliant. You win $40 on the Pass Line (eight wins), lose $8 on the Any Craps, and you are ahead $32. If any of the craps numbers appear, which they will four times in 36 Come-Out rolls, you lose $20 on the Pass Line bet but win $28 on the Any-Craps bet—which pays 7-to-1. You are now ahead $8! Add that $8 to the $32 you won on the Pass Line, and you are ahead $40 on the Come-Out rolls! Wow! Hooray!

Now here it comes—"it" being why this is a poor way to play: There are 24 other dice combinations that can roll (4, 5, 6, 8, 9, and 10) and on *all* those rolls, on each and every one of them, you lose your $1 Any-Craps bet. Uh-oh. You lose $24! You are only ahead $16 after the Come-Out rolls.

But you are still ahead, right?

Right…except. Had you played the Pass Line without hedging, you would have won $40 minus $20, which equals an overall win of $20—$4 more than the dippy, dopey, dumb hedging system.

Lesson? Don't hedge your Come-Out rolls.

Do You Hedge on the Darkside, Then?

Let's try a popular one on the Darkside and see what happens. You place a Don't Pass bet of $20, and when the Point is 6 or 8, you Place the 6 or 8 on the Rightside for $18. If the 7 shows, you win $2 ($20 on the Don't Pass minus $18 Place bet = $2). Now, if the 6 or 8 hits, you win a $1 profit. You win $17 using this hedge system.

A major problem comes with this hedge. When the Don't Pass bet makes it through the Come-Out roll, it is a favorite in the Point Cycle of the game. Against the 6 or 8, the 7 will appear six times while the 6 (or 8) will appear only five times. The Don't Pass bettor is favored to win $20. He wins six times, which equals $120; he loses five times, which equals $100. But if you hedged, you won only $17. So Darkside hedging won $3 less!

On all—all—such Don't Pass hedges, you will win less money. On the 5 or 9, you win $6 less; on the 4 or 10, you win $9 less. Look at that again: $3 less on 6 and 8, $6 less on 5 and 9, and $9 less on 4 and 10. So much for that Don't Pass hedge.

Now someone clever, or supposedly clever, might say, "Hmmm, what if I hedge on the Come-Out roll on the Don't Pass but leave the Point without a hedge after it is up? I think I got it!"

Okay, the Come-Out roll is the cudgel for the Don't Pass bettor. If he is betting $20, he loses $160 when the 7 and 11 show eight times, but he wins only $60 when the 2 and 3 show three times. Before he gets up on a number, he is $100 in the hole.

So our Don't Pass bettor hedges on the Don't Pass during the Come-Out roll by betting on the Any-7 bet. The Any 7 pays 4-to-1. So if the shooter rolls a 2 or 3, our Don't Pass bettor wins $20 minus $5, which means he is $15 ahead. He will win a total of three times on the 2 and 3 and be ahead $45.

But the 7 is going to roll six times. So what happens? It is a wash. The Any 7 wins $20; the Don't Pass bet loses $20. Unfortunately we are still losing on the 11—a loss of $40. So we are ahead $5 ($45 - $40 = $5). But there are those other 24 rolls to worry about, along with the 12. On each and every hit of a Point number or 12, the hedger loses his $5—which adds up to $125. We are ahead $5 but now lose $125. We are down $120—instead of the $100 had we not hedged our Don't Pass bet on the Come-Out roll.

Yuck!

The Iron Cross

One of our Golden Touch instructors and a member of our Five Horsemen craps team, Jerry "Stickman," did a complete study of another betting system called the Iron Cross. This system is often sold as a surefire way to win at craps with an 83 percent winning probability. Let Stickman show you the flaw of this very popular but dippy, dopey, dumb betting system.

"Over the years there has been a lot of talk about a betting system called the Iron Cross. The attraction to this betting system is straightforward—you will get paid whenever *any* number rolls, except for the 7. Imagine, when the 4 hits, you get paid; when the 5 hits; when the 6, 8, 9, or 10 hits—you get paid! Even when craps numbers hit—you get paid! You make money on the 2, 3, 11, and 12. If you do the math, you know there are only six ways to make the 7 out of 36 possibilities, so 30 out of 36 combinations result in a win—an 83.3 percent win rate!

"The Iron Cross bet consists of Place bets on the 5, 6, and 8 coupled with a Field bet. The Field bet wins if you throw a 2, 3, 4, 9, 10, 11, or 12. When the Field bet loses, one of the Place bets wins, giving the player a small profit—except of course if that nasty 7 appears. When that happens, the player loses *all* the bets.

"I can recall many times when I had a Pass Line bet with Odds and Placed the 6 and 8 and threw number after number without collecting anything. The Iron Cross bet will definitely eliminate that situation. The only time you will not win money is when you throw the 7. Sounds like an ideal situation, doesn't it? And it would be, were it not for the fact that when you throw the 7, you lose every single bet on the board.

"The question, then, is how good [or bad] a bet is the Iron Cross? Is winning better than 83 percent of your bets a good deal or a poor betting choice?

"Let's assume we are playing a random game. Conventional wisdom [and math] states that hedge bets cause you to lose more money. If you ordinarily bet $6 on the 6 and 8, you have $12 at the mercy of a 1.52 percent house edge. Multiplying the two, you are destined to lose about 18 cents on that $12.

"Now, if you add a Place bet on the 5 for $5, you add 4 percent or 20 cents. Add still another bet on the Field for $5, and you add 5.56 percent of it, or another 27.8 cents. You have more money at risk with higher house edges, so you will lose more money—period. There is no way around that.

"But what if you ordinarily bet $12 on the 6 and 8 for a total of $24 wagered, and you would rather bet $22 on the Iron Cross? Your bets would be $6 each on the 6 and 8 and $5 each on the 5 and Field. Here you are betting slightly less money and getting many more wins than before. What is the house edge on such a scheme, and what can you expect to lose per dollar bet?

"This much we know:

"1. The 6 and 8 have a 1.52 percent house edge working on $24;

"2. The 5 has a 4 percent house edge working on $5;

"3. The Field bet has a 5.56 percent house edge working on $5.

"Intuitively, the edge on the total bet of $22 should be between 1.52 and 5.56 percent. Betting $22 on the Iron Cross carries a 3.87 percent house edge when both the 2 and 12 pay double in the Field bet. Let's check the answer to the original question. Is it better to bet $12 each on the 6 and 8 or $22 on the Iron Cross?

"Well, the 6 and 8 at $24 combined against a 1.52 percent house edge equals about 37 cents lost. The Iron Cross at $22 going against a 3.87 percent house edge equals about 85 cents lost—even though less money is at risk!

"So despite the fact that you are getting paid on 30 out of 36 rolls, the 'tax' on those winnings amounts to about 2.5 times more money. This is not a good bet. No matter how tempting it seems, prudent players will avoid it."

Other Hedges

Yes, there are other hedges, but none of them are worth much. All just give the casinos much more of your money. The wise thing for the wise player is to make the wise bets. The dippy, dopey, dumb bets should be left to the ploppies.

Trend Betting

The most popular form of dippy, dopey, dumb betting at craps concerns perceived trends in the game. The player sees the shooter hit the same number a few successive times and he thinks, *Wow! This number is hot!* and he throws out his money on the number—whichever number it is—

even if it is a number with a monstrous house edge. The belief is that such a trend will continue.

There are other trends—opposite ones. Our player hasn't seen a number in a long, long time and thinks, *Boy, that number is due to appear soon! I haven't seen it in the last half hour.*

Now all logical thought concerning randomness assures us, as the math certainly assures us, that trends in randomness are not predictable above and beyond the normal probability of a number's appearance. In short, if the 12 has a one in 36 chance on any given roll, as time goes by the appearance of the 12 will get closer and closer to its probability.

The 12 will not do it smoothly. There will be periods when the 12 comes up frequently; there will be periods when you'd think the dice can't make a 12. But the math will win out. If you think you can jump on that 12 and ride it into a mansion for you and your family—welcome to the poorhouse. That 12 isn't going to cooperate with you as you go about trend-betting. You'll just join all the other trend-betting losers.

Randomness precludes predictability in craps. Hot trends, cold trends, mixed hot and cold trends, hot tables, cold tables—you name it, and they *don't exist.*

Trends in a random game can be seen only in the past. If you could bet backward, then you'd never lose because you saw the trend already; going forward and predicting trends is totally different. Trend-bettors are big losers at craps because they will jump on bets that are totally stupid to make. Do not join their company. The only real trend that trend-betting achieves is the losing-your-money trend.

CHAPTER 5

Paying Off the Bets, or, the Moron Factor

I've got to thank my Golden Touch instructor Billy "the Kid" for saying to me, "Frank, it isn't just that craps players make really bad bets. Many don't even know how those bets get paid off by the dealers, what the order of payoffs are. Experienced players are morons in this area too. It drives the few good players insane when other players screw up the game. You need a chapter about that in your book."

I have found out through painstaking research (actually just watching hundreds of my fellow craps players at the tables) that Billy is right. Not only don't most craps players know the true house edges of bets and what those edges mean, but they have no idea of the order in which all those bets are paid off or taken by the dealers—the good bets, bad bets, and the in-between bets.

In fact, I haven't seen any articles or sections of craps books relating to this question either. I think all gambling writers have tended to assume that experienced craps players know such a thing. Evidently they don't. Keep in mind that the bets are paid off in a way that protects the casino's money from the bad guys. You'll see that the order makes sense in that light.

So here we go. Everyone should read this section and memorize it. All craps players will be better off doing so.

1. A number hits, the dealers immediately take the losing bets off the table. These losing bets are usually of the one-roll variety, although they can be Hardway bets as well.
2. The "contract" bets are paid off—meaning the Come bets—from inside out. These bets are paid off from the stickman around to the dealer.
3. Place bets are next paid off—inside out as well—from stickman to dealer.
4. Next all the Crazy Crapper bets are paid off. These are paid off on the side of the table where the dice landed. So if you are on the opposite side from where the dice landed, just be a little patient. You'll get your payoff.

Now what if a Point is made? Then the dealers deal with those Line bets first. They take the Don't Pass and then pay off the Pass Line bets. The bets are paid off from the dealers to the stickman. The stickman watches the payoffs on the side where the dice landed; the box man watches the payoffs on the side of the shooter.

Okay, so many players have no idea of the above, but these players also have no idea of when and how to bet. They merely throw their chips onto the layout and scream their bets aloud. Often this is done when the shooter is about to throw the dice (bad manners!) or when the dealer is paying off someone else's bet.

Listen to an irate Billy "the Kid" on this issue: "It drives me crazy when players throw bets out when a shooter is about to roll the dice. Don't they know the traditional rules of the game? No, they don't; they are morons, ploppies of the first order. How about when they nag the dealer about paying off their Hardways or Proposition Crazy Crapper bets? The poor dealers have to keep telling them it is not their turn to get paid yet. The players look dumbfounded. They have little idea of the fact that there is an order to the payouts. What do they think, the bets are just paid off in a random fashion? I call this the moron factor. Come on players; at least learn how to play the game properly even if you make the dumbest bets."

Billy continues: "You know how many arguments occur when players do this stupid stuff? Do you know how many other players get confused and start yelling for their payouts—out of order too? It's like craps players come into the casino and immediately lose about 50 points on their IQs. It's maddening. But if you do know how to play craps properly, you will get maddened too. I've gotten to a point where I will leave some tables because the players are driving me nuts."

Billy has his list of dos and don'ts. So here are some other things to understand about the game that too few players actually know or do:

1. Do not buy in when a shooter has the dice. Wait for the dice to be in the middle of the table.

2. Instead of buying in fully, throwing the game to a dead stop as the money is counted and the chips are placed on the layout, just place the exact amount you want to bet on the felt. If you are betting a $60 6 and 8, then put out $120 in cash and say, "$60 6 and 8!" The dealer then places your bet very quickly and the game continues at a good pace. This is important for controlled shooters who are looking to get into some kind of rhythm.

3. When your Place bet wins, you wait for your turn to be paid off and then you have the option of saying the following: "Same bet," "Press my bet" (meaning double it), "Press my bet *X* amount," "Turn my bet off," or "Take my bet down."

Billy also thinks a lot of players just don't know how much their bets pay off. "It is crazy that someone would make bets and not know what the correct payout is. How stupid can you get? If you are making a bet, then you better know how much you should get paid. It can drive you to drink listening to someone trying to get the dealers to explain to them that the bet they made is being paid off correctly. Why the heck did they make the bet in the first place if they didn't know how much it paid off?"

Now that you have read this, you should never make any of the above mistakes again. Of course, anyone who reads is probably not the person this chapter is addressed to. What that means is simple—the ploppies will always be with us, and, as Billy the Kid warns, "Beware of the moron factor!"

CHAPTER 6

The Captain's 5-Count

How do you position yourself to take advantage of hot rolls without losing a fortune betting on every single shooter and every single roll of the dice? How do you get the same amount or more in comps with less risk? The legendary Captain from Atlantic City developed a method called the 5-Count, which takes both these questions into consideration.

On our site, www.goldentouchcraps.com, is an interesting article discussing what the 5-Count can and can't do for smart craps players. One of our Five Horsemen, Skinny, has done a series of articles on the strength of the 5-Count, using University of Massachusetts mathematician Dr. Don Catlin's study of the 5-Count as his basis. The 5-Count cannot magically transform random rollers into controlled shooters—nothing can do that but practicing how to control the dice—but the 5-Count can find controlled shooters better than any other method, if those shooters are at your table. The only method better than the 5-Count is to know who the controlled shooter is in advance!

When the brilliant Captain was discovering his great 5-Count playing method, he knew he had three imperatives:

1. Reduce the number of random rolls you bet on to save your money;
2. Increase the likelihood that the shooters you do bet on will win you money;
3. Increase your comps based on *body time* as opposed to *risk time*.

The 5-Count accomplishes all three of the Captain's imperatives based on Dr. Catlin's study.

1. It eliminates almost 57 percent of the random rolls. You will be betting on only about 43 percent of the random rolls.
2. It gets you on the controlled shooters (the Captain called such players *rhythmic rollers*) at a higher frequency than *bet-all* players. If there is a controlled shooter at the table, you will be on him with the 5-Count 11 percent more often than bet-all players.
3. It increases comp value because of body time. You are usually given credit for 100 percent of the time you are at the table, but you are risking your money only 43 percent of the time. Indeed, you can get a *monetary edge* by betting this way. That means even against random rollers, with your small losses subtracted from your comps, you might still be ahead of the casino. The 5-Count also makes you look just like all those players who wait for some qualifying event to enter the game.

So what is the 5-Count? It is the method we use to decide which rollers to bet on. It starts with a Point number on the Come-Out roll (4, 5, 6, 8, 9, or 10) and ends with a Point/Box number. Throws between rolls No. 1 and No. 5 can be any number, except if the shooter sevens-out. Let's take a look at the various scenarios:

Example One: The Basics

Shooter's Roll #	Number Rolled	Count	Bet
1	7	0-count	0
2	*4	1-count	0
3	11	2-count	0
4	6	3-count	0
5	3	4-count	0
6	*8	5-Count	Betting begins

Example one is the bare-bones 5-Count. The shooter is on the Come-Out roll and rolls a 7, which is a winner but is not the start of the 5-Count because it isn't a Point number. (Remember that Point numbers are also called Box numbers.) His second roll is a 4. The 4 is a Point/Box number and is also his Point. Now he rolls an 11, the 2-count; then a 6, the 3-count; then a 3, the 4-count; and then an 8, another Point/Box number, which completes the 5-Count.

Example Two: The Holding Pattern

Shooter's Roll #	Number rolled	Count	Bet
1	11	0-count	0
2	7	0-count	0
3	*6	1-count	0
4	5	2-count	0
5	9	3-count	0
6	11	4-count	0
7	3	4-count and holding	0
8	2	4-count and holding	0
9	*10	5-Count	Betting begins

Example Two shows what happens when other than Point/Box numbers are thrown after the 4-count. This causes a *holding pattern*. Roll six, which was an 11, established the 4-count, but then the shooter rolled a 3 and then a 2—both of which are not Point/Box numbers—which causes the 5-Count not to be completed. The 4-count is holding until a Point/Box number is rolled. Finally, the shooter rolls a 10, which is a Point/Box number, and the 5-Count is completed.

Example Three: Shooter Makes Point

Shooter's Roll #	Number Rolled	Count	Bet
1	4	1-count	0
2	3	2-count	0
3	4 (point!)	3-count	0
4	7	4-count	0

Shooter's Roll #	Number Rolled	Count	Bet
5	11	4-count and holding	0
6	7	4-count and holding	0
7	11	4-count and holding	0
8	3	4-count and holding	0
9	*9	5-Count	Betting begins

Example Three shows what happens when a shooter actually makes his Point during the establishment of the 5-Count. His first roll is a 4, the 1-count; his second roll is a 3, the 2-count; and on his third roll he hits his Point, the 4, which is the 3-count. Now he is on the Come-Out again. He rolls a 7. Because it is a Come-Out roll, that 7 becomes the 4-count. Now the shooter rolls a string of non-Point/Box numbers (the 11, 7, 11, 3) before he finally hits another Point/Box number, the 9. The 5-Count is now completed.

How to Bet with the 5-Count

Now that you know how the 5-Count works, you have to decide how you are going to structure your betting. Remember that the 5-Count is the Captain's way to eliminate approximately six out of every 10 random rolls and save you a bundle of money. So how do we bet on the shooters who get through the 5-Count?

The best way is to make minimal Come bets and take the full Odds. The Odds bet is a wash between the casino and the player. If you can afford to take the Odds, do so—if you are a frequent player, the Odds bet will wind up being an even proposition between you and the casino.

Please Note: *Dice controllers should consider always taking Odds even on random rollers, because taking Odds makes you look like a regular player. Very few Lightside players don't take the Odds.*

If you go up on three Come bets of $10 each, your risk is 1.4 percent of $30, or 42 cents.

So here is one example of how to use the Come bets in our most conservative way. You will put up a Come bet after the 5-Count is completed. This placement is favorable to you because there are eight ways to win on the initial placement of the Come bet (7 and 11) and only four ways to lose (2, 3, and 12). You have a 2-to-1 edge on this placement. If the shooter makes a Point number, your bet goes up on the number, and you take Odds.

Now you place another Come bet *if you wish*. If the shooter sevens-out, you lose the bet on the number and win the bet just placed on the Come. If he rolls another Box number you go up on that number if you wish and take the Odds. If you wish to go up on a third number, you simply put out another Come bet. If the shooter has actually made his Point, then you make a Pass Line bet. We will use $10 betting units. You can translate these into your betting units.

Example Four: Come Betting

Shooter's Roll #	Number Rolled	Count	Bet
1	4	1-count	0
2	11	2-count	0
3	5	3-count	0
4	6	4-count	0
5	*8	5-Count	$10 Come
6	9	Come bet goes to 9	Take Odds on the 9 $10 Come
7	8	Come bet goes to 8	Take Odds on 8 Put up new Come bet if you wish to be on three numbers

You can also go up on the Come before the 5-Count is completed, doing so after the 3-count or 4-count, but put Odds only after the 5-Count is completed. The longer you wait, the better for your bankroll. However, many players don't feel comfortable waiting for the full 5-Count if they are going the Come-betting route. Dom and I prefer to go up after the entire 5-Count is completed.

Example Five: Place Betting

Place betting with the 5-Count is very simple. When the 5-Count is completed, you Place the 6 and/or 8. If you wish to bet on the 4 and 10 or 5 and 9, make sure these are buyable, with the vig paid *only on wins*.

Shooter's Roll #	Number Rolled	Count	Bet
1	7	0-count	0
2	8	1-count	0
3	12	2-count	0
4	6	3-count	0
5	4	4-count	0
6	2	4-count/h	0
7	*9	5-Count	Place bet the 6 and 8; buy the 4 or 10 if vig is paid on winning bets only. Be up on no more than three numbers.

That Is Yours, This Is Mine

The 5-Count is the only shooter-selection system that has been proven to work in a massive study of 200 million simulated shooters. Check out the report on our website, www.goldentouchcraps.com. It makes you look like a regular player but keeps your risk quite low.

And there is also an added benefit, which we alluded to earlier. Sometimes the 5-Count can actually give you what we call a monetary edge over the casino—even against random rollers.

What About Going Up on the Darkside Right Away?

Some players, trying to outthink the brilliant Captain's 5-Count, think that going up on the Don't Pass or Don't Come before the 5-Count is finished is a way to play almost every roll with little risk. Not so. The very moment you put that Don't Pass or Don't Come bet, the casino's edge is 8-to-3 over you because the casino will win eight times on the 7 and 11 and the Don't bettor can win only three times on the 2 and 3. So you are just giving the casino more cracks at your bankroll going up before the 5-Count is finished. In fact, going up on the Don't Pass or Don't Come right away is the same as betting on all shooters and all rolls.

If you like to play the Darkside Don'ts, then wait until the 5-Count is finished, then bet a Don't Come (or Don't Pass) and when up on a number, take full Odds. The 5-Count works the same for Darkside random players as for Lightside random players. Every player should use it.

What the 5-Count Isn't

Some ploppies mistakenly think that the Captain used the appearance percentage of the 7 to the other numbers as the foundation of the 5-Count. He wasn't looking at averages or short-term results, not at all. He was looking at the totality of the game to save us money over extended periods of time. These ploppies then state: "How stupid the Captain is. With five rolls or more before you bet, the 7 is more likely to occur."

No it isn't.

The 7 has about a 17 percent chance of occurring in a random game at any time—now and forever. There is no more likelihood of the 7 appearing on the ninth roll than on the first roll than on the 50th roll. Players who think a number is more likely to appear because it hasn't appeared in a while are mistaken. In a random game, a number does not have more of a chance to come up than its probability indicates. It takes some time to see that this is so...*but it is so.* Ploppy critics try to outthink the Captain, which is a waste of their time...and ours.

The *Exact* Math

In the above discussion of the 5-Count, I did not use fractions. However, to be precise, Professor Stewart Ethier did a mathematical study of the 5-Count against *random rollers*, and here is what he found: the 5-Count players bet on 43.5 percent of the *random rolls* and did not bet on 56.5 percent of the random rolls. He took four rollers as examples so we could see what he means.

Roller No. 1: rolls 6, 8, 11, 9, 7-out (5 rolls: 5 no-bets)

Roller No. 2: rolls 4, 4, 7, 12, 3, 7, 9, **4, 6, 6, 8, 3, 11, 7-out** (14 rolls: 7 no-bets, 7 bets)

Roller No. 3: rolls 3, 7, 6, 10, 9, 6, 2, 8, **4, 9, 2, 5, 5, 8, 7, 6, 2, 5, 7-out** (19 rolls: 8 no-bets, 11 bets)

Roller No. 4: rolls 11, 9, 7-out (3 rolls: 3 no-bets)

Roller No. 1 survives five rolls but does not achieve the 5-Count. You do not bet on Roller No. 1. Roller No. 2 survives 14 rolls, achieving the 5-Count on the seventh roll. You bet only on his last seven rolls in bold. Roller No. 3 survives 19 rolls, achieving the 5-Count on the eighth roll. You bet only on his last 11 rolls in bold. Roller No. 4 survives three rolls but does not achieve 5-Count. You do not bet on Roller No. 4.

Professor Ethier summarized what his mathematical analysis found: "In the example, you eliminate two of four rollers, or 50 percent of the random rollers. Long-term percentage is 48.6 percent. In the example, you make no bet on 23 of 41 random rolls, or 56 percent. Long-term percentage is 56.5 percent. To state the converse: in the example, you bet on two of four rollers, or 50 percent. Long-term percentage is 51.4 percent. In the example, you bet on 18 of 41 rolls, or 44 percent. Long-term percentage is 43.5 percent."

Stewart Ethier is professor of mathematics at the University of Utah and has long had an interest in craps. For example, he wrote "Improving On Bold Play at Craps" in the journal *Operations Research*.

CHAPTER 7

The Question of Credit

They have the highest house edge of any machines in the casino. In fact, no one has ever come out ahead playing them—ever. They loom in the hallways and lobbies—brightly lit machines with no conscience that neither ask for nor give quarter, or quarters for that matter. Many a player will rush to them and start pressing buttons, hoping to make a quick withdrawal. And the players pay a hefty, hefty price on these machines, because no one has ever won on them. No one has even broken even on them. Ever!

I'm not talking about your garden-variety slot or video-poker machines. I'm talking about those ATM Credit Card Advance machines, sprinkled all over casino creation, that charge unconscionable interest rates of upward of 3 percent on a single withdrawal, often adding fees of up to and over 10 percent of the total money withdrawn. (Fees? Fees? Isn't the interest the fee?) Casino players who use these machines are making the dumbest possible move they can make—dumber than splitting 10s at blackjack, dumber than betting Big Red at craps, and dumber than playing Sic Bo.

What's worse, using those currency-sucking monsters is so unnecessary! In fact, no smart casino player should ever give them a look much less a mention when right in the casino sits a flesh-and-blood human being who will give you money, who *wants* to give you money, whose *job* is to give you money—money for free, with no interest and no fees—and he or she will also give you anywhere from seven to 45 days to pay it all back, depending on how much you borrow. Now, casino players can't ask for anything better than that other than a win the very next time they play. Yes, I am talking about casino credit.

Every casino has a special credit department whose sole reason for existing is to give away money. (Okay, let's not be naïve. They give it away in the hopes that you'll lose it in the casino. But that's so obvious I don't have to say that, do I?) The upsides to getting casino credit are numerous and obvious. The downsides are small and even more obvious.

The first benefit to a casino credit line is that you don't have to carry wads of cash when you travel by car, bus, train, or plane to your favorite casino venue. The second benefit to credit is that the money you have in your gambling bank account can sit there for up to six weeks gaining interest before you have to pay back the casino what you owe it. (You do have a gambling bank account, don't you? Money tucked aside that is used strictly for playing purposes? If not, start one now, even before you get credit.) If you win, you pay back your marker immediately. If you lose, the casino takes it out of your account. Contrast this with those awful credit-card-advance machines that immediately dock your account and rip their pound of interest flesh from your economic carcass as well.

A third, generally unspoken, unpublicized benefit to getting casino credit has to do with how you're perceived after you have, use, and pay back a credit line. Although I could get no casino executives to state for the record that "credit players" are viewed in a more favorable light than "money players," the fact is that they are. The casino assumes that credit players are willing to lose the amount of their credit line (which may or may not be true). A simple mind experiment can prove this.

Two players enter a game and both cash in for $1,000. Joe gives cash, and Joan takes out a $1,000 marker against her credit line of $10,000. Both Joe and Joan now lose their $1,000 in short order. Who would you bet on to go for a second $1,000—Joe, the cash player, or Joan with the $10,000 line? I pick Joan because I know (or think I know) that she has $10,000 in play money she's willing to gamble. I have no idea how much Joe has. For all I know, that $1,000 was for his kid's braces and he's in a powerful lot of trouble when his wife, Big Gert, finds out that little Lulu is still going to resemble Bugs Bunny when she hits junior high next year.

Casinos also think that credit players are more motivated players. In fact, this is probably true. My experience tells me that credit players tend to come to casinos more frequently than other players. Casinos like that.

Interestingly enough, between 4 and 10 percent of table-game players have established credit lines, and anywhere from 15 to 30 percent of the table-game drop, in Atlantic City at least, comes from these players. Casinos that attract big action tend to have more credit players than casinos that attract small to moderate action.

Even more interesting, only about 1 to 2 percent of slot players have established credit. Why so few? Because many slot players don't know that credit exists for them as well. But it does. In the future you are going to see a big push to get credit for slot players from the casinos.

How do you get that credit line? Easy! Just call your favorite casino and ask it to send you a credit application. Most casinos in a given venue use similar forms. In Vegas, the forms tend to be modest. They'll ask for your name, address, phone number, social security number, and the bank account you'll use for your credit line.

On the other hand, Atlantic City desires more information. Most casinos there will want to know your full name, address, phone number, where you work or if you're self-employed, your yearly income, your outstanding indebtedness, the name of your bank, and the account you want to write your markers against. Some Atlantic City casinos will go one step further and ask to know your net worth.

You'll then sign a release form that will allow the casino's creditcheckers to make sure you have enough money in the specified account to pay back the amount of the credit you're requesting. This is an important item. When you apply, make sure you have more than enough in one account to fully cover the entire line of credit you want.

The casinos will then do a credit check to make sure you're a good risk. The whole process takes about a week.

What are your chances of being turned down?

Stated one casino credit manager who wished to remain nameless: "I'd say that approximately three-fourths of the people who ask for credit get it. The only area where there might be some difference of opinion between us and the patron is on how much credit we should give. Firsttime credit applications are often for sums that we feel might be a little too high. If someone asks for $10,000, we might say, 'Let us give you $5,000, and we can readjust that figure in the future.' The people we turn down are usually people who just have a history of not paying their bills.

Remember, we're giving a loan for up to six weeks with no interest, and we want to make sure we're going to get that money back."

What percentage of the money borrowed by players is not returned? The figure varies from casino to casino and state to state and is a closely guarded secret, but I estimate that less than 3 percent of the total money borrowed by credit players is not paid back in a timely fashion.

After your credit is approved, your next trip to the casino will probably see you take out your first *marker*. A marker is a promissory note that can be drawn directly against your bank account. In fact, it looks like an oversized generic check, which is exactly what it is.

Once you're at the table of your choice, you'll say to the dealer, "I'd like to take out a marker, please." The floor person will be called over, and he or she will ask you, "For how much?" Once you tell the floor person how much you want, you'll probably be asked for your player's card. In such a case, the casino floor person will fill out most of the information on a marker form and ask you to sign it. If you don't hand in a player's card, or if the casino is very busy, the floor person will give you a small sheet of paper where you'll write your name, address, phone number, the name of your bank, and how much you want to take out. Then you'll sign your name.

It usually takes two to five minutes for the marker to arrive. When it does, you'll sign it, the floor person will put it on the table, and the dealer will count out the appropriate number of chips (credit players in Las Vegas and some other venues will get the chips even before the marker arrives). Slot players will usually do their transactions at the cashier's cage.

That's it. You're in the game. It's a lot faster than the ATMs and a lot more economical.

How and when you pay back your marker is a product of how you did at the tables. It is customary to pay back all the money you borrowed at the end of your trip if you won. If you don't pay after a winning stay, it is considered a very bad thing, called *walking with the chips*. Casinos frown upon players who "walk" because they feel (rightly) that not only have you won money from them at the tables (fair and square), but you've taken a loan that now will get you interest for however long it sits in your account before the marker is redeemed (unfair and not square).

Some high-rolling, self-employed business people have attempted to use their casino credit lines as short-term business loans at no interest. If casinos discover you doing this, they will not only cut off your credit, they'll say bad things about you behind your back and you won't get credit at other casinos when the word gets out that you're a "chip walker." So never walk with the chips.

How much time do casinos give you to pay the piper? If you borrowed up to $1,000, you usually have seven days to pay up. If you borrowed between $1,001 and $5,000, you usually have 14 days; and if you borrowed $5,001 or more, you have between 30 and 45 days. Each state will have slightly different timetables, but the above is representative.

But what if you borrowed $1,001 and lost only (only?) $500 of it? Here you have a choice. You can pay back the $500 that is left and wait the two weeks for the casino to collect the rest, or you can simply write a check for the other $500 on the spot. (Some casinos want first-time-credit players to do this until it is firmly established that they are not risks.)

I know why players would want to get credit, but why would casinos want to give it? Some players believe that casinos give out credit as a part of a plot to get them to play for bigger money than they can afford and for longer periods of time than they should. Although this is not the reason casinos give out credit, it is a pitfall that players should be aware of and is the one big downside to casino credit. Your credit line should be in keeping with your budget. Don't take out a $10,000 credit line if you are a $5 player with a gambling bankroll of $500. The temptation to plunge into your credit line for more money might just prove too great to resist on a bad day or night.

Casinos give out credit as a customer service, a loyalty inducer, and a convenience. Players should be aware that markers are money in the bank—your bank—and although they are interest free, they aren't obligation free. Should you lose in the casino, you will be expected to pay back what you borrowed. Make sure you can afford to do so.

But given the other alternatives of carrying wads of cash and/or borrowing from those bent-nosed ATM loan sharks in the lobby, establishing casino credit is the intelligent way to go.

CHAPTER 8

Some Frequently Asked Questions

ere are some frequently asked questions about the *random* game of craps. These questions might have answers you weren't expecting. At the end of the book are questions pertaining to controlled shooting and advantage play at craps.

Question: *Some people say there are two aspects to the basic game of craps. What are they?*

Answer: There is the Come-Out aspect, where the Pass Line bettor is hoping for a 7 or 11 and not the 2, 3, or 12 and where the Don't Pass bettor is hoping for a 2 or 3 and not a 7 or 11. That's part one. Part two is the Point Cycle where the shooter must make a Point before the 7 shows for the Pass Line bet to win. Combining parts one and two, which you must ultimately do, the house edge is 1.41 percent on the Pass Line and 1.36 (or 1.4) percent on the Don't Pass.

Question: *Can you bet only one side of the game at a time? If you are betting the Lightside, do you have to have all your bets on the Lightside and not be able to bet the Darkside?*

Answer: No, you can have some Rightside bets up and some Darkside bets up at the same time. Doing so doesn't reduce the house edge, but there is no restriction on which side of the game you can bet at the same time.

Question: *What about only betting on one number? Is that stupid to do? Can't you miss out on big rolls this way?*

Answer: After the 5-Count, going up on only one number is a smart way to play. Yes, if someone has a big roll, you might not hit very often, but when those cold rolls occur you will lose only one bet. The bottom line is this—it doesn't matter! You will lose the house edge on the bets you make, whether you experience a hot roll, a cold roll, or a mediocre roll this moment. You save yourself money by betting on fewer rolls; simple as that. You get to stretch out your money over time just betting one bet.

Question: *Can players* not *shoot the dice?*

Answer: Players don't have to shoot the dice. They can pass up their turn if they wish—which is called *passing the dice*. But one of the thrills of the game is taking those dice in your hand and trying to beat the house.

Question: *How come you can't move the dice from one hand to the other in the air? Why is it you can do things with only one hand?*

Answer: It is much easier to substitute fixed dice into a game when you can move dice from hand to hand above the table. Making players use one hand helps to thwart this practice. Obviously, really skilled cheats can get around even this rule.

Question: *What is a crossroader? What is a railbird?*

Answer: A crossroader is a cheat or criminal. A railbird is a person who stands next to you at a craps table and tries to steal your chips from your rail. When you aren't protecting them or when you are shooting, the railbird scoops a couple up. The worst railbird I ever heard about was a man from Greece at Bally's in Vegas—this was in the 1980s. He was stealing black chips ($100) from a gentleman next to him and stuffing the chips into his pants. He was caught. The police were called in, and he was taken down to the station and told to drop his pants. Nothing. No chips. Then it dawned on the police where the railbird was stuffing the black chips he had stolen. Guess those black chips must have blended in up there.

Question: *What is an independent trial game?*

Answer: Each decision is independent and is not influenced by any decisions that occurred in the past. A popular way to say this is, "The dice have no memory." In craps you could have the 12 come up five times in a row, and the odds of it coming up a sixth time are the same as they were for it coming up the first, second, third, fourth, and fifth time. What happened before has nothing to do with what will happen now. Craps is a random game. There will be streaks, but they are not predictable. If you could bet backward on what just happened, then all streaks are predictable, but we can't bet backward. We can only go forward. There is no predictability going forward. Most casino players just can't seem to get this through their heads. This has hurt more gamblers than you can imagine. Many gambling writers keep pushing this idea to the detriment of those poor souls who read such scribblings.

Question: *What is a dependent trial game?*

Answer: In blackjack, if all the aces come out of the deck, then there will be no blackjacks. What happens now is dependent on what happened in the past. That's what makes card-counting possible. You keep track of what has just happened to make your betting and playing decisions on the next hand. In a random game of craps, this is not so.

Question: *Is dice control an independent or a dependent trial game?*

Answer: That depends. If you are dealing with a skilled dice controller, he is changing the probabilities of the game. So the past performance of such skill definitely tells you something about the future.

Question: *Are casino dice really not biased? Shouldn't there be some imperfections in them? Couldn't the casinos put in fixed dice too?*

Answer: They are unbiased, and each side is the same as all the other sides. The pips do not weigh any more than the plain areas. So the six-pip side weighs the same as the one-pip side. Sure, casinos could put in fixed dice, but what would they be fixed for? The casino has small to hefty edges on all the bets, so why take a chance on being caught? Also, if the 7 were the fixed number, that 2-to-1 edge on the Come-Out roll would be more than enough to make the casino sweat buckets. Also, it is likely that doey-don't players might have a field day as well. No, casinos would be stupid to cheat—as players would be stupid to cheat. Cheating isn't worth the risks.

Question: *What is a tub craps table?*

Answer: You take a bath as you play. Just kidding. It is a very small table about the size of a bathtub, handled by one dealer, with players seated around it. You won't find many of these in the casinos. Most craps players don't feel the tubs give them the real feel of the game.

Question: *How come shooters say they want the same dice when one die goes off the table? If the game is random does it make a difference?*

Answer: It's a harmless superstition based on the idea that because he hasn't sevened-out yet, the dice must be doing the shooter some good service. He is afraid that if the dice get changed, the 7 will show up. And it will—about 17 percent of the time! (One 7 in six rolls = 16.67 percent!)

Question: What *are some of the other superstitions of craps? Do any of them have any truth?*

Answer: The most popular superstitions at the game of craps are the following ones. Keep in mind that individuals add their own superstitions too, so you might hear someone yelling some incoherent thing at the table, which to him will ward off the coming of the ominous 7 or bring it on if he is a Darkside player.

Popular Craps Superstitions:

1. *When the dice hit someone's hand, the roll will be a 7.* Not so. In a random game, the 7 comes up 16.67 percent of the time, whether the dice hit another player's hand or his head or the back wall. But it is considered impolite to hang your hands over the table. Is there truth to this myth? For controlled shooters, yes, there is. Dice that hit the hands of another player will be random even though a controlled shooter is shooting. So keep your hands to yourself.

2. *Late bets thrown onto the layout or to the stickman after the shooter has been passed the dice will bring out the 7.* No, these bets will only anger the shooter and everyone else at the table. Controlled shooters could lose their concentration in these cases, so for them, the late bets can be a distraction. You don't want to be distracted if you are a controlled shooter.

3. *If a good shooter is throwing the dice, throwing money on the table to buy in will make the 7 appear.* No, it won't. But it will slow down the game and annoy everyone, as the box person has to stop the game to count the money and give the player his chips. By the way, you want to take a controlled shooter out of his rolling zone? Stop the game dead by buying in when he is rolling.

4. *Never speak to or touch someone who is having a good roll.* This is manners again. Let the shooter shoot. You can cheer if you want, but don't slap the shooter on the back or rub his arm or talk up his nose with your beer breath. If you are dealing with a controlled shooter, pounding his back and shouting up his nose or in his ear is not a good thing. Think of a baseball hitter with a fan standing next to him yelling, screaming, and pounding. We doubt the player will hit the ball.

5. *Never mention the number 7 when a shooter is shooting.* This has no real effect except that players fear the very word *seven* while the game is in progress. Some players call the 7 "it"; some players call the 7 "the devil"; some call the 7 "Satan's ass." There are many more. Take your pick. Again, not saying "seven" is considered proper manners at the craps table. Some Darkside Don't players love to shout out the word "seven" while the shooter is throwing. These Darksiders evidently do not fear their imminent death when they do this.

6. *A woman who has never shot the dice before will have a good roll the first time she shoots the dice.* Men believe this for sure. It is called the *Virgin Principle.* Hey, Luck is a lady tonight, right?

7. *A man who has never shot the dice before will have a bad roll.* It's like the first time with sex; most men just don't know what they are doing, and the "roll" ends pretty quickly. Neither the Virgin Principle nor the *Testes Tanking* theory has any validity.

8. *Never open a table when you are alone or play when you are alone at a table.* Very few craps players like to play alone at the table. Many controlled shooters do, in fact, prefer to play alone or with one or two other people. I guess for the average player, being alone makes them feel lonely; they like the camaraderie of other players. Craps is a communal game.

9. *A Darkside player at the table will increase the appearance of the 7.* Not so, but these players really get to many Lightside players. Most Lightsiders might not even allow a friendship between themselves and a Darksider—their rivalry is worse than the New York Yankees and Boston Red Sox.

10. *If the dealer passes the dice to you with the 7 showing, then the 7 will be rolled soon.* Because the 7 comes up about 17 percent of the

time, any idea will show some validity because it will happen enough times to make it seem real. I could say, "If you touch your nose while a shooter is rolling, the 7 will come up." That has as much of a chance of being accurate as the dealer passing you the dice with the 7 showing.

11. *Counting your chips while a shooter is rolling will bring on the 7.* Hopefully you actually have some chips to count! Unless the dice have eyes, they can't say to themselves, "That creep is counting his chips. Okay, bub, a 7 is coming right now!"

12. *There is no way to beat the game of craps.* For random rollers throwing out all manner of stupid bets, yes, this is true. Even the best bets will lose over time for random rollers. That's just the way it is. The only way to beat the game of craps is to become a Golden Touch Craps controlled shooter.

Question: *Do all casinos have the same rules and payouts for craps?*

Answer: Unfortunately, no they don't. Ignoring the various differences in Odds bets, payouts can be different for some of the Crazy Crapper bets as well—either for the better (meaning less bad) or for the worse (meaning more bad). Some casinos want you to bet the table minimum for those same Crazy Crapper bets; other casinos allow $1 on such bets. Same goes for the Field bet. All casinos want you to hit the back wall and not take several decades to throw the dice. Some casinos don't allow setting the dice; these casinos are run by drooling knuckle-dragging executives. Some layouts have circles for Hop bets; most do not. Some layouts have the Big 6 and the Big 8; most do not.

Question: *Are all craps tables the same? Length, height, width?*

Answer: No. Some tables are 10 feet long (a few); some are 12 feet long; some are 14 feet long; some are 16 feet long (a few). Some tables have hard surfaces, some have what we call traditional surfaces, some are bouncy, and some are super bouncy. The layouts come in various fabrics; also their colors can be quite different—some vibrant, some dull. Some tables have seats for two box people. The width of tables can differ too. When you play, just note how close or far the Pass Line is from you, and that will usually give you some idea of the width of the table. The height of the tables can be quite different too; some tables are so high that shorter players have to get on their toes to shoot the dice. Some tables are shorter. The only thing that seems to be relatively consistent is the height of the layout from the floor—usually about 28 inches, give or take.

Question: *Is online craps the same as casino craps?*

Answer: If the game is random, the game is random—either online or in the casino. You do miss out on the cheering and moaning of the other players, but the results will over time be just like the random casino game. However, you can't control the dice in an online game, so you are just playing into the house's edge with every bet.

Question: *Craps has been called a man's game. Is this true?*

Answer: Yes, it is, if you go by total numbers. There are far more men who play craps than women—about 90–95 percent to 5–10 percent respectively. However, these numbers actually mean that women are getting involved in craps more than they did in the past when it was almost impossible to find them at the tables other than as companions of their male escorts. We have found that in Golden Touch dice control the women are better natural shooters than most of the men.

Question: *I've heard the term "natural" at craps. What does that mean?*

Answer: The 7 or 11 are the naturals on the Come-Out roll, just like a two-card 21 is a natural at blackjack and a 9 is a natural at baccarat. It means an instant winner.

Question: *I have a friend who had an interesting experience playing craps at a small casino in Wisconsin that I would like to share with you. This casino opens its one craps table only on weekends. Because it is the only craps table in the area, the rules are somewhat harsh with 2X Odds. It is a $5 table. Anyhow, my friend was doing well that evening with Pass and Come bets and full Odds. By 1:20 AM he had all the numbers covered with the Pass Line and Come bets. He had "built his house" as he says and was having a good session. The casino closing time is 2:00 in the morning.*

The pit boss stepped up to the table and said, "Three more rolls." My friend asked him what he was talking about. The pit boss replied that the table was closing after three more dice rolls. My friend said that the table will close when the devil shows up. Nevertheless, the next three rolls had no seven-out or win on the Pass Line, but the table closed and all my friend's bets—Pass and all the Come bets with Odds—were returned to him.

If Pass Line and Come bets are contract *bets that the player cannot take down under any circumstances, does the casino have the right to take these bets down?*

Answer: Well, contract bets (bets you can't take down or call off) aren't like contracts in the real world. They are just the rules of the game, but the casinos can change those rules if they wish. There have been times when I have had my bets returned, Pass and Come with Odds, because something happened at a table (once a guy got sick all over everything—truly disgusting). Next time your friend (or you) is at the table and there are three rolls left—take all the Odds down and put up a monster Come bet on that last roll. You have a 2-to-1 edge at that moment, because there will be no number established where the edge would then swing back to the casino. You'll win on the 7 and 11 with eight possible ways to hit them and only four ways to lose. It's a great bet. In fact, go there every night and make that bet!

Question: *I have a question on bets with big house edges, like the Field bet and the Hardways. If I am betting black on the Pass Line (with 5X Odds) and I play the Hardways for five bucks, how is it that bad? The house edge on the Pass Line for a $600 bet is 0.3 percent, which is two bucks, and the house edge for a Hardway for five bucks is 11 percent or 55 cents; why is it so bad?*

Answer: Hardways being good bets? Or not "bad" bets? Let me answer your question by way of analogy.

In some pig-vig casinos, you can buy the 4 or 10 for $35, paying the $1 vig up front. The house edge is 2.8 percent on this bet. However, if you put out $35 for the 4 *and* $35 for the 10 at the same time, the house will collect *$3* for the bets. Now, how big a deal is that one extra dollar? The casinos that do this are multimillion-dollar businesses. How important is one single, stinking dollar to these people?

But that dollar is important because it adds up. So your loss of 55 cents is cumulative—and I'll bet you bet more than one Hardway at a time. Why do that? If you feel compelled to bet an extra $5 or $10 or more on Hardways, then put your money on the Pass Line and face a much smaller house edge—a much, much, much smaller house edge.

Those smaller cents make a lot more sense to me. Hey, if that one extra dollar is good for the casinos, then saving 55 cents should be good for you!

Question: *While playing craps at one Atlantic City casino on a Friday evening, I placed the 6 and 8 and told the dealer to piggy-back an extra dollar on each bet for the dealers. I managed to hit a few of each before sevening-out. The dealers were appreciative. The very next afternoon in the same casino when I asked to set up the same bets, it caused quite a stir. Both the box person and pit boss stepped in and said that bets could "only be placed for the dealers" (which meant that they would be taken down on a win) and could not ride on top of my bet. One of them made some allusion to it being against the Casino Control Commission's rules. I said that I'd been allowed to make such a bet in their casino the night before—but it was no-go.*

When the box man added the comment that he wasn't about to risk his job for a dollar tip, I decided not to push it. Of course it soured the feeling at the table, and I left shortly thereafter. So what's the story? I know that you often suggest this very arrangement, and I've not had it questioned when using it elsewhere.

Answer: It's your bet when you put it on top, and you can decide what you want to do with that dollar when it wins. You can keep it or give it to the dealers. You could have just said to the pit boss, "Fine, that dollar is my bet now." The box person and the pit boss are completely wrong, and there is no Casino Control Commission ruling on how you can tip. These guys were either ploppies or deliberately lying to you. (Why? I have no idea.) You could have taken the tip down and said, "I like to tip the dealers all the time, but I like to tip them the way I like to tip them. Take the tip down."

The box person who said he wouldn't risk his job for a $1 tip should be suspended for being an idiot for not knowing these bets are perfectly legitimate. He should also have his mouth duct-taped for uttering such an imbecility to a player who tips! I am sure the dealers think this guy is a jerk of the first order.

Question: *I have purchased some dice from an Internet dice store and noticed something funny about one of them. I am practicing the Hardways Set, so I place the 5s on top and the 3s toward me. I noticed that one of them has the spots on the 3-pip side that start in the upper right instead of the upper left. Wouldn't this make a mess of the 3-V set?*

Answer: There are two types of dice used by the casinos. It seems to me you got one of each from this craps store. The most common dice set with the 3-V on top will have the 3s in a V shape with the point of the V pointing to you, a 5-spot on the left, and the 1-spot on the right facing you. The other set will not have that. It will have the 2-spot on the left and the 6-spot on the right. Turn the dice into a pyramid and that 5:1 now comes up, with the base of the pyramid facing you. Different casinos use different dice—usually the first kind, which is Type A—but some casinos use the second kind, Type B, and a minority of casinos will alternate both types. They just don't mix and match as you did. Let us recommend that you get new casino dice to practice with. Go here for more information: www.goldentouchcraps.com/dice.shtml.

Question: *Is it better to carry cash or get credit to take out markers?*

Answer: Depends. If you are staying at a casino or you play a casino quite often, then getting credit is probably a good idea. Walking around with wallets, pockets, or purses full of money isn't that great of an idea. Even in the high-class casinos, thieves are hunting those wallets and what's in those pockets and purses. The reverse is also worth thinking about. If you are a controlled shooter and you are playing incognito, obviously you don't want credit because then your name will be known. I guess it boils down to a personal decision. Dom and I have credit at some places we play and no credit at other places we play.

Question: *Do casinos use shills at craps?*

Answer: Shills play games to encourage other players to join in. You probably won't find these casino employees anymore at craps, although they are still used somewhat in poker.

CHAPTER 9

The Greatest Random Roll in History

ince 1940, there have been only four verified, witnessed shooters who have rolled 100 or more numbers before sevening-out. The Captain rolled 100 numbers in 2004 and 147 numbers in 2005, Stanley Fujitake rolled 118 numbers in 1989, and Pat DeMauro rolled 154 numbers in 2009—the all-time record.

Although both Fujitake's and DeMauro's achievements came from random throws; the Captain's two 100-plus rolls came from controlled throws.

Here is Pat's story:

She Had The Golden Touch

The odds of getting a royal flush in Texas Hold'em poker are 649,738-to-1. The odds of being struck by lightning in a single year are 700,000-to-1. The odds of dying in a plane crash are 11,000,000-to-1. The average state lottery player faces odds of 35,000,000- to 50,000,000-to-1. The Megabucks slot-machine jackpot comes in at about 50,000,000-to-1. The Mega Millions lottery has about 150,000,000-to-1 odds. And the odds of winning the Powerball jackpot are 195,249,053-to-1.

So when Pat DeMauro stepped to the craps table at Borgata Casino in Atlantic City on May 23, 2009, she had no idea that she would do the gambling equivalent of walking on water—and this was only her second turn with the dice in her life.

After four hours and 18 minutes of rolling those bones, Pat DeMauro hit 154 numbers before sevening-out. Now hold your breath, because her accomplishment, according to mathematics professor Stewart Ethier, editor of *Optimal Play: Mathematical Studies of Games and Gambling*, was one in 5.59 billion. Make sure you spell that as one in 5.59 B-I-L-L-I-O-N.

Pat beat the two all-time craps records of the last 70 years (records that we know about, anyway)—Stanley Fujitake's formerly longest roll of three hours and six minutes (118 numbers) in 1989 and the Captain's roll of 147 numbers in 2005. Think of the billions of craps rolls during the last 70 years, and what Pat DeMauro accomplished boggles the mind and the math.

And it came out of nowhere, like a barrel full of lightning strikes.

On that night, Pat DeMauro and her good friend John Capra decided to give craps a whirl with their last $100. "We figured we were staying for a few days, and we didn't want to lose too much. It had been a tough night for both of us, so we figured we'd team up and play $100, and if we lost it we would get something to eat and then go to bed."

According to John, "Pat had been playing slots, and I had been playing three-card poker. I was down about $700, and I didn't want to take a beating in one night, so I told Pat to come to the craps table with me and roll and win us some money. She had rolled once before, several months before this. I was looking for Lady Luck."

He found Lady Luck at a $10 craps table, and luck's name was Pat.

"We each put down Pass Line bets of $20," said Pat, "while the man to the right of the stickman took the dice. There were just four people at the table. He established his point and sevened-out right away. We were down $40."

"We didn't take Odds," said John. "Because we wanted a couple of turns with the dice."

The dice were passed to John. He passed the dice over to Pat. "You shoot," he said. "If we lose now, we call it a night."

Pat took the dice and established her point. "I was feeling awkward," she said. "I was uncomfortable. John just told me to relax, throw the dice down the middle of the table and hit the back wall, and not to think of anything else. He'd handle all the betting from this point on."

"I put all of our money on the table now," stated John. "This was it. If she could hit the Point, we were in the game. If not, we were done for the night."

In a couple of rolls Pat did hit her Point. And that started the greatest roll of all time. Pat soon recognized a change in her feelings as well. "After about 12 rolls I started to feel a kind of momentum. I was getting in a zone. I wasn't nervous at all. I just threw the dice down the middle of the table and hit the back wall."

"Pat started to rub her hands before each throw," added John.

"I just kind of got into that habit, and I just kept doing it," laughed Pat. "That became a part of my form. Rub my hands, throw the dice. Rub my hands, throw the dice. I didn't deviate from that."

Within 45 minutes, the table was jammed with players. John explained, "The table had at least 18 people on it; they were pressed in sideways. People were even pushing me to get onto the table. Some of the other players yelled not to disrupt the shooter as players tried to force their way next to her. Not disturbing the shooter is a tradition in craps. Everyone knew a good roll was happening with all the cheering, and many, many players wanted to get in on it."

"Within an hour and a half, a huge crowd started to gather behind the players at the table," said Pat. "I just didn't bother looking at the people behind the players. I would have become distracted. By this time I was in like a dream world."

Most of the players at the table were small bettors, buying in for between $100 and $200. There were several green-chip players but no high rollers. Across from Pat at the other end of the table were three young Asian women just learning the game. "That slowed things down somewhat," said John.

But no epic roll goes swimmingly at every moment in time. One new dealer found it difficult to make the payouts. "He would screw up," said John. "He'd pay the wrong players, and then we'd have to have that straightened out. That took a lot of time."

By the two-hour mark, the layout was totally covered with bets. John explained how the game started to grind down almost to a halt. "With each number she rolled, players increased their bets, and more money was thrown into the middle for the Proposition [Crazy Crapper] bets too. It was really slow by now. But it didn't affect Pat at all. At one point I yelled out, 'Come on, Patsy!' and everyone at the table picked up the chant."

"I remember hearing the 'Come on Patsy!' chant with each roll," said Pat. "It was like being at a ballgame. People playing in the other pits were standing up to see what was happening."

One energetic guy in a Yankees hat and T-shirt became the self-designated announcer of the table. He'd shout out the numbers and do commentary. John said, "Even when Pat's dice hit someone's hand or bounced off the table, she never sevened-out even though superstitious players at the table called off their bets. As the Yankees guy saw that nothing could stop her from hitting numbers, he yelled, 'You are bulletproof!' And her roll continued. It's funny. I am a Red Sox fan, and he is a Yankees fan, but I told him, 'We are on the same team tonight!' He laughed and agreed."

By the three-hour mark, some of the bigger bettors were wagering black and even purple chips. The game slowed even more because many of the players were now throwing out Hop bets, and all of the 18 players were pressing their bets and betting on almost every number.

"What is really weird," said John. "Pat maybe hit four or five Points during the whole roll. She rolled maybe two or three 7s during her Come-Out rolls. She just rolled the other numbers over and over again. The dealers were making some money too. Many of the players were tipping them."

In addition to that, another weird betting pattern existed. "No one," said John, "and I mean *no one* made Come bets. From the very beginning everyone was a Place bettor. I've never seen that before, and I have been playing craps for 40 years."

Of course, the Borgata executives streamed down in force to observe the game. "They were all friendly," said Pat, "except for one guy who was very stern. He took the dice and examined them. I don't think he ever smiled."

After the four-hour mark, one executive was heard to exclaim, "This must be some kind of record." Suits were on the phones and scurrying in the pit by this time.

And then, as always happens in the game of craps, the dreaded 7 was rolled. "I couldn't see the number, the table was so long," stated Pat, "but I heard the stickman shout out, 'Seven out! Take the line, pay the don'ts.'

Everything went dead for about five seconds. No sound. Just silence, like the end of the world. Then the table exploded into applause."

"It was like a standing ovation at a Broadway show," said John. "It seemed to go on forever."

Because John had been doing all the betting, except for Pat's Pass Line bet, Pat stepped back from the table to take a breath, and then the casino executives, with their public-relations vanguard and their videographers along with several security guards surrounded her. "They had Dom Perignon champagne for me. Then they whisked me away to the high-roller pit. I got to tell you I was exhausted and confused with all the attention. They handed me a [release] paper to sign, which I did."

The Borgata executives knew a good thing when they saw it. After Pat signed the paper, Borgata's publicity machine went into high gear telling the media world of her monumental achievement.

I received urgent calls from the *Wall Street Journal*, *Time* magazine, and the *Newark Star Ledger* asking me to comment on Pat's amazing night. My first word was always "historical," then "the greatest roll in craps history."

John summed up his thoughts: "Pat's roll made several high rollers about $30,000 each. There were several other players who made in the teens. According to a Borgata executive, the casino lost about $185,000. He told me that if there had been some really high rollers at the table, Borgata would have dropped between $2 and 3 million. But it wasn't that kind of table. It was mostly small bettors and some brand-new players who had to be helped along. Still, it was fun."

So what does Pat DeMauro attribute her world-record roll to? "I had positive energy. I was relaxed. And I was lucky."

CHAPTER 10

Dice Control: The Only Way to Beat Craps

You'll learn all the elements of dice control from the upcoming chapters. Practice, develop your throw, and you could become one of the select craps players who can actually beat the game. It can be done.

***

Most players who have read about craps probably know who Dominator is. Aside from being the world's greatest dice controller, he is the codirector of Golden Touch Craps dice-control classes and a partner in Golden Touch sports-betting service and our blackjack, poker, and video-poker advantage-play classes. But very few people know much about his story. Because Dominator is working with me on this book and because I have spent time in many of my books writing about myself (a topic that fascinates me), here is a short autobiography of the Dominator.

I come from a family of Italian immigrants. As a child I was taught that the only way to succeed was through education, but I had this gambler's streak in me. Actually the focus on education by my parents instilled in me a desire to study, practice, and learn from people as much as I could. I finished college and then went into business for myself. I always loved to gamble, but I would gamble only on games that I had a chance of winning with skill.

Back in the fifth grade I would pitch nickels against the gym wall with my friends. You won if you could land your nickel closest to the wall. This is where my throwing touch, what I now call my Golden Touch, was first honed. I would stay after school and practice throwing against that gym wall until the gym teacher would kick me out, and then I would practice against my garage wall at home. I was an avid baseball player as a kid, practicing baseball for hours with my cousin Jim. Then at night I would practice flipping baseball cards. It got to a point where none of my friends would flip cards with me or pitch nickels with me. Unlike casinos, my friends didn't have an inexhaustible bankroll to spend on more nickels and more baseball cards.

The first craps game that I ever played was in the back room of a men's club when I was about 18 years old. I was standing at the table with a friend, watching the game, when my friend took $10 from me. He threw it on the table, said something at the guy with the stick, and I lost my $10 in a split second! I said to myself never again would I gamble on a game where I didn't have an edge.

I received a math degree and I have a fairly good memory. I wanted to learn how to beat the casinos, so I decided to learn how to count cards at blackjack and shuffle track. I read many books on both subjects and decided to hit the casinos in Atlantic City once every three months. I did this until 1997, when craps became my main game as the game of blackjack was getting harder to beat with the advent of shuffle machines and bad games. I had read Frank Scoblete's early craps books and articles, and I knew that there must be a way to learn how to control the dice. I was fascinated by the Captain, whom I have now talked to, and I wanted to learn what was then called "rhythmic rolling."

Although Frank is the main craps writer in the country and his books and articles are largely responsible for the advent of controlled shooting in the casinos, he was not teaching seminars. He was just doing in the casinos what I wanted to do—actually winning at the game of craps! His teacher had been the Captain. Of course, I didn't know him in the mid-1990s. To me, Frank was and still is the star of gambling writers.

But his books had affected more players than just me. And one [systems seller] saw rhythmic rolling as a way to make some serious cash. The very first seminar offered in dice control was PARR, created by controversial systems seller Jerry Patterson in the mid-1990s. Patterson knew a good thing when he read it, and he had obviously read Frank's works, for he changed the Captain's term "rhythmic rolling" to "rhythm rolling" and dubbed his course Patterson's Advanced Rhythm Roll (PARR). A young engineer nicknamed Sharpshooter quickly joined Patterson, and they started teaching a method for controlled shooting. I took one of the early courses of PARR. It was 90 percent lecture and a lot of wasted time, but it did actually teach a valid throw that was, when Frank saw it, remarkably similar to the Captain's.

Suffice it to say that once I had the basics of what to do with my throw, I practiced and refined what I had learned. I spent months analyzing and learning at home. I practiced every day. I helped PARR advance in its teaching techniques and met most of the original crew of Golden Touch shooters through PARR. All of the great shooters who helped to create Golden Touch Craps had done what I had done. They had gone home and practiced and perfected their throws. PARR had given us the basics of what to look for, and we were like bloodhounds after that—determined to refine and perfect the controlled throw.

It took me some time, but I found I had the ability to control the dice and gain an edge, but I wanted more knowledge. I felt that there was more to this game of craps than just the physical technique I had created. As a young athlete I knew that there were times in sports where I was "zoned" in. I felt like that sometimes at the craps table but not nearly often enough to suit me. My challenge was having that "zoned" feeling all the time that I threw the dice. I had always studied Eastern methods of meditation, so I started to think about ways I could incorporate some of the meditation techniques I learned into craps. I knew with proper mental discipline and physical technique I could turn dice control into the art form that it has now become. As any athlete knows, once you have mastered the physical skills of the game, the mental components become very important.

Am I a professional gambler? I don't know. Frank and I spend up to 100 days per year in casinos, but I also own businesses in several states, and the two of us run the Golden Touch franchises, and we also do casino jamborees.

Okay, that's a short history of me.

* * *

Morphing from the words "rhythmic rolling," which was coined by the Captain, controlled shooting has become the latest casino fad. You take the dice into your own hands, and by setting them and throwing them correctly, you try to turn the edge in your favor. There may be a couple of million craps players in America, but very few can actually control the dice. I would be surprised if there were many who were economically successful at the skill, because it takes more than just physical technique and mental toughness and calm to beat the casinos. It takes a lot of wisdom too, especially when it comes to betting. The horrible truth about the majority of would-be dice controllers is this—they are acutely poor bettors, betting Crazy Crapper bets as if these were going out of style.

What does that say for their chances of actually beating the casinos at the game of craps? It says the casinos must be licking their lips with this kind of silly wagering practice. Indeed, some of these characters might have some influence over the dice when they throw, but if they make these kinds of high-house-edge bets, they are long-term losers. It is very hard for gamblers to become advantage players, because the thrill of betting their hard-earned money overcomes their intelligence and discipline.

Certainly, many real craps advantage players do exist. I know plenty. These are long-term winners, too—some have been winning for a couple of decades now. Dice control is not an impossible skill to learn—it just takes practice and desire. It also takes the knowledge that you will not win every time you get the dice. Indeed, most of your turns will probably be losers, but your winning turns will make you a profit overall. That is the way to take money from those giant casinos.

* * *

Dice players go all the way back to the dawn of history, and even then you probably had shamans and scammers controlling the dice as the onlookers asked the gods for advice. We know that dice control was practiced in the 20th century with carpet rolls, helicopter shots, and stackers. When dice became the favored game in the casinos, the house structured the game to win more decisions or to tax a player's win. To make sure it would win, the house also put foam-rubber pyramids on the walls of the craps table, and the shooters had to hit those pyramids. Doing so would make the game random, and a random game completely favor the house. Then they also put into effect all those high-house-edge bets that the ploppies wager to assure the casinos a profit on the game—a rather *large* profit.

There were probably craps players in the 1950s and 1960s who had developed controlled throws and were able to get small edges over the house. However, the first man to articulate the kind of throw necessary to beat the modern game of casino craps was the Captain. He—along with the greatest dice controller I ever saw, a woman nicknamed "the Arm," and one of his "crew" members, Jimmy P.—won millions from the casinos between 1978 and the mid-1990s, when the Arm retired due to severe arthritis. Jimmy P. passed away at that time, too. The Arm passed away in 2007.

The Captain's throw is the model of the controlled throw that Dominator and my company, Golden Touch Craps, teaches. There are other kinds of controlled throws. The Arm, for example, had a throw that was uniquely hers. I have never seen a throw like it. Although many of us have attempted to duplicate it, no one has yet succeeded. From our research, however, the Captain's throw seems to be the best-suited for the modern casino craps table. The other eccentric throws we have seen, except for the Arm's, just don't have the power of the Captain's throw. Dominator and I have personally seen hundreds of self-styled controlled shooters, and those who attempt other throws just don't seem to have the goods.

This book, the most complete guide to craps and dice-throwing the correct way is an all-encompassing craps book for all players who are looking to learn the game and also move into the advantage-play category.

Most of the Golden Touch Craps dice-control instructors have done a minimum of 20,000 recorded controlled throws in their at-home practice sessions. All the instructors have passed the Pro Test® dice-control test using the new software program *SmartCraps* in 50 to 500 rolls. In fact, most of us practice every day. And that is where the real learning takes place—at home, at practice, intensely working on your technique.

You will find that you'll read sections of these advantage-play chapters over and over again. You will not find the answers on pages that you read once, put down, and never refer to again. So take your time, read through the material completely, and then focus on those sections that give you the help you need to start learning a controlled throw. Then purchase some dice and either make a practice box or buy one from Golden Touch Craps at www.GoldenTouchCraps.com. As my wife, the beautiful AP, says, "If you want to learn, you do need the tools."

An interesting side note concerns women. Although about 95 percent of craps players are men, Golden Touch has many women shooters in our fold. We believe that women are by and large natural shooters and benefit much more readily and rapidly from instruction and practice. We are not quite sure why this is so. It could be that women naturally have better control of the muscles necessary to make a good craps throw. It might be that the women attracted to craps are extremely hard-working. It might just be a mystery.

* * *

The Captain: *I guess it's now pretty well known that you can beat craps if you learn to control your shot and bet intelligently. You have to do both things to win at the game. If you play as recreation, not professionally, you will find yourself at tables with random shooters who will lose you money. Most of them you will have to eliminate if you wish to have your skill overcome the house edge and the edge these other players give the house by their random rolling. Most rhythmic rollers will not have edges in the double digits; that's a lot to expect. But if you can achieve between a 5 and 10 percent edge and you eliminate those random rollers, you should be able to make money at this game.*

Craps is a great game. I have been playing it since the late 1930s. But craps is more fun when you have an edge. Most gamblers have no idea of how to win, and the casinos cater to those gamblers because they lose hundreds of millions of dollars. You will also have to appear as if you are a normal casino gambler when you play. Casinos are not going to want to see you destroying them on regular visits. I would recommend that you play at many different casinos or make sure that your friends at the tables are random rollers.

Even if you were to be an extraordinary shooter with a 10 percent edge, the game can still be humbling. You will have good days and bad days.

You must get ready to lose in order to be able to win. Losses should not throw you into a tailspin. You must be able to manage your money so that you aren't worried about your money. Those bad days can hurt you if you allow your emotions to get to you. Rhythmic rolling requires a clearness of mind and an understanding that what you are doing in the casino is a contest between two powerful forces—the casino and you. The casino has the game; you have the skill to beat that game if you can control your emotions and if you allow yourself to shoot as you have trained yourself to shoot. Some [athletes] are great in practice, but when the time comes to actually do it in the contest, they lose their heart or get intimidated. Don't let that happen to you.

I know and Frank and Dominator know that craps can be beaten. The only question for you is this—will you be able to beat the game?

CHAPTER 11

What You Need to Know Before You Throw

Before we get into the intricacies of the controlled throw, it is important to understand what a good craps player must do at a table to blend into the woodwork. Being a good craps player starts with knowing the proper etiquette. Please reread Chapter 5 and learn exactly how the game of craps is played. Nothing is more upsetting to savvy players and dealers than someone who throws in late bets or slows down a game.

Craps players are very superstitious and believe that someone having a good roll needs to get the dice back quickly to keep the rhythm going. There is some truth to this—a good controlled shooter, like a good pitcher in baseball, wants to get into a rhythm when he rolls, and poor players can disrupt the game, causing a controlled shooter to lose his focus. Because you don't want your focus distracted by flying chips and late buy-ins, neither should you be the cause of such distractions for others.

Tipping the Dealers

The majority of a dealer's income is from tips (also called *tokes*). How tips are distributed among dealers varies from casino to casino. One of the tips that dealers appreciate is a tip on the Pass Line for them. Just place a $1 chip next to your Pass Line bet and say, "Dealers on the line." The reason that dealers like this bet concerns the math of the game of craps. The house has a very small edge here, and the dealers will win the bet quite often. Or place the chip on top of your Pass Line bet and say, "Dealers are on top of my Pass Line."

Many players like to Place a Hardway bet for the dealers. If this Hardway hits, the dealers will take the win plus the tip and throw it to the box person, who will deposit the chips into the dealer's toke box. *This is not a good bet* for you or the dealers, but some dealers like the idea that they can get 9-to-1 or 7-to-1 payoffs.

You can also put a tip for the dealers on top of your Place bet. This is an excellent way to tip. Again, just put the money down in the Come area and say, "Put this $6 on top of my 6 or 8 for the dealers." You can also say that you are *in control* of that bet. Being in control of the bet means that if the bet wins, the dealers will take only the winning bet but not the original bet like they do in the above examples. By tipping this way, the dealers can make money during a good roll while you are risking only that one bet.

Some casinos will pay off $4 for a $3 Place bet for the dealers on the 6 and 8. If so, it is preferable that you make your bet in this denomination, as it will give the dealers an actual edge at the game. You should probably Place twice as many bets this way as you would if you were betting the 6 or 8 for $6.

Also there are now casinos that will allow you to tip $1 as a Place bet for the dealers and pay those dealers 2-to-1 if the bet wins. What a huge edge these players give those dealers in such a game on the numbers 5, 6, 8, and 9. Again, when making these bets, always say, "I control the bet."

Tipping for random rollers obviously has no effect on the outcome of the game. Random is random. Novice players should not go tip crazy, as you are facing a house edge no matter how you bet, no matter what you do. So tip only intermittently, probably every time you shoot if you are at a crowded table, or every 15 minutes or half hour.

But for a controlled shooter, one who will be taking care with his stance, set, and throw, getting the dealers on your side from the beginning is a smart move. You want the dealers to desire a long roll from you because they are in the action when you shoot. Smart dealers will make sure that the other players, the ones who haven't learned how to actually comport themselves at the table, don't interfere with your throw. So tipping is a definite "yes" when it comes to being a successful controlled shooter. But keep in mind—your skill level must be good enough to overcome the fact that you are making these tips. That is something you must factor when you compute your overall win rate.

Those of you who have worked in the service industries that rely on tips know how hard it is to make a decent living. Good craps players, known as "Georges" if they tip, are the lifeblood of dealers. I am a tipper because as a young man I worked as a waiter, and it was rough when you worked your butt off and got almost nothing in return.

I have only one caveat about tipping dealers and it is this: dealers are supposed to be professionals, and they had better be. They should be pleasant to everyone at the table. Whether a player is a likeable individual or a ploppy makes no difference. Like an actor playing a role on the stage, the inner state of the dealer is irrelevant to his performance. Dealers should never be sarcastic; they should never look bored (even if they are bored); and they should never crosstalk to the other dealers, thereby ignoring the game and the players.

In short, the craps table is the dealer's stage, and he better perform his role professionally. His award will be a tip, which is the Academy Award for good service.

Talking to the Shooter

Some craps players think that if they shout in the shooter's ear it will make the numbers appear. This is not so. Shouting in a shooter's ear will merely cause him to lose some functioning in that ear. If the shooter is a controlled thrower, shouting at him might just take him out of his rhythm. It's one thing to cheer when a number is made; it is quite another thing to scream at the shooter as he sets the dice, aims, and throws. Silence was golden when you were a little kid; well, that silence is even more golden at a craps table. No matter who is shooting, be he a random flinger of the dice or a master dice controller, keep your mouth closed until a Point is made. Then you can clap.

The Golden Touch Philosophy of Craps

If you take the dice in your hand, shake them up, and wing them down the table where they bounce off the back wall and cascade all over the place, the game of craps can't be beaten. The casino created rules to randomize the game, the biggest rule being that the dice should hit the back wall of pyramids. So you must obey the rules of the casino, and that means two things: set the dice quickly and hit the back wall on your throws.

It's important to realize that most players today will set the dice and take as much or more time to arrive at a decision as do controlled shooters. When you practice your dice sets and delivery methods, you will find that as time goes by you will be able to deliver the dice just as fast, if not faster, than the average random roller. Although you might shoot just as fast as or even faster than a random roller, the casino and other players often think you take too long. Your care seems to extend time in the minds of those around you, whereas the ill-preparedness of the random roller seems to make it appear that he shoots fast. Talk about Einstein's relativity of time!

If you are a novice, just getting started, take care with your roll. Such care could be the foundation of ultimately learning how to actually control the dice and get an advantage over the house. Don't fall into the habit of winging and flinging.

It is important to realize that as a controlled shooter you must obey the casino's rules. You have not been given a dispensation because you have an advantage over the house. You should set and deliver the dice in a normal time frame, and you must hit the back wall. The throw you will learn in this book is meant to hit the back wall of the craps table. Of course, some casinos think they have a rule that all players must lose. There is no such rule. If a given casino gives you a hard time about how you throw the dice or the fact that you seem to win more than you lose, you might consider going to a different casino.

Having a Partner

Although it's perfectly okay to be a lone-wolf craps player, having a partner who is a good dice controller is a very helpful thing. First of all, playing with a partner allows you to have two known dice controllers at the same table. That increases your chances to come home a winner. But it also allows you to help him with his throws and him to help you. Even the very best players can get into bad habits, and it's often hard to see what you are doing wrong. A playing partner helps.

The Golden Touch team The Five Horsemen—composed of Dominator, Stickman, Nick-at-Night, Skinny, and me—will play all over the country together. We are friends and teammates. Each of us has a sharp eye and can help the other if our throw is off on any given session or trip.

Facts and Opinions

Craps players are loaded with opinions about how to play the game, and they are more than happy to vociferously share their non-winning strategies with you. Unless they advocate dice control, there is no system, plan, bet, hedge, or prayer that can change the game into a positive one for the player. Almost all craps players are long-term losers. That's a fact. The only craps players who can win in the long run are those who have perfected the ability to change the game by influencing the outcome of a dice roll.

Unfortunately, there are many players who persist in making poor betting choices even after they have acquired some ability to alter the game. If your dice-control ability gives you a 5 percent edge (which is a large edge) when you roll, and you persist in making bets that have higher house edges—you will also lose. That's a fact too. As a dice controller, you have to make the bets where the house edges are low enough for your skill to overcome. Unfortunately, there are dice controllers who have the skill to change the game but do not have the discipline or intelligence to bet properly.

Make those bets that are beatable by someone with moderate dice-control skill. Follow the math of the game whenever in doubt about whether you should make a certain bet or not. The facts are right; the opinions of craps players are often wrong—in fact, they are almost *always* wrong!

The *How* of Dice Control

Pick up two dice. The perfect throw—a throw the casinos will not allow you to use very often—is one where the dice land, *don't* hit the back wall, and just die on the numbers that you set—as if Velcro were attached to them. We call this a *kill shot*. It's the shot the Lee Brothers dice team uses *once per session*. It is a tough shot to learn—actually it is an almost impossible shot to learn—and the casinos are adamant that this shot is against their rules. Indeed, some casino personnel have become salivating lunatics about shooters not hitting the back wall because they think that true controlled shooters are always looking to land kill shots.

This is utter nonsense, but many casino personnel buy the nonsense. Our Golden Touch shot is geared to hitting the back wall. Period. If we miss, the chances are that the shot is merely random, just like the wingers and the slingers.

If you glued two dice together, you know that the only numbers that could show would be those numbers already showing. Unfortunately, the mean casinos will not allow us to glue the dice together in a real game, so we must use energy and rotation to duplicate, however remotely, what gluing the dice would do. The physics theory of degrees of movement is what we use to try to keep our dice glued together. Any moving projectile—and as the dice are in the air they are moving projectiles—has six degrees of movement. By putting rotation and backspin on the dice, we are trying to eliminate three of those degrees. Eliminating half of the degrees of movement will give us a better chance of having an extended hand or hitting certain specific numbers more than probability indicates for the random game.

Thrown correctly, the dice have a gentle backspin. This backspin does several things. It keeps the dice together, it prevents the dice from randomizing in the air, and it acts as a break when the dice hit the table. We want the dice to hit flat, to dissipate as much of their energy as possible but still have enough energy to make it to the back wall, which they'll hit softly, and where they'll die. You know the dice have hit flat because you will often hear a "smack!" when they hit the layout (if it isn't too noisy in the casino).

Dice control goes from the almost perfect—your dice sets, stance, grip, and throw—to the imperfect: when released gravity acts upon the dice, energy flows from the dice to the tabletop, where it returns in a lesser form and pushes the dice to the back wall. All these reactions cut away at your almost perfect dice. If you have a 100 percent perfect setup to the throw (or close to it), the dice will not react at the back wall 100 percent perfectly. From hand to final decision, the dice lose much of their perfection. But you don't need to be perfect to get an edge at craps, just as you don't need to throw a strike with every pitch to be a great pitcher.

The Golden Touch technique will give you the best chance to start your dice throw almost perfectly and end it with an edge over the casino when the dice come to rest. You will be taught to have a little more forward momentum than backward momentum caused by the backspin. That slight forward thrust will be enough to assure that most times the dice will hit the back wall but not hit it so hard that the impact randomizes the throw. We want the dice to hit and die.

So, the things you can do almost perfectly, you must learn to do them. The time spent on the stance, dice sets, grip, and delivery will ultimately determine how good you're going to be. You must learn the physical elements of dice control to have any chance of beating the game. After that, you must train your mind.

CHAPTER 12

Physical Elements: Where to Stand, How to Stand, When to Scan

I f you were a pitcher in baseball, do you think you'd have a better chance of striking out a batter throwing the ball from second base to home plate or from the regulation pitcher's mound? The closer you are to home plate, the faster your pitch will be and the better chance you'll have of beating the batter. So the pitcher's mound is where you want to be. You don't want to pitch from second base. The same holds true for dice control. The closer you are to the back wall, the better it is for your throw. The less energy you impart to the dice, the less energy they have to bounce and randomize when they land on the table and hit the back wall. The farther away from the back wall you are, the more difficult it is to control the dice. If you shoot from the back wall to the other back wall, you are maximizing the distance and energy and creating greater problems for your control. You have to impart far more energy into the dice to get them up and out to the back wall, and you must put more spin pressure on them to slow them down before they hit the back wall. All this utilization of energy merely makes it harder to control the outcome of your throw.

The Stance

Golden Touch recommends that you stand one of the following four ways:

Stick Right One (SR1):

Shooter is standing Stick Right One.

Stick Right Two (SR2):

Shooter is standing Stick Right Two.

Stick Left One (SL1):

Shooter is standing Stick Left One.

Stick Left Two (SL2):

Shooter is standing Stick Left Two.

These are the closest points on the table to the back wall. In general, it is better to play at shorter tables than at longer tables because the distance to the back wall is also shorter.

First, we recommend that right-handers stand at Stick Left (SL) and left-handers stand at Stick Right (SR). This allows an easy pendulum swing, and the release of the dice will be as close as possible to the back wall. Only if these positions feel completely uncomfortable should you stand on the opposite side. Give yourself a few weeks of practice before you decide you can't handle our first recommendation, because this is the best way for most shooters to throw. What you want to gain is consistency. Being able to throw from both positions is not a badge of honor. Using the baseball analogy again—not too many baseball greats can hit from both sides of the plate. The same goes for dice shooters. Find the position that feels the most comfortable, and practice from that position. Master one position before trying to master a second position.

When you are standing at the table, your non-shooting arm can simply grip the table like so:

Shooter standing with hand on rail.

You can also put it flat down if you wish, like so:

Shooter standing with arm resting on rail.

The preferred stance has the hand on the rail rather than the arm resting on the rail, as you'll have to get up over your arm as well as the rail to perform your throw.

In any athletic endeavor—and throwing dice certainly is an athletic endeavor—your stance is very important. A baseball player at home plate gets into a stance that will help him generate power through his hitting zone. So must the careful shooter develop a stance at the table that is relaxed, comfortable, and above all, stable. Your stance should give you a feeling of control at the table. Your stance should be comfortable and give you free arm movement for your pendulum swing.

If you are right-handed, let's start with the basics from shooting from Stick Left (SL). The basics of this stance are the same for a left-handed shooter shooting from Stick Right (SR). So if you are left-handed, just change the words to "Stick Right."

There are a two ways you can stand.

The Upright Stance: Your stomach is up against the rail. Stand with your feet about shoulder length apart. Stabilize yourself by putting your left hand on the rail. Lean over as far as you can. Dominator and I will actually get up on our toes when we shoot from Stick Left to reach over more.

Next, pick a spot on the table where you want your dice to land. This spot should not be in the corner but about six to seven inches from the back wall on the straight part of that back wall (at times table conditions will change where you land the dice). Now support yourself, breathe out, hold your breath, go into your pendulum swing, and hit that spot!

Shooter standing upright at the table.

The Bender: Your feet are still about shoulder length apart. Instead of stabilizing yourself in an upright position with your hand holding the rail, you are bent over with your left elbow on the rail.

Shooter bending over with arm across the chip rack.

Pick the stance that is most comfortable for you, but make sure your throw is actually better from that stance. You might even have a mixture of both stances. The most important things are that you are comfortable and that you can swing your arm in a free manner.

The Opposition Stance: The stances for a right-hander or a left-hander shooting from the nonpreferred positions of Stick Left or Stick Right are a little different. Instead of standing with your stomach against the rail, you are standing with your right or left side/hip against the rail, square with the back wall. This is important to remember, as you need to be as square as you can be. You need to lean over the table so you have to put more of your weight on your right leg if you are standing Stick Right as a right-handed shooter, and your weight would be mostly on your left foot if you are a left-handed shooter standing Stick Left.

Dominator: *I actually have to lift my left foot off the floor as a right-hander standing Stick Right. Using either your right or left hand as a support, grip the chip rail and lean over, and pick your landing spot on the table. This spot should be about six to seven inches from the back wall,* *away from the curves in the table. Obviously, the taller you are the better off you are in this position.*

Your back swing will not go back as far because it starts to hurt. The arm cannot do a full pendulum swing from this position. Again you want to lean over the table as far as you can. But even by leaning over, your pendulum swing might still be on an angle to the back wall, causing your dice to travel on an angle. Because of this, using this nonpreferred position makes it harder to control your toss. You need to compensate for this angle by putting slightly more rotation on the dice.

Through practice you will be able to gain some control from this stance and position at the table. But always try to get your preferred position to throw from.

After a year or two, you might decide to practice from both sides of the table—but you must first be successful from one side before you tackle a second side.

Shooter from Stick Left in Opposition Stance.

Question: *Why don't you recommend shooting from the end of the table? I have seen many dice setters shoot from there. Why is it a poor choice?*

Answer: If you were to take the number of home runs that a great home-run slugger hit, how many would be to center field? The closer the fence is to you, the easier to hit a home run, and the less power you need. The closer the back wall is to you, the easier it is to control the dice. If we could just reach out and place the dice, that would be the perfect throw. You would hit whatever number you wanted. As you start to move back, you start to load the dice with energy, and all that energy must be dissipated before the dice stop. The more energy in the dice, the tougher it is to dissipate the energy. If you are at the farthest point of the craps table, you have to load the dice up with much more energy than if you are standing next to the stickman. The more energy, the harder it is to control the reactions with the table and the back wall. Now, you might have seen dice setters throwing from the end of the table, but they were probably just setting the dice and not throwing with any ability. Deliberately putting yourself in the worst spot to throw the dice will just make it that much more difficult to control your throw. Players who claim they can do this, and maybe some can, would be better off moving closer.

Scanning the Dice

When you are the shooter, you should be in the game at all times. Do not allow anything to disrupt your focus. After you have thrown a number and the dice are in the middle of the table, watch them. Note the sides of the dice. Think in terms of how you are going to arrange them when they come to you. Remember that each side and its opposite form a 7: the 5-pip has the 2-pip opposite it, the 4-pip has the 3-pip opposite it, and the 6-pip has the 1-pip opposite it.

Most stickmen will not bring the dice to you with sevens showing. Often they will just bring the dice over to you with the number you just hit or, in the case of really savvy stick people, with the dice set how you like to use them. Those latter stick people are the best, because you don't have to set the dice at all. You just have to grip them, pick them up, aim, and throw.

If you watch the dice, you will know which spots are where, and making your set will be that much easier.

CHAPTER 13

Physical Elements: Dice Sets

S ome pitchers have one pitch, maybe a blazing fastball. Some pitchers have a good curve as well. The great pitchers also add a third and fourth pitch. Some might have even more. Each pitch a pitcher throws has a different setup in his hand. A curveball is not set up like a fastball. A knuckleball is not set up like a screwball.

In craps, the *set* of the dice (also known as *dice set*)—that is, the initial configuration of each die to the other—is very important. You set the dice to increase the likelihood that your throw will bring about certain numbers or eliminate other numbers. Because most craps players are Right bettors— they bet with the shooter and against the 7 on the Point Cycle of the game most of our discussion of dice sets will be those used by Rightsiders. In this chapter we will also discuss dice sets that can be used by both Pass Line and Darkside bettors to increase the likelihood of the 7 either on Come-Out rolls or to quickly seven-out during the Point Cycle of the game. We will also show those sets that are not recommended by us but that are used to increase the high-house-edge numbers appearing.

You must practice these sets at home because you want to be able to set the dice quickly. A word of caution is merited here. Do not attempt to learn a multitude of dice sets. That would be overkill. You might want a Come-Out set and, *at most*, three different Point Cycle sets. Many of our Golden Touch instructors use just one set at all times. This works well for them, as they simply concentrate on the task at hand and they don't worry about this or that specific number—other than avoidance of the 7. Some Golden Touch instructors use up to four sets, one on the Come-Out and several during the Point Cycle.

Unfortunately, there is a tendency on the part of some dice controllers to constantly change their sets when their throw is off, thinking that such changes will be beneficial. Indeed, in the short run of a throwing session, a set change might help, but this is like taking an aspirin for a heart attack—it's a temporary solution in a critical situation. If your throw is off, the problem is probably in your grip, where most of the problems occur. In the long run, it is the excellence of your throw that will determine whether you win at craps or lose. In fact, most sets that are discussed in the dice literature just aren't worth making, as they try to hit numbers with high house edges. The degree of ability you need to accomplish those throws is way too high for most controlled shooters to bother with.

Because the appearance of slowness exists with careful shooting, the one thing we don't want to happen is for the box person or floor person to think you're taking too long with your dice sets. So practice your sets at home; let them become second nature to you. We are sure that you have seen shooters set dice and take forever to line them up. Don't let that be you. When the dice are in the center of the table, as bets are being paid off, look at them and begin to visualize how you are going to turn the dice to make your set.

Our advice is to learn the Hardway Set first. Then you can add the All-Sevens Set. After that we recommend the 3-V. However, many great shooters just stick with the Hardway Set. The point about sets is simple—you use them to make money. There is no reward for the shooter who uses the most sets; the only reward that exists in craps is winning money at the table. You must also realize that although there are many possible sets, most of them aim for high-house-edge bets that are difficult, if not impossible, to beat in the long run.

Are Golden Touch Shooters Slow?
Frank's Study
"Controlled shooters take too long to deliver the dice, and that's why the casinos get annoyed." You hear this sentiment, or some version of it,

from casino box people, pit people, dealers, and even from dice control-lers themselves. In Golden Touch we caution our students to set the dice in two or three seconds.

Many dice controllers fear that if they take too much time with the dice, the casinos might get really annoyed and ban them from setting their numbers as they wish. I never want such a fate to befall me or any other controlled shooter at craps.

So, I was once talking to the Captain and discussing this issue of dice setting and "taking too long" with the dice, and he said, "How do you know controlled shooters take longer to deliver the dice than random rollers? How long is a craps roll on average? How long does it take for a random shooter, after the dice are put in front of him, to get a decision? From point A, the pushing of the dice to the shooter, to point B, the two dice stop and the stickman calls out the number, what is the average length of time? Is there a difference between the controlled shooter and the random rollers in total time elapsed?"

I had no idea. The Captain thought there might be a small difference, very small. I figured there would be a big difference. But neither of us knew for sure. In fact, neither of us could even make an educated guess at the answer.

As far as I know, no scientific study has ever been done concerning the difference between, say, careful shooters (defined as anyone who uses dice-setting techniques) and careless shooters (defined as those who pick up the dice, shake them, kiss them, blow on them, talk to them, promise them improbable things, and then wing them down the layout where they bounce, bump, and bang all over the place). So I decided to do one myself. Here's what I found, checking my watch as I watched the shooters:

There was very little difference between careful and careless shooters from starting point A to decision point B. The average careful roller takes between 5 and 10 seconds from the time the dice are passed to him until a decision is rendered. The average careless roller takes between four and 10 seconds.

I took 10 shooters that I considered careful rollers and 10 who were careless shooters, and I then tried to answer the following questions: When the dice are pushed to the shooter and the stickman takes the stick away, how long does it take for the dice to get into the air? When the dice leave the shooter's hand, how long before a decision is rendered? What's the total elapsed time for the event?

Here's what I found: There was only a two-second difference between careful and careless rollers in the initial stages of the shoot. Careful rollers took two to four seconds, the actual setting of the dice, before they shot. Careless rollers just picked up the dice. Most of the careless rollers, however, shook the dice in their hands from two to three seconds, whereas the careful shooter, as soon as the dice were gripped, shot them. So, believe it or not, the delivery stage, while slightly longer for the careful shooter, was not that much longer.

The biggest difference I discovered concerned some careless shooters who never bothered to actually pick up the dice but just took them and flung them a nanosecond after they touched them. This accounted for the one-second overall difference in the lower average time for careless shooters on the figures here.

However, because the careful shooters' throws were soft, when the dice arrived at the back wall, they tended to die faster than the dice of the careless shooters, whose dice, propelled by much greater force, took extra time to settle down.

If we were to take a typical roll, here's what it looks like from both the careful and careless shooter's viewpoints and the range of times we could expect to see:

Careful Shooter

Dice are delivered by stickman

Careful shooter sets the dice (2–4 seconds)

Careful shooter aims (1 second)

Careful shooter's dice arc and gently land—decision (2–3 seconds).

Time range: 5–8 seconds

Careless Shooter

Dice are delivered by stickman

Careless shooter picks up the dice (1 second)

Careless shooter rattles dice in his hand (2–4 seconds)

Careless shooter wings them down the felt—decision (2–3 seconds)

Time range: 5–8 seconds

Although the overall time is the same, the pattern of each event is different. Also, all the controlled shooters I watched shot from SR1 or SL1 or once removed from either. The random rollers shot from everywhere. There might be a second gained or lost there, but I couldn't factor that in.

So, based on my admittedly highly unscientific study (yes, I just used my wristwatch, and the number of people I "clocked" were not much of a sampling), I'd say that controlled shooters don't have to worry about "taking too much time." They don't slow the games down; they just try to slow down the casino's profits on them when they roll. And who could possibly get upset by that?

The Two Games of Craps

There are two cycles in a craps game: the Come-Out Cycle, which is when the shooter gets the dice and establishes his Point number, and the Point Cycle, where the shooter tries to make his Point or, for Darksiders, hit that 7. Many controlled shooters like to set for the 7 on the Come-Out roll. You already have a 2-to-1 edge on the Come-Out with six ways to make the 7 and two ways to make the 11, versus four ways to lose on the 2, 3, and 12. (We aren't counting the Point/Box numbers in this part of the game.)

Increasing the number of 7s thrown is a great way to increase your edge in this part of the game. You have nothing to lose by trying to increase your edge during these throws because you can't lose the dice. Setting for the 7 on the Come-Out is a great way to make some money and to see how your throw looks. There are six ways to make a 7. If we have practiced our controlled throw, we can set for the 7 on the Come-Out roll and increase our advantage during this part of the game. The Come-Out use of an All-Sevens Set is a good way to try to put some money on your rail before you play the part of the game where a bad throw can eliminate you. The Come-Out roll is also great practice on the table. You can get an idea of the bounce of the table.

There are some members of our Golden Touch team who use the same set for the Come-Out Cycle and the Point Cycle and never change sets during their turn with the dice. This type of play might also be good for you. Changing sets might distract you from the mental job at hand—beating the casinos. So if changing sets disrupts your focus, then use a Point-Cycle set throughout your roll.

Come-Out Sets

In the controlled shooting literature, we read of random rollers being called "chicken feeders," because their form often looks like those old farmers flinging out the grain for their chickens. The only time when a chicken feeder or random shooter has a mathematical advantage over the house is on his Come-Out roll when he is establishing the Point number; that is, if he is betting on the Pass Line.

A Pass Line player will win his bet immediately if a 7 or 11 is thrown. He has eight ways to make these two numbers, six ways on the 7 and two ways on the 11. The player has four ways to lose on this Come-Out roll: once on a 2, once on a 12, and twice on a 3. The other 24 combinations of 4, 5, 6, 8, 9, and 10 are Point numbers.

So the Come-Out heavily favors the players. By using an All-Sevens Set, you can increase the appearance of the 7 during this part of the game—with no risk of sevening-out, obviously.

As you study these dice sets, think about the axis that the dice rotate on. Imagine a rod through the center of both dice, on which they spin. This axis of rotation has to be the same for the sets that are described, but what number is on top or facing you as you set the dice doesn't have to be what is illustrated.

All-Sevens Set

**The sides of the
All-Sevens Set.**

**The All-Sevens Set
in the air.**

As you can see, the All-Sevens Set has a 7 on each side of the dice made up of a 4:3 on two sides and a 5:2 on the other two sides. The side faces are also a 7, with 6:1. The axis that this set revolves on is the 6-spot and the 1-spot. You can have any number facing you, either the 4:3 or the 5:2, but you must set the dice with the 6-spot and 1-spot on axis. If you practice throwing and keeping the dice on axis in the air, you will start your turn at the tables by throwing 7s. What better way to begin than by putting money in your rack?

Starting with an All-Sevens Set is a wise thing to do. The Come-Out roll is a practice roll because you will always get the dice back. So not only can you judge the table, but also you give yourself the opportunity to take more throws if those 7s come up. Now, if you prefer to use the Come betting method on yourself during the Point Cycle of the game, then you would not use the All-Sevens Set on subsequent Come-Out rolls, because you don't want to knock your Come bets off the numbers.

The Yo or World Set

The Yo or World Set.

This set will produce an 11 or a 3. These are very high-house-edge bets, coming in with an 11.11 percent casino advantage. There are very few dice controllers who have such a keen delivery that they can make betting on these numbers worthwhile.

The Yo or World set has for its axis the 4-spot and the 3-spot. This set gives you two sides that are 6:5 for an instant winner on your Pass Line bet and two sides that are a 2:1, for a loser on your Pass Line bet but a win when betting the Horn, a high vig bet with a 12.5 percent house edge.

Avoid the sets that try to hit the high-house-edge numbers. You'll be like a hamster spinning your wheel and getting nowhere. The numbers you are going after are worthless in the long run because you can't control the dice well enough to get edges over 13 percent consistently. When you are going after the 6s and 8s, or even some of the other Point numbers, your throw should be able to bring in the money. The high-house-edge bets are for suckers. Most dice controllers who make these bets are falling into the casinos' trap.

Point Cycle Sets

Hardway Set

This is the best set to begin your dice-control career, as it offers the best protection against the 7. It is the best set to use when you are practicing because you can tell what your dice are doing much more easily than with other sets. It is not, however, a good set to use for particular numbers unless you are trying to hit Hardway numbers—which have high house edges. The Hardway Set is so named because all four sides of the dice have Hardway numbers. As you can see in the photos, the Hardway Set has on its axis the 6-spot and 1-spot.

Now, a simple rule of thumb is to put the 6-spot die to the left and the 1-spot die to the right (or vice versa—but always do it the same way each time). The 6:1 is your axis of the dice. Always do this, and the Hardway Set is easy to make. Now, all you do is make sure you have 3:3, 5:5; 2:2; and 4:4 as the combinations showing. With the 6-spot die on the left and the 1-spot die on the right and with any Hardway number showing, you can now be confident that your set is the set that keeps that nasty 7 away.

The Hardway Set from different sides.

If you take the dice and turn each one a quarter-turn, always starting with the Hardway Set, you will see that you cannot form a 7. The 7 will occur only when you double pitch, double yaw, or double roll.

The dice flip twice—a double-pitch 7.

The dice do a double yaw.

The Hardway Set is excellent when you start controlled shooting because it protects against the 7 better than any other set. It is not a badge of honor or skill to move away from the Hardway Set to other sets just to say that you use other sets. Many of the greatest Golden Touch shooters still use the Hardway Set exclusively. However, to get that added protection against the 7, you decrease your ability to snipe out other numbers. It's a trade-off but certainly a worthwhile one.

3-V Set

The 3-V set is used to hit the specific numbers 6 and 8. I first introduced this set in 1991 in books and articles. It is the set Dominator and I use most often. It requires strong axis-control.

The different sides of the 3-V Set.

As seen in these photos, the typical way to set the 3-V is to have the 2-spot and 5-spot on axis on one die and the 6-spot and 1-spot on axis on the other. Then make sure that the four sides of the dice have 3:3, 4:4, 5:1, or 6:2 all the way around. Most players have the 3s on top, forming a *V* or an inverted *V* (a pyramid). Some shooters prefer to put the two 4s on top. Again, the configuration you use is up to you—as long as all the dice are aligned correctly. Any of the four sides on top will work as long as you have the axis numbers right. This is a popular set to use to hit the 6 and 8. Another way of quickly setting the 3-V set is to start with the Hardway Set with the axis numbers being 6 and 1, left to right. Then turn the left die two clicks and then turn the right die one click. Using the *V* sets is for the more advanced and consistent throwers who tend to keep their dice on axis more often. One word of caution: use the same sides up all the time. You want to get into an unthinking rhythm when you roll. I always have the 3s in a *V* at the top. (If the dice are of the *B* variety, the top will be a pyramid shape with the 3-spots.

The 2-V Set

The 2-V set for hitting 4s and 10s.

The 2-V is the sister to the 3-V set. This set is used to hit the 4 and 10, as these are the primary numbers on the face of this set. The reason most people do not use this set is because unless you can afford to *buy* the 4 or 10, which are the primary hits with this set, the house edge of 6.67 percent is far too great on the Placing of these numbers. The 3-V set, with its primary numbers being the 6 and 8, is a better set since the house edge on placing the 6 and 8 is only 1.52 percent.

Look at the photos here, and you will see the normal setup of the 2-V set. This set has for its axis 6:1 on the left die and 3:4 on the right die. Make sure that the four sides of the dice have 2:2, 3:1, 5:5, and 6:4 all the way around. Again, any one of these four sides can be on top.

> **Please Note:** *There are some casinos in the country that allow the placing of the 4 and 10 without taking any vig from the bet. That means the bet is paid off at its true odds of 2-to-1. In a casino such as this, using the 2-V and betting only the 4 and 10 (along with the Pass Line) would be optimal.*

Other Sets
Straight 6s

Straight 6s: Trying for the high-house-edge bets of 12, 2, 4, and 10.

The Straight 6s has as its axis 4:3 and 4:3, with 6:6, 5:5, 2:2, or 1:1 on the four sides. This is not a recommended set, because you are trying for the highest house-edge bets. A 12, for example, has an almost 14 percent house edge.

Cross 6s or 6-T

The Cross 6s or 6-T set has as its axis either 5:2 and 3:4 or 2:5 and 4:3. With the 5:2, 3:4 axis, the four sides are 6:6 (with the 6s forming a *T*, hence the name), 3:5, 1:1, or 4:2. With the 2:5, 4:3 axis, the four sides are 6:6 (with the 6s forming a *T*), 4:5, 1:1, or 3:2. You can see that you pick up a 5 or a 9 as a primary hit using this set, but again you have very high-house-edge bets on the other faces.

Cross 6s or 6-T.

Primary and Secondary Hits

To understand sets completely, you need to understand the difference between primary hits and secondary hits. This will help you decide which set to use and whether you want to change sets in the heat of battle.

A primary hit is when the dice stop after hitting the back wall and the number thrown is one of the four sides of the dice that you set originally.

The Hardway Set with a quarter pitch.

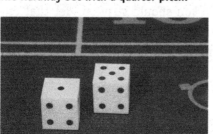

The Hardway Set with a quarter roll.

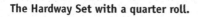

On the Hardway Set if you roll a Hardway number, you have a primary hit. A secondary hit is when one die or both dice land on one of the other sides of the dice a quarter pitch, yawl, or roll plus or minus from the original set. An example of this using the Hardway Set is when you land with the number 8 composed of a 5:3. Take a look at the two illustrations below showing the Hardway Set and what happens with a quarter pitch.

The left die turned a quarter-pitch to the 5, and the other die was on the 3. Another example of a secondary hit with the Hardway Set is landing on 6:3. In this case the right die rolled to the left one-quarter turn and stopped on the 6 while the left die was on the 3 of the original Hardway Set. In the first example the dice rolled on their axis numbers, while in the second example the dice rolled off axis. You must document how many secondary hits you get, because secondary hits are as good as primary hits. You still haven't thrown a 7 with a secondary hit using the Hardway Set, which is why the Hardway Set is the best set to avoid the 7.

On the 3-V, the primary hits are 5:1, 6:2, 3:3, and 4:4. However a single flip or roll can start bringing up 5s and 9s. The 3-V Set requires that you be more consistently on axis than does the Hardway Set, and those shooters who prefer the 3-V tend to have many more on-axis rolls than do Hardway shooters. However, if you are a little off using the 3-V, that 7 will tend to materialize because it is not that far away.

Question: *Do you have to keep the dice on axis in order to win?*

Answer: No, you don't. The Hardway Set is not predicated on keeping the dice on axis as the dice can roll, pitch, or, in my language, flip and flop without that 7 showing. However, the better shooters tend to keep their dice on axis more than randomness indicates. We want to try for those primary numbers, the ones we are setting for, and keeping the dice on axis is the key to achieving that goal. So, to sum up, you can win without keeping the dice on axis, but you should strive to get that on-axis kind of control nevertheless, because that will give you a bigger edge over certain numbers that you set for.

CHAPTER 14

Physical Elements: Grabs, Pickups, and Grips

R andom rollers just pick up the dice and throw them down the table. That's fine for players who have no chance to win at the game. But for the Golden Touch shooter, picking up the dice properly is essential. It is the beginning of the stage of our throw where body and movement occur.

If you are using the preferred Three-Finger Grip (discussed shortly), you can put all three fingers on the front of the dice first or—much easier—just grab the dice with your middle finger and thumb, pick them up, come down with the ring and pointer fingers, and proceed.

There are different approaches to grabbing the dice. Your hand can come over the top, and/or you can come in from the sides.

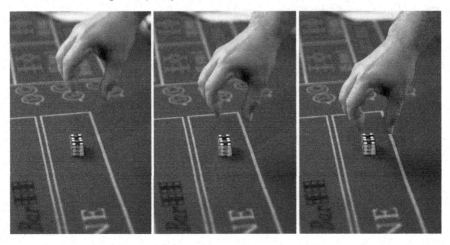

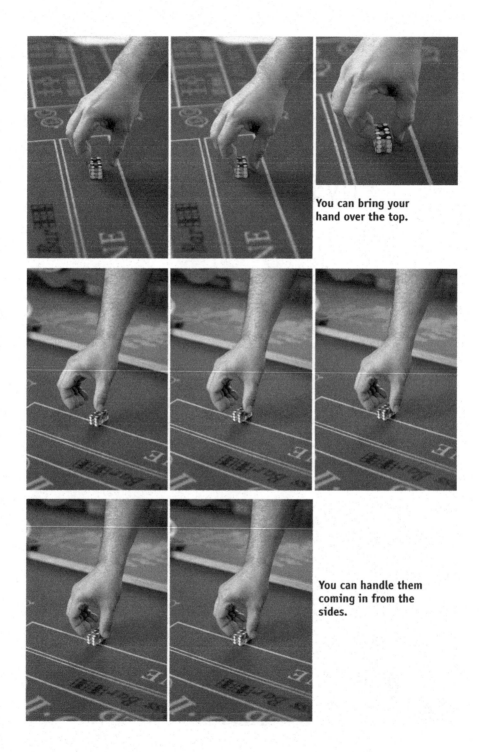

You can bring your
hand over the top.

You can handle them
coming in from the
sides.

Sometimes the dice might split as you are holding them. If this happens, just take your outside fingers and gently close the dice together.

The dice are splitting on this shooter.   **Shooter uses his index finger and his ring or little finger to bring the dice together after they split.**

Grabbing the dice will become second nature to you with a little practice. However, if you find that the dice feel uncomfortable in your hand, put them down and start again.

Grips

The most important element in the pre-throw is how you *grip* the dice. The objective of the Golden Touch grip is to make sure that the dice leave your hand together. We don't want one die lagging and one die leading. We look to make as close to the perfect throw as possible—both dice together, spinning in exactly the same way. The grip is the key to getting those dice to leave your fingers properly.

Most of the problems you will encounter with a controlled throw will come down to your grip on the dice. Your toss starts with the grip, and to have a chance at an excellent throw, your grip must be perfect. After the dice are released, you don't have any control over them, so the more perfect they are at the point of release, the better chance you'll have of switching the edge from the casino to you. Any little deviation of finger placement will alter the flight of the dice in the air and cause your dice to not travel on a perfect plane down the table.

Gripping the dice with too much pressure will prevent the dice from rotating freely. With a tight grip the dice will stay on your fingers too long. You should practice so that you can grip the dice without thinking about finger placement or tightness. You should practice your grip every day because it is the first big step in a controlled throw and first steps are the most important.

A little exercise can help you. Cut a piece of 12"×15" cardboard or quarter-inch plywood. Cover this rectangle with felt by gluing or stapling the felt on. You now have a smaller version of a craps tabletop to practice your dice grip. Have it next to you while watching television or at your desk at work. One of our students brings it into his car and will practice his grip at stoplights. Of course, we don't recommend this car practice, unless you have very good insurance.

Which Grip to Use

Your grip will be determined by your finger size, body type, and performance of the dice in the air. Your grip must feel comfortable. The dice should feel as if they belong in your hands with the grip that you choose. There are some grips that are better than others in terms of the physics of dice control, but if these premier grips are uncomfortable for you, then you must settle upon a grip that works for you. No two shooters are exactly alike, just as no two baseball pitchers are exactly alike, so ultimately the grip you choose to use will be the premier grip for you.

You might not be able to use certain grips because of a physical problem you might have. For the longest period of time, one of our great instructors had to use the Two-Finger Grip because of a tendon problem he had in his fingers. He got his tendons corrected, and now he has gone back to the Three-Finger Grip, which is the grip that gives you the most control over the dice.

For women, the length of your fingernails is an important consideration in determining which grip you should use. Men and women with big fingers might not be able to keep the fingers straight across the front of the dice without a little overlap on the sides of the dice. If this is the case, you will have to use the Two-Finger Grip. The same holds true for a lady with long fingernails. If you have long fingernails and you want to use the Three-Finger Grip, you will have to use the pads of your fingers versus the tips of your fingers to achieve the grip. Again you might have some overlap on the sides of the dice, so the Two-Finger or One-Finger Grip might be for you. (You can also cut your fingernails!)

Pads or Fingertips?

The perfect grip will exhibit each of the following characteristics:

1. Very little finger contact with the dice
2. Very little force needed to get the dice to leave your hand
3. The dice stay together in flight
4. The dice feel comfortable in your hand and you have control
5. Both dice should be perfectly still in your hand during your pickup and swing
6. No splitting of the dice
7. All four sides of the dice should be square with the table and walls
8. The force that you apply to hold the dice should be minimal
9. The dice are released from your fingers with little drag
10. Your fingertips should be like a fulcrum
11. The dice should travel down the table in a perfect arc

You should strive to use the tips of your fingers on the front of the dice. Using the tips of your fingers gives you the least amount of finger contact on the dice. This allows for the smallest amount of drag and friction upon release of the dice. If you grip the dice with the pads of your fingers, you obviously have slightly more finger contact on the dice.

One-Finger Grip

The One-Finger Grip is so named because it uses your middle finger and your thumb to hold the dice.

One-Finger Grip using fingertips.

One-Finger Grip using finger pads.

Your index finger needs to be perfectly centered between the right and left die with equal pressure, and your thumb needs to be centered in the back with equal pressure. You can use either the tip of your middle finger or the pad of your middle finger, but the important thing is that your middle finger is perfectly centered with equal pressure on both dice.

Some controlled shooters who cannot use the premier Three-Finger Grip use this grip. It can cause some instability in the dice when they are released because the ends of the dice will sometimes wobble. Wobbling is bad, as it causes the dice to hit on their sides—which tends to random-ize the roll. Also, the dice will have more of a tendency to split when released. Splitting is also bad.

The pickup for the One-Finger Grip is easy.

Dice rest on the table.   **Middle finger and thumb grab the dice.**

Two-Finger Grip

If you have large fingers, you might find that the upcoming Three-Finger Grip, the best of all the grips, just isn't for you. Many large-fingered shooters then go to a Two-Finger Grip. Here you use two fingers, usually your ring and middle fingers, to grip the dice. Your index and pinky are off the dice completely.

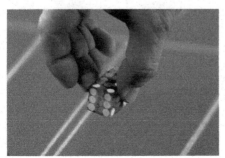

Two-Finger Grip with pads.

Three-Finger Grip

The premier grip, and the one that satisfies all the elements shown above, is the Three-Finger Grip. In the Three-Finger Grip, your index, middle, and ring finger are on the front of the dice, and your thumb is on the backside of the dice. The only finger that is not being used in this grip is your pinky. Do not have your pinky touch the dice at all during the pickup, grip, or delivery of the dice—because that will literally throw off your throw.

The holding of the dice with the Three-Finger Grip is actually pre-formed with your middle finger and thumb. Your index finger and ring finger are simply placed along the front of the dice and act like wings of a plane and a fulcrum for the dice to rotate on as they are released. You must make sure of a few things with your finger placement using the Three-Finger Grip. Your fingers have to be perfectly straight across the front of the dice, and you must make sure there are no splits in the dice at the bottom. A split will cause the dice to move away from each other in the air. The farther away they move, the less control you'll have over them. Freedom is good for human beings but very bad for dice! Although we say that the middle finger and thumb are holding the dice, the pressure differences between the three fingers on front are not that great. Softness is the key.

 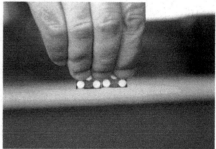

Fingertips on the front of the dice.   **Finger pads on the front of the dice.**

Picking up the dice for the Three-Finger Grip can be done in a number of ways. I pick them up with the middle finger and thumb and then, as I aim, I bring in the ring and pointer to their positions. Dom usually picks up the dice with all three fingers on them at once. Either pickup is just fine.

Picking up the dice with middle finger and thumb.

The index and ring finger are placed on the dice.

Dice are gripped all at once.

The Three-Finger Grip keeps those dice perfectly aligned and allows them to leave the hand together. The spin of the dice is created equally, and they move through the air together. This is not the easiest dice grip to learn, but it is, for most people, the best grip to use. It should be the first one you try to master. Give yourself time to learn it and use it. Do not get discouraged if you find that several days or even weeks are needed to really master this grip.

Four-Finger Grip

The Four-Finger Grip is the Three-Finger Grip plus one. Some people just can't get the pinky to stay out of the way with the Three-Finger Grip, so they incorporate the pinky in the grip. You slide over the pointer and place the pinky on the dice as well. Obviously your fingers will be wider than the dice, perhaps even a little on the side, but with the proper softness, the dice should be able to leave your hand with equal energy.

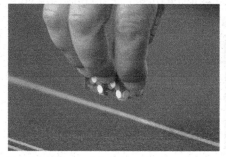 

The Four-Finger Grip.

Ice-Tong Grip

This grip is called the Ice-Tong Grip because you are picking up the dice on one side with just your thumb and on the other side with your index, middle, or ring finger. You are using just two fingers, and the look on the dice is like an ice tong.

The Ice-Tong Grip.

Very little force should be used in holding the dice together. This is a problematic grip, and we have not seen very many shooters who actually can control the dice enough with this grip to get an edge. The dice can easily shift in your fingers. The release of the dice is also problematic, as they rarely stay together and their landing is quite hard. The dice will usually split and go their own ways after they hit the back wall. Although this is a very easy grip to master, it is not a recommended one for real controlled shooting.

The Stacker Grip

You are stacking the dice one on top of the other in this grip. Your thumb would be on the left side of the dice holding both dice in the middle. Your middle finger would be on the right side of the dice directly opposite your thumb. And finally your index finger is on top of the dice.

The Stacker Grip.

The idea behind this grip is to make the bottom die stop and land the way you set it. The top die should force the bottom die to stay put when it lands against the back wall, and then the top die falls off. Knowing what face is on the bottom will allow you to bet certain numbers that are made with that die face. It might also be possible to land the dice in such a way that the top die falls off and lands on certain faces as well. This is a very difficult grip to master and is not recommended.

Diagonal Grip

You can use your two, three, or four fingers with this grip. The difference is the way that you start the grip.

The Diagonal Grip.

Instead of the four sides of the dice being square with all four sides of the table, the dice are held on an angle. You actually are grabbing the dice on their edge, which makes this a very problematic grip. You are always trying to have the dice land on the table with as much of the surface of the dice as you can. When you have more surface of the dice landing, it releases more energy to the tabletop, and that will give the dice less energy when they hit the back wall. If you start your toss on an angle, the dice might end on an angle with very little of the surface of the dice touching down first. Dice that land on the edge will cut down your edge and usually take it away altogether.

Thumb Placement

How should your thumb be positioned on the back of the dice? It really doesn't matter if you use the edge of your thumb as shown in the pictures. Neither does it matter if the thumb is not exactly straight but somewhat slanted. Many shooters' thumbs cannot be placed straight on the back of the dice. For example, Dom has a straight placement, whereas I don't.

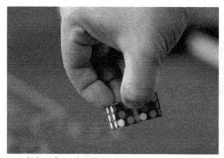

Straight thumb placement.

Crooked thumb placement.

You can also decide whether to use a pad or tip placement for the thumb as shown in these pictures.

Thumb edge on the dice.

Thumb pad on the dice.

The important thing is that the thumb contact should be *equal* on both dice. With all of the grips, how far up or down on the dice your thumb is can change the amount of rotations that you get on the dice after release. As a rule of thumb (pun!), your thumb should be about halfway down the backside of the dice. Even though the One-Finger Grip is recommended only as the second grip of choice, it is a very important grip. This is because the No. 1 grip that you should be trying to use, the Three-Finger Grip, uses the One-Finger Grip to actually hold the dice. So practice gripping the dice with these two fingers and see if you can hold the dice together without them coming apart in your fingers. Try wiggling them back and forth between your fingers. If you can do this without the dice separating, you are on your way to creating your Golden Touch.

Grip Adjustments

You should always carry a set of dice with you. Let your fingers and the dice become friends. Just picture a young person who wishes to develop his or her ability at baseball. What do they do? They always have a ball with them. They throw the ball up and catch it; they throw the ball against the wall and catch it. They play with that ball until its feel, its essence, becomes second nature to them. Dice controllers must do the same thing. Your fingers and your dice should become one.

Now when you are actually at a table and shooting, we don't recommend adjusting your grip too much because to do so causes you to think too much. Too much thinking about your grip will throw you off focus. Hamlets are not good dice controllers—they reflect too much. But there are some adjustments in grip that can be made with very little thinking.

1. If you feel the dice slipping out of your fingers during your pickup or your follow-through, you might need a little more contact on the dice. Again we recommend that you have very little contact on the dice to have the least amount of drag on them. But if you feel them slipping, try moving your thumb down a very little bit and possibly moving your fingers down a fraction as well.

2. If your dice are not coming out of your fingers with any backspin or are moving flat down the table, then you have to adjust the position of your thumb. Remember that backspin is important in keeping the

dice together. Backspin will remove some of the force of the forward momentum and is a necessary component of a successful throw. So if you need more backspin, move your thumb down the back a little lower than your fingers.

3. If your dice are spinning with too much rotation, then move your thumb up on the dice. Too much backspin is not good because the dice will have more energy to release as they land on the table, and the dice will be more random as they land. We want the backspin to almost cancel out the forward movement but not eliminate it, because we want the dice to touch the back wall.

4. Another problem could be that one die may be lagging behind the other or one is traveling higher than the other, as they are moving down the table. Again this is a grip problem. Here is a quick checklist that you can go through to remedy this:

   A. Make sure that your fingers are parallel with the table and straight across the front of the dice. Some people have problems with either their index finger or their ring finger not being exactly equal to the other two fingers on the dice. Use a mirror to check for this when you practice at home.

   B. Make sure that you have equal pressure across the dice and, if you are using the Three-Finger Grip, that your middle finger is perfectly centered on both dice.

   C. You can put your three fingers on the dice tabletop and make sure they are straight before you put them on the dice. Remember that your fingers will be bent somewhat to stay on the dice in a straight line. Unfortunately, we were not born with fingers all the same size.

   D. Make sure that your thumb has even pressure on the back. Your thumb can be holding the dice with its edge, but you must have the same amount of your thumb's skin contact on both the left and right die.

5. Another problem might be that your dice are ending up in either corner of the table, traveling down the table in a banana-type angle. This problem usually means that your backspin and follow-through are not on a straight line. Try using the Don't Pass Line as your guide or runway—as long as the Don't Pass Line is actually heading for the flat

part of the back wall. When your dice land in the corner, or what we in Golden Touch call the *mixing bowl*, your dice will tumble and roll off axis, and chances are you will see the dreaded seven appear. The mixing bowl randomizes even the best of throws.

6. Perspiration and any oils that you have on your hand can affect the outcome of the roll because of drag or slippage. Always wash your hands before you go to a craps table to remove any oils. Some of us also use a little deodorant that we carry in our pocket in a pillbox. About three shooters before we get the dice, we will rub a little deodorant on our fingertips and then wipe off the excess on our slacks for perspiration-free fingertips. But please don't do this in view of the casino personnel. Just slip your hand in your pocket and do it there.

CHAPTER 15

Physical Elements: The Throw, the Backspin, the Bounce, the Back Wall

The Throw

Next we come to the dynamic section of the *Physical Elements*, the delivery of the dice to the back wall. How you grip and throw the dice, how the dice spin, how they bounce, and how hard they hit the back wall will determine just how close to perfection we can get.

Here are the steps:

1. You grab the dice and put your fingers straight across the front so that they are perfectly even.
2. In the back, your thumb can be about 40 percent to halfway down the dice, and your thumb must be centered evenly between the two dice.
3. The bottom of the dice should be level with the tabletop.
4. The front of the dice should be square with the front wall.
5. If you start your throw on an angle, it will end on an angle and not give the dice enough surface area to release energy to the tabletop.

Dice perfectly aligned with walls and felt.

You want the dice to be squared to the felt and the walls of the table, and then we aim and gently bring the dice back and then forward, and we release.

Dice being brought back in pendulum swing.

Dice coming forward in pendulum swing.

Let's go over this again. You **grab** the dice; **grip** them properly; **pause,** making sure that the dice are square; **aim;** then gently bring them back, then forward with a smooth and continuous **pendulum swing;** and you **release** them.

You want your arm to go back enough so that it will have enough forward momentum but not too far back that your arm will bend in. You don't want to push to release the dice; you want the dice to come out on their own from your hands. If your grip is light, a gentle forward motion should release them properly.

The Arc of the Dice

After the dice are released from your hand, you want them to usually attain a 45-degree angle in the air. This is the perfect angle for a normal dice table. However, on softer tables, you have to take the angle down a bit, or the impact will cause the dice to bounce too high.

The dice reach a 45-degree angle in the air.

Backspin the Dice

After the dice are released, they make their way to the back wall. Golden Touch advocates a gentle backspin for the dice. This backspin will do three important things:

1. Keep the dice together in the air
2. Act as a break when the dice hit the table
3. Help to dissipate the energy of the dice

You do not want the dice hitting that back wall with too much energy. With too much energy, the dice will move more, bounce more, and become closer to random. The closer to random the dice are, the less control you have exerted over them.

You grip the dice and do your back swing and forward swing and then release the dice into the air in a smooth, natural manner. The backspin of between two and six revolutions will occur naturally. If your three front fingers and your thumb are properly placed, you should have little trouble achieving a natural backspin. The thumb should be about halfway down the back, and the three fingers should be on the top one-quarter of the dice.

The Bounce

When the dice hit the table, the biggest problem begins. The perfect or almost perfect throw now starts to deteriorate rapidly as the dice make their way to the back wall. You want the dice to travel on a 45-degree angle on most tables. Then, when they come down, you want the dice to hit solidly on the felt so that first hit takes away a lot of the energy from the dice. In your practice sessions you will actually hear a loud "smack!" as the dice hit squarely. You want the entire surface area of the dice to

Dice hitting squarely on the table.

hit the tabletop. That is why everything must start with the dice being square to the table and the front wall.

Then, the dice make their way to the back wall.

You want to hit the back wall on one bounce. By the time the dice actually arrive at the back wall, you want their energy to be almost completely gone. The dice should hit the back wall and die.

Dice hitting the back wall.

Dice die at the base of the back wall.

Let's go through the whole motion again: setting the dice, grabbing the dice, gripping the dice, aiming the dice, back swing, forward swing, release, proper spin and 45-degree angle, landing, one bounce, hitting the back wall, and dying.

Setting the dice.

Grabbing the dice.

Gripping the dice.

Aiming the dice.

Back swing.

Forward swing.

Release.

Proper spin.

45-degree arc.

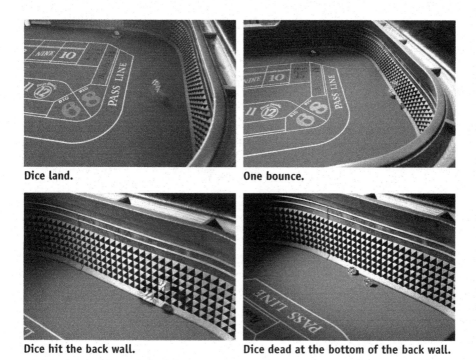

Dice land.

One bounce.

Dice hit the back wall.

Dice dead at the bottom of the back wall.

We do not want to hit in the mixing bowl, but rather where the back wall is straight.

The flat area of the back wall.

CHAPTER 16

Odds and Angles

You must master the Physical Elements of the Golden Touch throw to have a chance to beat the game of craps in the long run. However, because there is not one standard dice table in terms of length and design, and felts vary in their buoyancy, it is important to realize that each table presents you with a unique challenge, just the way each pitcher in baseball presents each batter with a unique challenge.

Tables come in all sizes and shapes. Some are long, aircraft-carrier-sized monsters of 14 to 16 feet. Other tables are 10 to 12 feet. Some tables are wide; some are narrow. You'll note that on some the Pass Line seems much farther from the back wall and on others it seems very close to it. Some layouts are like trampolines; some are dead, as if they have slate under the felt (which some do). When you shoot the dice on a hard table, they will die nicely. Do that same shot on a bouncy table, and the dice could very well sail off the table because the bounce is too big.

When you shoot at a new casino on a new table, you can do several things to ascertain how the dice react to the table. First and foremost, watch other players shoot the dice. Note the bounce. When you cash in to the game, put your hand on the felt and knock once or twice to see how the table surface feels to your knuckles. And during your Come-Out roll, a time when you can't seven-out, use however many rolls you can muster at that time to quickly ascertain the table's conductivity.

Exactly Where Should You Land the Dice?

Most accomplished shooters have a normal landing area for their dice on their practice rigs or their at-home craps tables. Their bodies are trained to land the dice this distance, and they do it without thinking or analyzing anything. This landing zone is usually 6 to 10 inches away from the back wall. The dice take one soft bounce and hit the back wall so softly that they die quietly on the felt without careening all over the place the way a random roll does.

Regardless of whether the table is wide or narrow; regardless of where the Pass Line is in relation to the back wall, you want to land your dice as far from the back wall as you normally do in your at-home practices. A *true-bounce* craps table will allow dice landed at 6 to 10 inches from the back wall to bounce almost perfectly, losing most of their energy on that one landing and gently touching the back wall without much of a rebound. However, many tables you will encounter do not have a true bounce.

If you land your dice in your normal area on your throw and you immediately notice that they hit the back wall too hard or too high or too lightly or not at all, you might have to change small things in your delivery for a bounce similar to your practice table.

Bouncy tables might need a landing of the dice farther from the back wall than your normal 6 to 10 inches. Your arc on these tables will also have to be lowered. You will find that with a lowered arc and a longer journey from bounce to back wall that you might be able to come close to a good throw. Usually, and don't be surprised by this, your throw on these tables will not be as good as your throws on true-bounce tables. However, not changing your throws on bouncy tables can be devastating for your control, so if you are going to play bouncy tables, you must take steps to make that bounce less damaging.

The reverse of a bouncy table is a dead one. You launch your dice in a 45-degree angle with your normal backspin. The dice hit the table ("smack!") and they die right there or close to it. They never make it to the back wall. The solution for this is rather simple. Land the dice closer to the back wall. You keep everything the same, except you add (maybe) one rotation of spin on the dice or slightly more power, and when they land a few inches from the back wall, they will touch down, hit the wall gently, and die. These "dead" tables are actually good for controlled shooting.

Chips Here, There, Everywhere

Many shooters become bothered when they see all the bets on the opposite side of the table, where they have to land the dice. However, a little logic here can be very helpful. With three or four players at the back of the table, there is still plenty of room available to land those cubes properly. Even if one player has his chips directly where you like to land your dice, just moving your landing area a half inch to the left or right of his chips should be all that is necessary to have your controlled throw work to give you an edge. Letting chips chip away at your throw because you get annoyed or rattled is much worse than having to land your dice a fraction of an inch over one way or the other.

If you are playing with several friends at the table and only two to four of them are shooting, you might want to have the non-shooters take up the positions at the landing zones. When you shoot, they do not place Pass Line bets. Your lane will be totally open for you then.

Some controlled shooters like to ask other players to move their chips, which is a bad idea. Asking players to move their chips can draw unwanted attention to you, so our advice is to learn how to aim! Dominator says, "Be a target shooter; be a winner, not a whiner." After you have been shooting for a long period of time, a year or two, chips should never be much of a problem for you.

What if the Pit Gets on You?

You can have the most dazzling controlled throw, but if you let your mind get away from you, you'll find that those seven-outs come like clockwork. Some casinos or casino dealers and pit people have a grudge against careful shooting and will say various things to you to throw you off your game.

"Hurry up with your set!"

"Dice setting can't change the game."

"Look at this, a pro, ha ha!"

"Make sure you hit the back wall hard."

"You must have taken one of those stupid courses."

You have two choices when faced with hostile crews. You can leave the casino and play at another casino that appreciates your action, or you can develop a thick skin and deaf ears. If the pit can't rattle you, they will usually stop their antics. Tips tend to shut up all except the most pathetic ploppy dealers, box plops, and floor ploppies.

CHAPTER 17
Betting Your Edge

O kay, let's repeat for emphasis: in a random game of craps, the casino has the edge. Memorize that sentence. And if someone tells you something else, flee from that person as if he has the plague, because in a sense he does. The plague of ignorance is manifest in the craps world, and many of the crapsters who profess to be experts are the most ignorant of the lot. Here are the facts: no betting system, no hedging system, no on/off method, no right-side, and no wrong-side strategy can give you an edge over the house in a random game. Players who think they can outthink the dice are poor thinkers. Authors and self-styled experts who claim that this or that betting or a money-management system can overcome a mathematical edge are authoring illusion.

Indeed, nothing can change the fact that in the long run, you will lose whatever the house edge is on the bets you are making—that is, if you play a strictly random game of craps. Yes, you will win some nights and lose others, but in the end, if you play enough, you will lose the house edge on the money you bet.

Those are indisputable facts.

Casino executives know these facts because they see the bottom line of their craps games, and those bottom lines don't lie. The math of craps is a devastating reality for the players and a delightful fact for the casinos.

Another little review here:

Many players have no idea how the casinos actually win money from them in the long run. They have vague inklings that something called "an edge" is working against them, but they don't really know what this edge

147

means. How you lose money is easy to see. You put a bet up, the 7 shows, and the dealer takes your chips and adds them to the casino's rack. You can understand you have lost that bet.

However, you also lose bets that you win! Check out the Place bets and the Crazy Crapper bets in the game. All of these are based on short-changing your win and paying you less money than the true odds should those numbers hit. You bet that nutty 11, and the house pays you $15 to $1 wagered if you win, but the true odds of the bet are $17 to $1. The house keeps the extra $2.

At craps you lose in two ways: On the Pass, Don't Pass, Come, and Don't Come, the casino wins more decisions than the players. On the Place and Crazy Crapper bets, the casino "shares" in your win by extracting its edge by not paying you at the true odds of the bet.

So you actually lose when you win!

The worse the Crazy Crapper bet, the more the casino takes from you. As a controlled shooter and one who is looking to play with an edge, the worst thing you can do is try to overcome the edges on the Crazy Crapper bets. That's like practicing for a marathon run and then jumping off a building to see if you can fly because you are in such good shape. The ground (and the house edge) will crush you.

The best bets for most dice controllers are the bets with the least mathematical edge for the casino, because they require the least skill to overcome. It is extremely difficult to overcome a 10 percent house edge. It is much easier overcoming a 1 to 2 percent house edge.

Please note: *What are the best bets? Just check out the charts in Chapters 1, 2, and 3. The low-house-edge bets for random rollers are the low-house-edge bets for dice controllers too.*

There is a question we ask the newest members of our Golden Touch dice-control classes: are you a gambler or an advantage player? The more you are an advantage player, the more you make the good bets, the less you make the bad bets. Gamblers just can't seem to refrain from making bad bets, and gamblers who pretend to be experts are doing players a grave disservice by recommending the poorest bets in the casino for would-be dice controllers. Keep this in mind: You can't win money on bets that you can't beat in the long run, and bets with double-digit house edges are losers for all but the most spectacular controlled shooters.

There is one slight change in betting that occurs when you have developed your skills to a great degree. In games with single (1X), double (2X), and triple (3X) Odds, you might find that Placing the numbers and buying the numbers are the better bets. The Come bet's power comes from the six times the 7 hits when first placed. If you are seriously reducing the appearance of the 7 by using a Hardway Set, you might consider making the Place and Buy bets as outlined above. But no other bets!

Establishing Your Edge

Exactly how you establish what your edge as a controlled shooter is actually not an easy task. The simplest method, and the method we recommend for beginners, is to use the Hardway Set and your SRR. The SRR, which stands for Seven-to-Rolls-Ratio, is a simple, handy way to see if you are indeed starting to change the percentages at craps to favor you by reducing the appearance of the 7. It is not the best or the be-all and end-all of craps edge assessing. It is merely a helpful tool as you begin your controlled-shooting career. The best way to ascertain your edge is by using the SmartCraps software created by Dan Pronovost, information about which is in the appendix. This software has revolutionized advantage analysis at craps.

Remember that the normal SRR for a random roller is 1:6, which means one 7 for every six rolls. That is, of course, an average. On a given night, you can see any manner of SRRs from random rollers, but over time the rolls will start to get closer and closer to the average—1:6.

Here are the minimum SRRs, rounded somewhat to overcome the house edges on the various Place bets. It is assumed that all the numbers are equally filled in with the reduction of the 7 (which is not necessarily what happens in the real world of casino play):

Minimum SRRs on Place Bets

Place Bet	SRR
6 and 8	1 to 6.2
5 and 9	1 to 6.5

Place Bet	SRR
4 and 10	1 to 6.7
Buy 5 and 9 for $30 with $1 vig on win only	1 to 6.2
Buy 4 and 10 for $25 with $1 vig on win only	1 to 6.2

Here is a representative sample of SRRs needed to overcome different Pass/Come bets with Odds. The assumption is the Come-Out roll and first placement of Come bets are random and that all numbers are equally filled in while reducing the appearance of the 7 during the Point Cycle. The percentages in the boxes are your edges:

SRRs Needed to Overcome Pass/Come Bets with Odds

SRR	No Odds	1X Odds	2X Odds	5X Odds	10X Odds
1 to 6.5	1.6%	3.3%	4%	4.8%	5.2%
1 to 7	4.5%	7.1%	8.2%	9.5%	10.1%
1 to 8	9.5%	14%	15.8%	17.9%	19%

Keep in mind that the SRR, although an attractive tool for beginners, is not the only or absolute criteria for a controlled throw. For example, a shooter might have a great ability to hit several of the same numbers on his roll, even though his SRR appears to be a random 1-to-6. There are 3-V shooters who hit several 6s and 8s and then seven-out quickly—yet these can be winning rolls for the shooter. So you have to take the SRR as merely an indicator. The best method for ascertaining your edge is SmartCraps software. Using both the SRR and SmartCraps can help even the newest shooter get some idea of what he's doing or not doing with the dice.

Practice, Practice, Practice

Ted Williams summed up his ability as a hitter in three words: "Practice, practice, practice." Your first several hundred or thousand rolls should not be recorded. Just watch your dice at all the stages and make sure your form and how the dice react is proper. When you think you have it down somewhat, begin to record your numbers. Do 1,000 rolls and record the numbers you hit. At the end of 1,000 rolls you will then assess your SRR.

Then, you will do another 1,000 rolls and see if you have improved. If you have been throwing correctly, you should see a slight to grand improvement by the time you reach 5,000 rolls.

> **Please Note:** *To make figuring your SRR easier and to see which numbers are hitting, shoot in multiples of 36; thus, 360, 3600, 7,200, and so forth.*

Do not attempt to do hundreds of rolls in one day. Fatigue can destroy the best shooter's SRR. Keep your initial sessions short, 15 minutes or so. You can do several sessions a day, but you want to make sure that you are on top of your game as you record the throws for your SRR.

Most Golden Touch Craps shooters have recorded about 20,000 rolls before they feel confident in their abilities with the Hardway Set. After this number of rolls, which might take up to six months to accomplish, you can then have a good idea of how far you have come. If your SRR is 1:6.5 or better, you are ready to take on the casinos. If your SRR is less than this number, you should practice more and also check all the elements of your delivery—the set, grab, grip, finger placement, back swing, forward swing, revolutions of the dice in the air, and how softly they hit the back wall. Any one of these things can cause an SRR to hit the dirt, so you have to be on top of each and every element.

Does the above sound hard? It should, because becoming a controlled shooter is not easy. It wasn't easy for the Captain; it wasn't easy for anyone who has become proficient.

Random Rollers

Famous philosopher Jean-Paul Sartre wrote in his play *No Exit*, "Hell is other people!" For a controlled shooter, losing at craps is definitely other people. There is no way to win in the long run against random rollers because the casino either wins more bets or takes a cut of the winning bets. This you already know. We'll repeat: no *betting system* can beat the random game of craps. Keep that in mind. Anyone who says a betting system can overcome the house edge is lying or crazy or stupid.

So our first piece of advice is not to bet on any random rollers. Play alone at the table or play only with fellow Golden Touchers.

Okay, we know what just about everyone reading this will say: "What, are you kidding? The only time I can get to the casinos, there are plenty of people playing craps. I have to play at tables with random rollers. I have no choice." Or you might say to yourself, "What are you talking about? I *am* a random roller!"

Or, you might be saying to yourself, "Yeah, I want to be an advantage player, but I also just love playing the game, and I am not getting up at 5:00 AM to get a table all to myself!"

All of us in Golden Touch Craps know that it is very hard to be alone at a table or to have only controlled shooters at your table. These are luxuries most of us will rarely get. Casinos will most likely become annoyed if you stand at a crowded craps table and bet only on yourself. They want you in the action so they can win your money. They don't want you waiting a half hour to an hour to regain control of the dice. So, because you must bet on random rollers to show that you are in the game, Golden Touch Craps uses three methods:

Method 1 for controlled shooters: How much to bet on random rollers in relation to how much we bet on ourselves or other controlled shooters

Method 2 for all players: Select whom you will bet on by using the Captain's 5-Count

Method 3 for controlled shooters: Have separate lines of betting for controlled shooters and for random shooters

The section on the 5-Count explains how to select which random rollers you will bet on. But when you know which ones you'll be risking your money on, how much should you bet?

Ideally, the Golden Touch controlled shooter should bet heavily on himself and other good shooters and very, very low on random rollers. Yes, random rollers can sometimes have long rolls. Luck does that. But overall, you will lose whatever the house edge is on the money you bet on these random rollers, long rolls or not. The lower your bets, the lower your losses on these shooters. Don't think that because some random rollers have good rolls that somehow these rolls are predictable—they aren't. Memorize this statement: You will lose the house edge on the totality of the money you bet on random rollers even if you get in on all their giant rolls. There are no ifs, ands, or buts about that sentence.

In order to be on a given random roller's long roll, you have to go up on *every one* of his rolls, which means...yes, you lose!

Let's take a look at recommended betting levels on random rollers:

Option #1: You bet Come and Pass Line bets at the appropriate time in the 5-Count sequences. These can be table minimum bets. You can go up on one, two, or three numbers. Taking Odds is your decision. We take the Odds because that looks more natural. On random rollers, the Odds bet is a break-even proposition in the long run, so it does not hurt to take them. You want to be betting about 4 to 10 times more on yourself than you bet on random rollers. I bet 10, 20, and 30 times as much on ourselves and on other Golden Touch Craps shooters as I will on random shooters. My average bet is between $400 and $500 when I first put out my money, and my Come bet on random rollers after the 5-Count is $5 or $10—on *one number* only. If you are on three Come numbers or a Pass and two Come numbers, your risk might be $15 to $30 ($5 and $10 table minimums on three numbers). That means your bets on yourself should be anywhere from $150 to $600.

Option #2: If you do not like the Come betting option but prefer to use Place bets (which have higher house edges), then you Place only the 6 and/or 8 for minimum amounts—trying to get that big difference between betting on yourself and other controlled shooters. In some venues, where you can buy the 4 and 10 for $25 and pay the vig only on a winning bet, then you can buy these numbers. But buy such bets only at these fig-vig casinos. There are also some venues where you can buy the 5 and 9 for $30 with a $1 vig only on a win. The house edges on such buys are 1.3 percent.

Okay, not everyone can afford to keep the ratio at 10 (or more)–to-1 for betting on random rollers. For you, a drastic realignment of your betting methodology might be in order. If you Place a $12 6 and 8 on yourself ($24 in action) along with a Pass Line bet with Odds, or use Pass and Come betting going up on three or four numbers, then you want to use only one Come bet at $5 (or $10) for a random roller. Indeed, my Five Horsemen colleague Jerry "Stickman" and I use one Come bet on random rollers. We'd also recommend that you forget the Odds bet on random rollers because you might not have the total bankroll necessary for the variance of such betting.

If you are a low roller, then one Place bet of the 6 or 8 is all you are going to make after the 5-Count is completed. Now, we know that some readers will say, "But I'm not getting enough action." But what that means is really this: "I am not losing enough betting this way!" You must keep your bets low on random rollers. That's the first law of winning money when you play at the tables with the random ones. They lose themselves money, and they lose you money. It's a law of the craps universe.

To really judge how much you are winning on yourself and how much you are losing on random rollers, some Golden Touchers use separate betting lines for random rollers and controlled shooters. In your chip rack, the top rack can be the chips you use for betting on yourself and other controlled shooters; the bottom rack can be used for the money you bet on the random rollers. If you are diligent and don't mix up the chips, you will be able to keep long-term records of how much you've won or lost on controlled shooters and random rollers. The longer you play the game of craps as a controlled shooter, the more stunning the difference between what you make on controlled shooting and what you lose on those random rollers will be.

CHAPTER 18

Money Management: The ½ and 1 Percent Solutions

I've discussed the best bets and the worst bets for controlled shooters to make; these correspond to the best bets non–dice controllers should make as well. In this chapter I am going to take a look at two types of betting strategies—conservative and aggressive—and some camouflage techniques for the truly skilled shooters. If you are a novice, you should avoid reading the camouflage techniques that more skilled shooters can use, because you might fall into bad habits.

The greatest enemy of controlled shooters is *overestimating* what your edge actually is and then playing accordingly. Too many dice controllers do this and lose their money. So it is better to underrate yourself than to overrate yourself. Always figure your in-casino performance will be slightly less than your at-home performance.

Stagnant versus Dynamic Edges

If you are a card counter in blackjack and the count goes to +5 because many small cards have come out, your edge is essentially stagnant based on what cards remain to be played. You can have a headache, you can be playing on marbled felt layouts, you can hate the dealer, you can hate the casino you're in, hate your spouse for annoying you, and maybe hate the whole world at large. No matter. If the count is +5, the count is +5, and there's no impact on it by other factors we just mentioned. In blackjack, your edge is stagnant and not dependent on the outside influences or world events.

If four aces have come out in a single-deck game, there is no chance of a fifth ace appearing; the casino edge is stagnant. Nothing can change that.

In a normal craps game, the house edge is also stagnant. No roll relates to any other roll—all are independent events. A 6 could roll four times, and the chances of it rolling a fifth time are the same as they have always been—five chances in 36 rolls. Stagnant.

As a controlled shooter, your edge is not stagnant; it is dynamic—ever changing based on a host of ingredients—and the reason for this is that you are dynamic. If the table is a little longer than you are used to; or shorter than you like; or somewhat bouncy; or very bouncy; or dead as a doornail (why are doornails dead?); or marbled; or decaying with old felt; or possessed of grouchy dealers and snooty box people or pit bosses who snarl and growl or loud, drunken, drooling players who insist on slamming your back in gratitude every time you roll a number or breathing their putrid breath up your nose, these can have a very profound effect on your throw and thus your edge. Just because you have established an SRR at home or have established a bona fide edge on SmartCraps does not mean that edge is precisely transferable to the casino game.

Just as some baseball players hit better in certain parks and worse in other parks, your results will change as the game, its conditions, and you change. Our betting advice is built somewhat on our recognition that you will have some days when you are on and some days when you are off.

As a card counter at blackjack, you can determine ahead of time how much you'll bet every time the count gets to +5. As a dice controller such a simple way of estimating your betting levels at any given moment in the game might not be the optimum way to wager.

Here's the problem by way of analogy. We know that Joe DiMaggio had a .325 batting average for his career. Now, do we use that to determine how we will bet his hitting in his first seven years? Do we use that to determine how we will bet his hitting in his last five years? If we say yes, then we are underbetting his first seven years by a lot and over-betting his last five years by a lot. And the problem is that they don't even out in the end. That's the dynamism of controlled shooting and any "athletic" event—although we can build a betting strategy based on statistics, those statistics can change drastically, owing to all manner of situations not inherent in the math of the game itself. A box person that harps about hitting the back wall even when the dice do hit the back wall could take a controlled shooter out of his game. Or he could make the controlled shooter even more intense and focused—shooting better than he has in his lifetime.

Creating a betting method for controlled shooting, therefore, must take into account the dynamism of the human beings who are doing the shooting. With that said, here are my recommendations. These are just general guidelines and do not cover every conceivable way to bet your advantage at the game.

Conservative Betting

Dom and I have seriously reconsidered our past advice concerning what percentage of your bankroll you should bet based on your edge. You will increase your bets as your bankroll increases. The following are merely rules of thumb. You will have to determine what kind of risk you can handle (another area where some players overestimate what risks their emotions can *really* handle). I stay at my percentage when I play. Dom will vary his a bit more. Of course, as our bankrolls have gone up over the years, both of us have increased our initial betting levels.

Most advantage players will establish their edge and bet a fraction of their bankroll into that edge. A blackjack player will bet his 1 or 2 percent advantage by betting 1 or 2 percent of his total bankroll (some will bet more, some less) and do this each and every time the game shows him to have that 1 or 2 percent edge.

It is the rare advantage player who will vary his bets astoundingly in those 1 and 2 percent situations, because the effects of a losing streak when the bets are too high can seriously damage his bankroll. So, most advantage players are fairly methodical in their betting styles. They are very much aware that even with their edges, it is possible to have losing streaks that eat away at their money.

The most conservative way to bet your edge at craps is to take your total bankroll (let's say that your bankroll is $30,000) and bet *approximately* 1/200 of it on Place bets during each turn with the dice (that is 0.5 percent). That means you can bet between $60 and $90 on the 6 and 8, plus your Pass Line bet if that is another number. If your Pass Line bet is a 6 or 8, then you stay up only on those two numbers. If you have a 5 for your Point, then your spread would be $150. You can determine how you want that spread to look.

As a Hardway Setter who is proficient, you will want to Place the 6 and the 8 for $60 each because the house edge is a mere 1.52 percent. In fig-vig games where you can buy the 4 and 10 and pay the commission only on a win (house edge is about 1.3 percent), you can buy those two numbers for $25 or $50 each and Place either the 6 or 8 for lower amounts as well. And what do you do when those numbers keep hitting? You do nothing but collect your wins.

Should you Place the 5 and 9? No. You must be a very strong controlled shooter to be able to overcome the 4 percent house edge on those 5s and 9s—and most novice shooters just aren't that good. If you are in a location that allows you to buy the 5 and 9 at $30 and pay a $1 vig on the *win only*, then you can bet those numbers at $30 each because the house has only a 1.3 percent edge on those fig-vig buy bets.

> **Please Note:** *A caution is advised here. As you get better and better with the Hardway Set, you might find that you tend to hit the even numbers (4, 6, 8, and 10) more often because your dice stay on axis. That would mean if you see those even numbers hitting, you might not want to buy the 5s and 9s in fig-vig games. Also, as your on-axis performance improves, you might want to see if SmartCraps recommends a different dice set, such as the 3-V.*

If you are not exactly sure as to what level your edge is at, then going with small Pass Line and Come bets and maximizing your Odds would be the best technique. As you get proficient, you may want to switch over to Place bets as the reduction of those 7s decreases the power of the Come bets on games under 5X odds.

The chart below can give you some idea as to the types of bets you can make depending on the size of your bankrolls. The key is to bet in proportion to your bankroll, whether you do only a 6 and 8 bet or whether you like to go with combination bets of Come and Place. By the way, betting only one number is no sin for a controlled shooter.

Before discussing aggressive betting, let's just go over the fact that controlled shooting is not a magic bullet.

Because you can have long losing streaks even though you are a proficient controlled shooter, having a large bankroll will prevent you from second-guessing yourself. I had a six-day losing streak during one of my trips to Tunica, before Dominator and I were banned from playing there. I played four sessions per day and shot three times at each session. I was so bad I didn't win once in all those turns with the dice—that's 72 straight losing turns with the dice.

How did I feel falling flat on my face? *Down* is too up a word.

I thought I had lost my touch. I lost a lot of money, and what was worse, our Golden Touch students were looking at me—students who had never seen me shoot in a casino before—as if I were a fraud. I could see it in their faces.

I went Point/seven-out so many times that I thought I'd change my name to Point Seven-Out Scobe. But I have the money to sustain me, even with 72 straight losses on my own throws in a row. Thankfully, some of those losses were not that big, because I did hit a number or two before sevening-out. My next five days were more typical of what I usually do—I won all my turns but two in those next five days, including a 50-plus hand. Then one week later I had another 50-number roll in Atlantic City. I also hit repeating numbers on my shorter rolls. I was back. I weathered the storm. But that storm could have destroyed a novice shooter and/or a shooter who did not have a large enough bankroll behind him. And Dominator has experienced the same thing.

Dominator: *During that exact same time Frank is talking about, I had terrible heel spurs on my feet. I could barely stand, and my shooting for two weeks, in Tunica and Atlantic City, was enough to make a grown man cry. I didn't lose every turn with the dice, but I lost enough that it could have gotten to me if I didn't know that I would get out of the slump. Having money behind you and knowing that you will come out of any slumps because even your worst shooting won't sink you helps you maintain some semblance of composure.*

Of course, a great controlled shooter can make a strong comeback. In a trip one month after my 72 straight defeats, I played 12 days and won

118 out of 144 turns with the dice. One of my hands was a 51-roll monster and several were in the 40-number range. So several 50-plus rolls right after those 72 straight losing hands and many other winning days as well can show you the kinds of ups and downs that are possible no matter how good you get. Controlled shooting works, but you do have to understand you will have those downs as well as those ups. You can't let the downs destroy you.

Aggressive Betting

Although many advantage players are flat bettors—they bet the same edge the same way over and over—most craps players have the desire to increase their bets when the going has been good. Against random rollers this is a disastrous method of betting, because your overall wagering on them is a losing proposition and you lose more money the more money you bet. On controlled shooters, the dynamism of their edge is such that positive progressive betting is not a foolish choice and can be used to get more money into the game in advantageous situations that are unfolding.

If a competent controlled shooter were to say to you, "I really love those tables and I have destroyed them," you might toy with the idea of throwing away the conservative strategy and go all out on him when he shoots. That might be a mistake.

Perhaps the best way to wager on this fellow is to go up with the standard conservative bets shown above, but when you win a certain amount, begin a gentle pressing procedure.

Or you can be more aggressive on all controlled shooters by using the 1 Percent Solution, that is, start out betting 1 percent of your bankroll instead of 0.5 percent. So your bet would be $1 for every $100 in your bankroll.

With $30,000 as a bankroll, your initial spread would be $300 using the 1 Percent Solution. You would have to determine how you want that spread to look based on the type of buy bets the casino allows. You could, if you wish, make one bet of $300 on the 6 or 8. Or one Pass Line bet with full Odds and then the remaining money on the 6 and 8, or one or the other.

The following chart shows what your total betting amount should be based on your bankroll.

Your Bankroll	0.5 Percent Spread	1 Percent Spread
$5,000	$25	$50
$10,000	$50	$100
$15,000	$75	$150
$20,000	$100	$200
$25,000	$125	$250
$30,000	$150	$300
$40,000	$200	$400
$50,000	$250	$500
$100,000	$500	$1,000

Raising or Lowering Your Bets

As your bankroll goes up, you will increase your bets. You will have to decide when to do this. Perhaps with every increase of 20 percent in your bankroll, you increase your bet by 20 percent. If your bankroll goes down by 10 percent, you reduce your betting by 10 percent. How you do this is up to you.

Please Note: *Some players think to themselves,* But if I lower my bets, then it is just that much harder to make a big comeback. *As a controlled shooter you think first of bankroll preservation, not of making a killing quickly to overcome a bad streak. Getting yourself wound up about making a spectacular comeback will usually result in your rhythm getting out of whack and your bankroll getting whacked.*

Betting Numbers on the Come-Out Rolls

There are two ways to handle the Come-Out roll when you are a controlled shooter or when you are betting on a controlled shooter. You can try for the 7s by using the All-Seven Set—with all your Place bets off. Many controlled shooters like to go for that 7 on the Come-Out.

The second betting technique is to just continue to use your regular set and try to hit those Box numbers that you are on. If you do set for the Box numbers, using the Hardway or 3-V set, occasionally the 7 will appear and wipe you off the board. That can hurt you. So if you think the mental anguish of seeing your bets being removed because of an inadvertent 7 on the Come-Out, then stick to the All-Seven Set and go for the normal Come-Out 7s.

The Captain prefers keeping the bets off on the Come-Out rolls because he considers the new Come-Out to be like the one-minute rest that is given to boxers between rounds. The Captain says, "You get to tone down a little and relax before going back to intense concentration. It's a nice pause."

Using the 5-Count on Controlled Shooters

Should you use the 5-Count on controlled shooters? The answer is yes *and* no. If a controlled shooter has been on his or her game, then going right up on such a shooter would be a sensible way to play. If the shooter is just starting a session or has been having difficulty, then using the 5-Count might be the wise move. A good saying to memorize: "When in doubt, use the 5-Count."

CHAPTER 19

Getting the Monetary Edge Over the Casino

The casinos have staffs of expert psychologists, psychiatrists, and public-relations people hunkering in underground bunkers where they figure out ways to fuel the players' desire to be loved, appreciated, and desired. These "psychos" are expert at making gamblers bet more, play more, lose more—and seemingly enjoy it more. All the casino bosses, shareholders, and executives laugh at the foolish gamblers trying to overcome Lady Luck's capriciousness. And the money rolls in!

Okay, that paragraph was a little over the top. Most of the "psychos" are actually above ground. The rest of that paragraph is thematically true, if not literally true.

The casinos beat gamblers with the house edge on their games, with their massive bankrolls, and with their ability to get the players to enjoy throwing money away. One of the best tools in the casinos' psychological warfare with the players is the area of comps—those supposed freebies given to loyal players. Comps are the biggest weapon in getting people to gamble more than they want and sometimes more than they ought.

Comps are used to make casino gamblers want to be recognized, loved, appreciated, lionized, and revered. All those red-chip players look at the comps of the green-chip players and are envious. Green-chip players look at black-chip players and are envious. Black-chip players look at purple-chip players who are looking at orange-chip players who are looking at gold-chip players who are looking at brown-chip players who are looking at billionaire types, who are treated as gods—and *everyone* wishes to be worshipped like that.

The big RFB comps—that is, comps for everything: your room, food, drinks, shows, limos, shopping sprees, airline fares, and exclusive parties— are the nectar of the gambling gods, and even the lowliest player wishes to partake in the repast.

And how dopey is that? Completely and utterly!

Comps are meaningless if you are losing your money to the casino. So what if they are giving some of your losses back to you in the form of comps—you are still a loser. But for some unfathomable reason, casino gamblers are in love with comps. They think, perhaps, that comps tell them something important about themselves, when in fact the casinos would comp a bum who bet and lost enough to "merit" it. In fact, I once wrote about the "million-dollar bum" who received incredible comps while on a winning streak at Treasure Island in the days when Steve Wynn owned that property. When he started losing...well, you can guess what happened to him and his comps when his bankroll went bust. My wife, the beautiful AP, talked to the dealers who dealt to this bum, and they described him as dirty and smelly and, as one dealer put it, "Ultimately a very sad case. He lost all his money back. But for a few days he was treated like a king."

Needless to say but necessary to say nevertheless, comps are a waste of time pursuing if they cost more to get than they return. If you are expected to lose $5,000 based on your level of betting, the fact that the casino might return $2,000 in the form of comps just means you are a $3,000 loser.

There is only one way comps can work for a player, and that is if the amount given to you by the casino actually makes up for *all* your losses and puts you in an advantageous monetary situation. In short, you are getting more back than you are giving. Advantage players who are actually making money *and* getting comps have the best deal, but second to that are 5-Count players who are losing less than what they get back from the casinos.

Let's go through how this works.

The formula for the *monetary edge* is simple: comps + win/loss = monetary edge. Most casinos will give back between 30 percent and 50 percent of your expected *theoretical loss* in the form of comps. Your theoretical loss is not your actual loss. On any given trip you can win and still be considered a loser—or you can lose much more than your theoretical loss as well.

The formula for comps: avg. bet X number of decisions per hour X number of hours of play X house edge = theoretical loss

Casinos rate craps players as facing about a 5 percent edge for 4/10 and 5/9 Place bettors, 1.5 percent for Pass/Come/Place 6/8 players, and a higher percent for those Crazy Crappers who make the horrendous bets at the game. It's a three-tiered system in many casinos, although some just guesstimate how much a player is betting and against what house edges. This guesstimate is usually around 3 to 4 percent.

Some few casinos count odds; most don't. Let's take a look at a typical 6 and 8 Place bettor.

$12 Place bet of 6 and 8 = $24 average bet

44 decisions per hour (decisions on 6, 8, and 7 only) = $1,056 wagered per hour

Casino edge 1.5 percent = theoretical loss is $16 per hour

30 percent comp return of casino theoretical = $4.80 per hour

40 percent comp return of casino theoretical = $6.40 per hour

50 percent comp return of casino theoretical = $8.00 per hour

Now watch what happens when you plug in the 5-Count. You face only 43 percent of the random rolls. Your theoretical loss of $16 is reduced by 57 percent, which equals a $6.88 loss per hour. If the casino returns 30 percent in comps, you have lost $2.08 per hour; if the casino returns 40 percent in comps, you are down a mere 48 cents per hour; and if the casino returns 50 percent in comps, you are *ahead* $1.12 per hour.

Just using the 5-Count has given you a monetary edge over the house when the house returns 43 percent or more in comps. The casino is giving you more money than you are losing against random rolls. With controlled shooters, you will have a *mathematical* edge in the game *and* a big monetary edge in comps. That's where the real fun is—winning the casino's money and caging all sorts of comps as well. It's David bopping Goliath in the head with the stone from his slingshot.

How to Increase Your Average Bet

Casinos love to use psychology against the players; it helps the bottom line. But players can also psych out the casinos in the comping game. We want the casinos to rate us as bigger bettors than we actually are and/or we want to get more comps than we actually have earned. Here are some helpful hints to achieve our goals:

1. **A Tip on Tips:** Always tip on top of your bet, whether Pass, Come, or Place bet. Keep that bet riding for dealers; never take it off or give it to them, but let them know that bet is theirs if you keep winning. By doing this, the bet counts as a part of your bet, increasing your average bet. If you tip any other way, the bet does not count as a part of your bet. Also, you are betting only a single bet that can win over and over again if you get on a hot streak. On other types of tips, the casino dealers take both the tip bet and the win down. To keep the dealers in action you have to make tip after tip after tip. You are spending more this way and receiving no benefit. So, if you are betting a $25 Pass Line bet and you want to tip, put $1 or $5 on top of it and tell the dealers that the "Red chip is a bet for you."

   You can also put a tip directly on a number and tell the dealers, "I control it." That means the dealers get to keep the win but cannot take down your bet. Some casinos will pay 2-to-1 on single-dollar tips on the box numbers. This is great for the dealers because they have an edge over the house on all 5 and 9; 6 and 8 tip bets.

   Do not waste your money by tipping on the Crazy Crapper bets. If the bet is bad for you, the bet is bad for the dealers too.

2. **Early Placements:** On the 4-Count if the shooter is on the Come-Out roll, you can put your Place bets up (if you are betting this way). You'll receive credit for them even though they won't be working on the Come-Out.

3. **Fake Play Time:** Always ask for a comp at least 10 minutes before you plan to leave a table. Let the rater think he has kept you at the table longer than you planned to be there.

4. **The *Big* Bet Ploy:** If you want to occasionally put up a "show bet" that is substantially bigger than your normal bet to get that in your rating, then do it on the 4-Count during the Come-Out roll. It will be up longer, seen more readily by the rater, and not be at risk. (You take

the bet down or reduce the amount when the shooter establishes his Point.)

5. **Comp as You Go:** If you are a marginal *RFB/RLFB* player and you are staying at a property, do not put everything on your room and wait until the end to find out what it will comp. Instead—*comp as you go*. Many times you will be able to get café and buffet comps up front and then get the total theoretical loss at the end of your stay to put against your gourmet food as well. Often the rater will say, "Are you staying here?" Tell the truth, "Yes, I am," then add, "But I don't want my wife (or husband) to know I am going to eat extra today!" That does work sometimes. Look for overweight pit personnel who have a better tendency to be sympathetic about all things involving eating.

6. **Overstay Your Welcome:** If you have stopped playing and have asked for a comp, stay at the table. Let them ask you to move. The fact that you are taking up a space will motivate "the computer" to work faster on your comps.

7. **Fly Me to the Moon:** If you are an RFB player and are interested in getting airfare for your play but have been turned down in the past, ask the casino to put you in a regular room and not a suite. Usually the suites are about five to 10 times more expensive against your comp points. If you stay in a regular room, you might reduce what the casino figures you have spent and it just might give you your airfare. And really, how many bathrooms and television sets do you need in a room? You don't spend very much time there, after all.

8. **Screw Psychology:** The "Casino Psychology Departments" use comps as a way to *get you* to measure your "self-worth" based on how many comps you get and what a big shot you are for getting them. No comp is worth the loss of money or sleep. Play your game, and the comps will come or they won't. Use these tricks too, because they can't hurt!

Please Note: *I saved this comping tactic for last. Why not ask the floor person what he is rating your play at? Then ask him to increase it. If you have been tipping and you've been a great player at the table, you might just find this simple technique works. It's worked for all of us in the Five Horsemen.*

Do comps make you a big shot in the eyes of the casino bosses or dealers? Absolutely not. They look with disdain on most players who are, after all, essentially giving their money away on games they can't beat. Who would ever be in awe of people like these?

CHAPTER 20

Money Matters

You are not playing with chips; you are playing with real money. If you win a bet, the money you won is *your money* now, not the casino's money. When you lose a bet, that money now belongs to the casino, not to you. As a smart advantage player, money matters.

The first thing you should do, if you haven't done this already, is set up a separate bank account for your gambling money. If you are a low roller, don't throw up your hands and say, "I don't have much money!" Because we'll shoot back with, "Then stay out of the casinos until you do!"

Your **401G** account (the *G* stands for gambling) can grow in three ways:

1. Weekly or biweekly deposits from your paycheck. It doesn't matter how much you earn; take 5 percent and put it in the account. If that means you don't go to a movie this week, then don't go to the movies!
2. All gambling winnings go into the account until you reach the "magic figure." We'll discuss the magic figure in a moment.
3. If you are already a high roller, then take a nice chunk of money and put it in the account. That's your gambling stake.

The 401G does several good things for an advantage player. You don't have to castigate yourself on a bad night (you'll have plenty of bad nights no matter how good you become) and say to yourself, "Gee, I could have used that money I lost for my kids' college educations." Your betting levels are determined by the amount of money in the 401G—as that

169

money goes up, your betting can go up; if that money goes down, your betting goes down. The idea is to never be wiped out of the game.

The "magic number" in a 401G is the amount you reach that allows you to take some of that money for other things like a new car, a new house, a new yacht, or a non-casino gambling vacation. How much is the magic number? That depends on you.

Keep in mind that you will consistently contribute to the 401G from your paycheck or business profits. Even if you are winning boatloads of money in the casino, your betting levels can be structured based on the ½ and 1 Percent Solutions.

Why are we advocating such *extremely* high amounts? Because as a controlled shooter, the last thing you want to think about is the amount of money you are betting. You want the money that you are putting into the game on yourself to be inconsequential—as if you were rolling the dice to win matchsticks or lackluster pebbles.

The worst thing that can happen in the mind of a controlled shooter is this: "Oh my God, I have a lot of money on the layout!" That will take you right out of your game. Unlike card-counting at blackjack where you just have to keep the count and the cards come out as they come out, in controlled shooting you create the edge. And the mind is a great part of that skill. When the mind wanders or worries, your throw is adversely affected, perhaps even destroyed.

The magic number comes about when you say to yourself, "I can't bet more than such and such because I get nervous." One of our GTC shooters, a great shooter, cannot bet a black chip. His biggest bets are $30 on the 6 and 8, and he'll buy the 4 and 10 for $25 only at fig vig casinos. Therefore, he can bet $110 as his top spread. When he goes over that, he starts to sweat...and his throw is affected. The fact that this man has plenty of money in his life is irrelevant. At $110, he's comfortable; at $220, he's not comfortable. This is where he stays. When his wins go over his magic number, he takes the money out and puts it in his regular accounts or he buys himself something.

And what happens when the account goes down? He reduces his betting.

Others develop a higher tolerance for bigger bets. Dom has a high tolerance for risk. I have almost no tolerance.

When Should You Quit?

As a controlled shooter, you quit a session when you feel tired—either mentally or physically—or if you feel upset. Controlled shooters get tired; random shooters can be exhausted, and it has no effect on their chances of winning or losing—they are losers whether awake, semi-awake, or comatose.

As a controlled shooter, however, you have a mental situation that random rollers don't have. Random rollers *hope* that they can win; they don't really *expect* to win. As a controlled shooter, you *always* expect to win—and losing hits you hard. We never get used to the 7 showing! When we play, we are stunned when we seven-out. If I never sevened-out, I wouldn't have time to write this book. During my epic 89-number roll in Las Vegas, I was surprised when I sevened-out. I thought I'd just keep rolling forever, I guess.

When I sevened-out, Dom said to me, "How did that happen?" In the Captain's 147-number roll, his seven-out came as a giant shock. The whole table thought, *How could* that *have happened?*

If you lose on several of your hands in a row, even if you are wide awake and seemingly perky—but deep inside you are somewhat down that you have displayed such poor form for the entire world to see—that's a good time to walk away and recompose yourself. Losses are harder for controlled shooters. That's just the way it is.

Some of our Golden Touch dice-control students have to wage a battle between the old gambler that they were and the new advantage player that they are becoming. The gambler wants action, action, and more action—that's more important than even winning. The advantage player wants to win money. The gambler wants to make stupid bets; the advantage player wants to keep those bets at low-house-edge levels so he can overcome them with his skill. Gamblers like to play long hours. For a controlled shooter, time is not a real factor; fatigue and mental upset are factors.

If you are now a gambler, you will find that following the whole Golden Touch routine might be very difficult for you. First, you'll try to figure out a better way than using the 5-Count on random rollers (the first mistake all new controlled shooters make); then you'll con yourself into thinking that there is money to be made on random rollers because some of them have winning rolls (the second-biggest mistake players make). You might also play when tired (the third-biggest mistake). You'll shoot the dice from the end of the table, because you desire action, action, and more action (a fourth mistake). The more mistakes you make, the closer you become to just another loser.

There are many skilled controlled shooters who are long-term losers because they haven't been able to tame that inner raging gambler. That inner gambler is a growling tiger looking to eat your bankroll. The Hindus call the inner self "the wild monkey." It is indeed. Amen.

CHAPTER 21

The P.O.W.E.R. Plan

You bought this book to learn how to play craps the educated way. You know that there is a better way to beat the casinos besides *hoping* for luck. Luck is fickle. One night she loves you; the next day she slaps your face and goes off with another. When playing against a casino edge, the slaps are greater in number than Lady Luck's kisses. Rely on luck in the casino and you are a loser. The casinos like that. They like that a lot.

There are educated ways to be a risk-taker, ways that make the risks you take have an ultimately positive expectation. Some of you have been risk-takers all your life. You started your own businesses or you moved away from your place of birth to a new community with the design of making life even better for yourself. This chapter—if you follow it—will not only help you to become an advantage craps player, but it will help you in everything you try to accomplish.

To become a winner at casino craps, you don't need luck in all her capricious fickleness, but you do need *skill*—physical and *mental* skill. Skill takes you from being a loser to a winner. You have already learned about the math of the game of craps, about how a controlled dice throw works and what you must do in your betting on yourself and on random rollers. You can beat the odds of this great game of craps if you follow our advice, but you cannot beat those odds if you read this book and then put it on your shelf and forget about it. Then you are just another loser—the casinos' favorite type of person. You are, in short, a ploppy; just another one of the millions of ploppies who go to the casinos each and every year.

The physical skill that you are reading about and practicing is only part of the equation of becoming a winning player. Actually, we believe that it is only 20 percent of what you need to become an advantage player. The other 80 percent is in your mind. You need to learn the techniques of controlled shooting, how to bet on yourself and others, and how to create and handle your bankroll, but that is only the beginning of the winning formula—the first 20 percent.

The 80 percent is what has made most Golden Touch experts big winners over the casinos. Think of the life that many of our Golden Touchers have—going to the casinos frequently, having everything comped, and then taking money from the casinos on a regular basis!

Dominator puts it this way: "It is everything that I ever wanted from the time when I first pitched nickels against the locker room wall and winning enough money to buy an ice cream cone after school, to now when I am pitching dice against the back wall of a craps table and winning enough money to buy anything I want."

Now ask yourself a question and answer it honestly: have you been an uneducated risk-taker? Have you gone to the casinos and risked money that you didn't have with the hopes of having a big score? Is your real strategy of play in the casinos one word—*hope*?

If it is, you are in a sorry state, because hope isn't enough to make you a winner. Emily Dickinson wrote, "Hope is a thing with feathers." Well, the casinos enjoy plucking those feathers. Everyone is plumed with hope when he enters the casino—slot players have machineloads of hope. Hope is a game plan that accomplishes one thing—it keeps the casinos in business. Oh, yes, you can still have hope as a controlled shooter, but to win you need other ingredients, important ingredients. You need preparation in the right techniques as shown clearly in this book, opportunity to use those techniques, and a realistic advantage game plan. After you have practiced your dice-throwing skill and you have your 401G set up, you visit the casinos with more than merely hope.

Some of you might ask, "Now what about this 80 percent mental thing? It sounds like hocus-pocus!" It isn't. It is what separates the risk-takers relying solely on hope from the educated risk-takers, separates the gamblers from the advantage players, and separates the losers from the winners. You need to add the proper mental attributes to your gaming plan and to your everyday life as well. The proper mental framework needs to surround you and, when it does, you will become an educated, successful person in addition to an advantage craps player.

What do all successful risk-takers have in common? First, they had an idea, and then they followed through on that idea. Yes, some of them failed the first time. That's right, most great achievers failed the first time, and many failed the second and third times too. Many Golden Touch dice controllers—men and women who now beat the casinos handily—have experienced rocky times in their early days of trying to win. The dice-control skill is not an easy one to master, and the mind can get depressed when confronted with establishing a point and quickly sevening-out time after time in real-life play.

From talks with the Captain, from our readings and personal experience, and from the experiences of our Golden Touch players, we have come up with our P.O.W.E.R. Plan—the 80 percent ingredient for winning after you have obtained the necessary physical techniques.

We strongly suggest that you accept this P.O.W.E.R. It will help to make you an educated risk taker.

The P.O.W.E.R. Plan

P Preparation

Practice breeds trust in your skills.

O Only

Live only in the present moment to control fear.

W Witness

Visualize only good thoughts, and imagine success clearly with your mind's eye.

E Energize your mind

Center yourself in body, mind, and spirit.

R Risk

Accept risk, thrive on it, and never second-guess yourself if you fail.

Each letter's meaning of the P.O.W.E.R. Plan opens up a world of opportunity and learning. It is not silly to grasp this plan as a method for creating the right mental attitude with which to attack the casino game of craps. Indeed, your life and your advantage play in the casinos will significantly increase for the better after you embrace the P.O.W.E.R. Plan.

Preparation:

Preparation is the key to any successful activity. For your shooting skills to be effective you must possess unconditional trust in your ability. This can be accomplished only with practice and recording of your throws so you know you have a winning SRR. After you have established that your skills are real and that you have an edge over the game of craps, you will realize the rewards. Common sense should tell you that before you can trust your skills in a situation involving risk, in our case gambling, your skills should be imbedded in your subconscious mind and muscle memory. Preparation and practice will then lead to *mindlessness*, a state of relaxation where you are just shooting dice and nothing else is occupying your mind. Preparation makes everything else fall into place.

Only:

Deal with your fear of loss by existing only in the present, the time that you have the dice. We all have fear, but fear usually deals with a future event or reflects on a past experience. Live in the present moment and believe in your abilities. By living for now and only now, what has taken place in the past doesn't mean anything. Say to yourself, "This particular time with the dice is a new time, and what happened last session doesn't exist."

Witness:

Witness only positive thoughts, but make those thoughts very specific when it comes to craps. Visualize, as you pick up the dice, not just any 6, but a 3:3 or 4:2. When you are going to make a big presentation in your work life, visualize how you want the meeting to go before you enter the meeting. Practice these positive images during the day, and you will begin to see the table cheering you, your rack filling with chips, and your life becoming happier.

Energize:

Energize yourself by centering yourself in body, mind, and spirit. Exercise your body and your mind every day. Take a daily walk, do push-ups, swim laps, anything that will maintain your body in a healthy way. Many GTC shooters practice meditation to center themselves. We recommend this and teach a powerful meditation technique in our advanced classes.

Risk:

You must be able to accept the risk of losing. Accept the fact that losing is a part of the game you are playing. Never stop or look back after action has begun. Some people so fear losing that it ties them in knots and makes them incapable of performing at their top levels. You are entering a high-risk situation when you are at a craps table. You must be able to accept this factor. Never play with money you can't afford to lose. Know your stop-loss in terms of your emotions. How many times do we get the dice and we are already down because of other shooters? Our thoughts are on that previous loss. Accept the loss and stay in the present. Your personal perceptions of risk versus reward are yours and yours alone. Know your comfort zone as far as your money on the table. You must be able to accept the risk. Commitment combined with acceptance of risk, centering, trusting, positive imagery, and living in the present will enable you to reach your goal of being a winner.

Let us talk some more about commitment. To have commitment you must:

1. Know what you want to accomplish.
2. Possess a real desire to accomplish it.
3. Develop a workable plan with which to accomplish it.
4. Set a reasonable time frame within which to accomplish it.
5. Never second-guess yourself if you fail.
6. Get up, brush yourself off, and continue to go for it.

Meditate every day. Meditation doesn't have to take long. As stated, in our advanced classes we teach a deep-meditation method. Making sure your body is relaxed is a prerequisite for accomplishment in skill-based activities. Ask any athlete. Ask any advanced dice controller too.

CHAPTER 22

When *That* Happens, *This* Is What You Do

Great hitters in baseball will have off days or even off weeks. Basketball sharpshooters will suddenly lose the touch and perform miserably. To be a great success, you have to understand that failure awaits you as well. Even the best fighters have gotten punched in the face! You take your lumps when you set out to perform a skill. It's easy to win—it seems like the natural order of things—but it's tough to lose.

As a dice controller, you want some handy tips that can get you out of a bad moment—or even a bad night. Here are the top tips to keep you from going down the tubes when your throw seems off. These are the main things that can happen to you when you try to beat the casinos at their own game.

1. **Dice go to the right:** Usually means that your pendulum arm swing is not straight down the runway of the table but is curving in the back. Or the dice are on a slant that causes them to curve when they hit the tabletop.

2. **Dice go to the left:** Usually means that your pendulum arm swing is not straight down the runway of the table but is curving in the back. Or the dice are on a slant that causes them to curve when they hit the table top.

3. **Dice split and go in two different directions:**
   A. Can mean you have uneven pressure on the outside of the dice. Check, if you are using the Three-Finger Grip, that your index and ring finger are not overlapping on the outside edges of the dice.
   B. Check that your middle finger and thumb are gripping the dice with equal pressure on the left and right die. If you have more of the surface of either your ring or thumb on one or the other die, splitting will occur.
   C. Make sure, when you pick up the dice, that you don't have a splitting of the dice on the pickup. The dice have to be perfectly together at the start of the pickup for them to land together at the end of your throw.
4. **One die leads another significantly:**
   A. Usually means that you are releasing one of your fingers before the other in your throw. Make sure that both dice are rolling off your front fingers, using your fingers as a fulcrum.
   B. Or it can mean that your fingers are not perfectly straight across the front of the dice during your pickup and release.
5. **One die hits back wall; one die doesn't:** Usually means that you are releasing one of your fingers before the other in your throw. Make sure that both dice are rolling off your front fingers together, using your fingers as a fulcrum.
6. **Dice bounce too high:** Lower your arc.
7. **Dice bounce too low or scoot too much:** Raise your arc to a 45-degree angle.
8. **Too much arc for most traditional tables:** Keep your arc at about a 45-degree angle on most tables. You will have to lower it a little at times due to the surfaces of some tables.
9. **Too much arc for bouncy tables:** You must lower your arc from the 45-degree angle to somewhere between 25 and 30 degrees. Use the results of the throw to indicate how much of an angle change you need. We call this going from the back side to the front side.
11. **One die is traveling higher than the other:**
    A. Usually means that you are releasing one of your fingers before the other in your throw. Make sure that both dice are rolling off your front fingers, using your fingers as a fulcrum.

B. Or can mean that your fingers are not perfectly straight across the front of the dice during your pick up and release. Make sure your ring finger and index finger are straight across the dice. Fingers will normally bend because they aren't the same length.

12. **The dice suddenly don't feel comfortable in your hand:** Put them down and start your grab again. If you throw the dice when they are split or not perfectly situated in your hand, your throw will be random. You can always make a bet to make it look as if you are putting the dice down because you want to change your wagers. You can also throw the dice off the table and then start again. Ask for the same dice to give yourself time to recouperate.

CHAPTER 23
Camouflage

You've worked long and hard to achieve success at dice control. You go to the casino and miss the back wall once, and suddenly the box person or floor person goes into a state of raging saliva-lathered dementia.

"You miss that back wall one more time, and I'm taking the dice away from you," he spews, his spittle flying into the air. "You hear me?"

You are a little confused. You have hit the back wall 14 times in a row with both dice. Other players have missed the back wall during your session, and the box person was not very upset about it. Why now?

On roll 20, one die misses the back wall, and the box person or floor person starts frothing. "Take the dice away. That's it! You can't shoot anymore!" The corners of his mouth are flecked with white goo. You wonder if he is exhibiting signs of having rabies.

Although this scenario has happened only a few times across the country, the fact that it has happened at all is indicative of two trends:
1. The casinos are becoming anxious about dice control and reacting strongly.
2. The casinos have mistakenly assumed that missing the back wall is the key to controlling the dice and changing the nature of the game.

With the exception of Tony Lee, the head of the professional dice-control team the Lee Brothers, dice controllers have not developed the almost-impossible-to-perfect "kill shot" at casino craps. The kill shot sees both dice miss the back wall, land flat, and, as if glued, stay on axis completely. Unfortunately, when almost all dice controllers miss the back wall, their dice are off and the throw is random. Casino bosses jumping all over a dice controller who misses the back wall are actually mistaken in their ire. They should welcome the missing of the back wall, as that makes the game virtually unbeatable for the controlled shooter.

Be that as it may, the casino executives who are hammering the player who occasionally misses the back wall with one or both dice is an unpleasant situation for dice controllers—and regular players as well.

It is important for dice controllers to hit the back wall for three reasons:

1. The Golden Touch throw works best when you actually hit the back wall.
2. It's not good to rile the casino personnel, because their lack of understanding of dice control will not stop them from thinking they have a complete understanding of the skill—and they'll react accordingly, and negatively.
3. You don't want to get hit in the eye with the froth spewing from a maddened box person's mouth.

In the event that you miss the back wall, you should immediately act as if *you* screwed up. "Damn it!" is a good start. A "Thank God it wasn't a 7!" is another good statement. If it was a 7, then say emphatically, "Every time I miss the wall, I seven-out!" On the very rare occasions when we miss the back wall, we quickly let everyone at the table know that we are upset by the occurrence. Should the box person also say something to us, we just nod our head in agreement and say, "I'm sorry." It's hard to get really angry with someone who is so forlorn for missing the back wall. Apologies are rarely rebuked. Eating crow can often allow you to continue shooting like an eagle at the table.

In point of fact, we don't want to miss the back wall, and we should feel somewhat ashamed, because that throw was probably just a random one. Funny, isn't it? The casino personnel yell at us for doing the very thing they want us to do—play a random game. Of course, not all box and floor persons are this dim-witted. The savvy ones don't get in a snit for an occasional miss. They know better.

Protect Yourself

Too many would-be dice controllers have become so enamored of their budding abilities or their self-assessed skills that they advertently or inadvertently draw attention to themselves at the tables. They conceive of themselves as big shots and want everyone to know that too. We have heard, or heard about, all of the following being said at the tables:

"Hey, great roll! Your dice are on axis!"

"What set are you using?"

"I'm setting for the 7 on the Come-Out."

"Your dice look terrific in the air."

"Your dice are glued together."

"You can beat this game with dice influencing."

"Make your dice bounce only once before hitting the back wall."

"Your dice are crooked in your hand before you throw. Straighten them out."

"The dice landed too far."

"The felt is too bouncy for my throw."

"I don't like hard tables."

"I'm off on my numbers because I rolled a 12."

"How much do you practice every week?"

"Move your chips; they are in my landing zone."

"No one talk at the table; I'm concentrating on my throw."

What's worse, some supposed dice-control experts actually give advice as other dice controllers, whether newbies or veterans are shooting—advice that is loud and easily overheard and understood by the casino personnel. Some ploppy teachers actually cart their students into the casinos to have "casino sessions" where they loudly proclaim how to do this, that, and the other thing. Some even keep written records of the casino sessions—right under the noses and *eyes* of the pit personnel, who eagerly watch and listen to what is happening. This is dumber than dumb and brings the wrong kind of attention to the shooters and to dice control in general. Dice controllers who are good do not want boisterous ploppies muddying our waters.

Several Las Vegas casinos have been angered by the bombastic broadcasts from a few of these ploppy experts. Boisterously discussing dice control at the casino craps tables is the worst kind of publicity. Taking students to the casino tables is not at all helpful; it has brought way too much attention to the truly skillful dice controllers as well. If enough frauds and hucksters talk the talk in the casinos, the pit is going to think something real is happening, even if these garrulous windbags haven't much in the way of actual dice-control skill.

Such behavior is not helpful to the Golden Touch shooters, who can actually get an edge over the game. Our students have been strongly counseled not to bring attention to themselves at the tables—although some of them, unfortuately, have not completely learned that lesson. The joy of being able to get the edge at the game sometimes goes to the heads of some novice dice controllers, who are in ecstasy when they see what their newly developed skill can bring them. What we don't want to bring them is the wrong kind of attention from the casinos.

You must protect yourself in the casinos from giving away what you are doing. The fact that you take care with your rolls is already a clear indication that you are not the typical player. Why add a body of new evidence—loud talk, dice-control chatter, dice advice—when very few players ever talk that way? That's harmful to all of us who want to continue to enjoy the advantage of having an advantage.

The 20 Commandments of Dice Control

1. Do not take longer than 10 seconds to set the dice, grab, grip, aim, and throw the dice. If you take longer than 10 seconds, the casinos will think you are slowing down the game, and that will bring attention to you. The good dice controllers average about seven to eight seconds from start to finish on their rolls.

2. Always hit the back wall, but when you don't, please give an indication that you have screwed up. Don't wait for casino personnel to yell at you. Apologize even before anyone can say anything to you. Do not argue with casino personnel—it is their place; you are the guest.

3. Do not discuss dice sets, dice throws, bounces, backspins, or anything of any depth at the craps table. You can discuss philosophy, religion, history, literature, science, or other trivial subjects, but stay away from any and all dice-control talk. Weighty dice talk can bring down the weight of the casino upon you, something you don't want.

4. Act as if you are a regular player at the tables. Don't be snooty. If someone has a good roll, be he a chicken feeder, the best of the GTC shooters, or anyone in between, cheer when he hits his Point. Feel free to yell out on random rollers, "Good shooting!" when they make numbers. The pit will see you are excited about a guy who really has no edge over the house. Make it look as if all shooters have the same chance to have great rolls and that you are rooting for all of them equally.

5. Do not give advice to anyone while the game is progressing. If a random roller asks you a question, refer him to the dealer with "Ask the dealers; they are the experts." This makes you appear humble. Humble is good. Also, praising the dealers never hurts. Everyone likes to be praised.

6. You might try to get in the line that your spouse or significant other or best friend is a slot nut who plays long hours when the two of you come together. It's good to be looked at as one of a gambling couple, the second of which (your wife, friend, son, daughter, etc.) is a big loser.

7. When you are having a good roll, do not become an egomaniac. Even if your dice are so perfect that you can call your number, don't do it. The time for showing off at the craps tables has ended. In the past, the great shooters could sometimes put on a show of skill (Dominator is the champion of such things), but that time is now over. Just act happy and excited, the way a normal craps player acts, when you hit your Point—and groan when you seven-out (which is actually quite easy to do).

8. If you are disputing a call, do so politely. Do not yell or speak sarcastically to casino personnel. You win no friends on the other side of the dice table by being obnoxious.

9. The dealers live on tips. Be generous with your tipping. You'd be surprised how stress-free most craps games are when the dealers think of you as a "George"—which means a guy who tips and is on their side. If you're on their side, they'll most likely be on your side.

10. Be friendly to the box persons and the pit personnel. Act like a regular gambler at the tables—except don't bet foolishly the way they do. If you see a "yo," don't bet the "yo" because that's for ploppy yo-yos!

11. If you happen to like the casino you're playing at, let the dealers, the box, and the pit know that you like them. That's good PR and also encourages them to continue to act in a manner that you enjoy.

12. Do not take notes at the tables. We have seen students taking notes while we are shooting the dice to determine how many rolls we did or for whatever esoteric system they think they are employing. You can record rolls using chips from your rack. Some of you take notes to see a trend. There are no trends in craps on random rollers, and GTC shooters have trends based on their sets—just bet as they do. (We know some dice controllers love to keep a record of their in-casino throws, not just how many—which can be done with chips—but the actual faces. This is a bone of contention. We don't like it; others do. We prefer just keeping totals.)

13. Do not do the fire drill at the table and fully switch positions back and forth. Again, friends who are gamblers and are shooting together do not do this, and you must not do this either. You can step back a little so your teammate can get a little closer to the back wall, but moving chips and changing positions will only draw attention to you. We draw attention to ourselves already because of the way we shoot. We don't want to draw any more attention. By the way, some casinos do not like shooters to have their arm cross the Crazy Crapper bets in the center of the table, so you might have to move back somewhat if you are in shooting position No. 2 so the No. 1 shooter can shoot from SL 1.5 or SR 1.5.

14. Do not ask other players to move their chips from your landing zone. Does a gambler ask someone to move chips to have a better place to land? *No!* Neither should you. You must practice to be able to hit different spots at the tables. We once saw a shooter actually go to the opposite end of the table from where he was standing and asked someone to move their chips. How ridiculous is that? He broke his own concentration, and you can guess what number came up with all eyes upon him! He became a laughingstock for the rest of the players.

15. Know how much you are going to get paid for a bet. Do not slow down a game because you are slow-witted on payouts.

16. Know what you are going to do after you get paid on a winning bet.

17. Make your presses at the right time and not out of order.
18. Keep the game moving. Make your bets all at once—don't wait until the last second to throw out a new bet. Never throw a bet out when the shooter has the dice or even when the dice are being pushed to the shooter. Even if the shooter is a random roller, it is a sign of respect not to jump in at these times.
19. Don't constantly keep calling your bets on and off. This just angers the dealers, and a gambler just doesn't do this very often. Gamblers will occasionally call their bets off, but it is not an ongoing practice. On random rollers, it doesn't matter what numbers he hits—it's random!
20. There is a final commandment that might be needed in the near future—or right now if you are reading this book several years after its publication. During the Come-Out roll, you might not want to set the dice at all. Because you can't seven-out, just gently roll the dice down the table and take your chances with the math on a random roll. You have a 2-to-1 edge on the Come-Out roll, and this might be the time to act like a regular shooter. To give you more time at the tables, it might be necessary to act like a random shooter at times when doing so will not hurt you too badly.

CHAPTER 24

Team Play

There are two ways to set up team play. The first way is controlled shooters getting together and playing at the same table, but wins or loses are not shared. We call this type of team play table take-over. The second way is more detailed. It is when an actual team is established with a team bankroll and wins or loses are shared. We call this type pro-team play. We have played on both types of teams.

There are some similarities in both types of team play.

The main reason for team play is to have a better opportunity to win. With a lot of great hitters in a lineup, it is easier to score runs. With a lot of good dice controllers at the table, it is more likely someone will get hot. It is a great feeling knowing that the table is loaded with careful shooters who have practiced their throws. You are therefore betting on the best.

Let's look at the similarities of both types of teams:

1. Everyone should be friends and be able to leave egos at the door. The team is established to win. If someone is off in his shooting, he will give his spot on the table to someone else (usually after a table switch). No egos here. Just like on a sports team, the ball—or in this case the dice—should be given to the person who is hot. Remember the word *team* isn't spelled with the letter *I*.

2. The best team has six or more shooters where two shooters stand SL1 and SL2, two shooters stand SR1 and SR2, and two shooters stand at the hook protecting the landing zone of the shooters. They make sure that there aren't any chips in the shooter's landing zone.

3. Each shooter takes two turns at his spot. If after two turns he sees that he is not on, he should move and have one of the shooters who is protecting the landing zone move into the shooting spot. (This way of changing places can be very dangerous. Proceed with caution here. You can always take a break and come back a little later with players in different positions.)

4. Each member of the team should know what each team member sets on his Come-Out roll. If he sets for a 7, then Come bets are not a good idea.

5. No coaching is acceptable at the table. Any major flaws that a team member sees should be discussed away from the table. Remember, no egos!

Now let's look at the differences in team play. These differences come into play for pro-team play. Here egos really need to be left at the door because money is usually divided up equally.

Organizing a pro-team:
A leader needs to be voted in, and his or her say is the final word. Aspects of team play can and should be discussed, for example, what Come-Out set is going to be used, how the betting is going to take place, etc., but the final decision is made by the team captain.

Team Captain's responsibilities:
- Keeping track of the money
- Deciding who is going to take up what position at the table
- Deciding when a particular team member should move out of the shooting position he is in so a different team member can shoot
- Setting up practice sessions at home
- When the final betting strategy is determined for the team, the team captain will make sure that strategy is not changed during the game

1. A bankroll needs to be established with all team members contributing equally. Money now gets involved, so have everything written down so that there won't be any misunderstandings.

2. The shooter's sole responsibility when he or she shoots is to make numbers and not worry about betting. The shooter will bet only the Pass Line and take odds. That is it! There shouldn't be anything else on his mind except the task at hand, which is hitting numbers.

3. The betting style has already been established. The important factor here is that no one on the team is betting the same numbers as the other members of the team for obvious reasons. Because this is team money that is being bet, we don't want to have double exposure on a number. If Come bets are being used then the shooter knows that they can't set for a seven on the Come-Out roll. A decision needs to be made by the team to work or not work the Odds on the Come-Out roll.

4. If Come betting is the strategy, then each member of the team, except the shooter, will have a Come bet. There should not be more than four numbers bet at any one time for the initial part of the shoot. So if there are more members on the team, some team members will not be betting. If a roll lasts for a while, then more numbers can be wagered until all numbers are covered.

5. The amount that is wagered at any given session should be determined before that session begins and should be a factor of the overall bankroll. 10 percent of the bankroll is a good percentage. Remember, not all sessions will be winning sessions.

6. Determining when the money will be split is important. You might decide that the money should be split at the end of the day, win or lose, without any money left in the bankroll. Then the next time the team gets together, a new bankroll is established. Or the team might decide that members will take just a portion of the win and leave the other portion in the bankroll so that the bankroll will grow. One way is not better than another.

7. You must set up beforehand when the initial bets will be increased. You must decide at what Point will you press the Place bets and increase the Odds on the Come bets. The team needs to also decide at what point they should increase the number of bets on the table. A good rule of thumb is to use a factor of three. When the team has three times the money that it has on the table in its rack, then a press on the Odds or Place bets would be justified. An example of this is if one bettor is Placing the 6 for $30, then the 6 would not get a press until

there is $105 dollars ($35 win times three) in that bettor's rack. Some bettors will be pressing before others, depending on the numbers that are hitting. These wins should be placed in the front portion of the rack so that the team captain can see and estimate the amount of money that has been won. When the team captain estimates that three times the outlay on the table is in the rack as profit, then the team captain, and only the team captain, will give a signal for another bet to be placed on the table.

8. Every team member should have the respect and confidence of every other team member. You don't want to lose friends because you don't like the way they handle themselves at the tables.

Dom and I have played on both types of teams, but the one that we enjoy the most is the *table takeover team*. When shared money becomes involved, unless all guidelines are established and adhered to, problems can grow and friendships can evaporate. The Five Horsemen enjoy playing high minimum tables so that we tend to have the majority of the action in our own hands.

CHAPTER 25

Frequently Asked Questions by Dice Controllers

Question: *Frank, I read in one of your books over 20 years ago about "buying" the Don't Come 6 and Don't Come 8 from Darkside players. Explain that again.*

Answer: Some Darksiders get nervous when their Don't Come (or Don't Pass) bets go up on the 6 and 8 because they feel their edge isn't big enough on these numbers, so they take them down. They are totally mistaken in this belief, as they are winning even money on a bet where their edge is 6-to-5. They have the better of it now. So should you be at the table when one of them starts to call out, "Take my Don't Come 6 [or 8] down," offer to take over the bet for him. If he doesn't want that, then offer to buy the bet from him. Because the bet pays $5 for $5 instead of $5 for $6, if his Don't Come is $10, give him $11. You still have an edge on the bet by using this method.

Question: *Some casinos want you to have a bet up on the shooter who goes before you. That means you can't use the 5-Count because if the shooter doesn't make it through the 5-Count and you haven't made a bet, you lose your turn with the dice. How do you handle this?*

Answer: Just make a table minimum Pass Line bet when the shooter has his Come-Out roll. Your expectation for $5 is a 7 cent loss; for $10, it is 14 cents.

Question: *I like to progressive bet when I am winning money, but I do not like to go from $30 on a 6 or 8 straight to $60—that's too big a jump for me. What do you suggest?*

Answer: We used to recommend a progressive system that would often confuse the dealers. So now here is what we recommend—just wait an extra winning roll on the number and then do a full press from $30 to $60; if you wish to go up after that, you can do a half-press to $90. The dealers all understand these presses.

Question: *You guys say not to play the first or last days of a trip. What is the reason behind this?*

Answer: There is a tendency to want to let it all hang out and go for a big win, thinking, *I'm leaving. Let me get some more time in.* There is a good chance that your rhythm might be off; so might your shot. I schedule those last-day flights for early in the morning with the night before being my last playing session. The first day has to do with being fatigued—the enemy of a dice controller.

Question: *There are so many experts on dice control and on craps strategies that it is hard to tell the difference between the real experts and the pretenders. Give me a guide?*

Answer: There are gambling-book writers pushing idiot betting schemes that can't overcome the house edge. These schemes all have exciting names, too (just like the bad bets at craps have exciting-sounding names), "the Bombardment System," "the Echo Effect," "Momma's Dice Dessert," and "Bloated Blubber-Mouth's Barbecue Bash." And the Internet is host to hundreds of deluded writers who post on various gambling message boards. It often happens that new or self-deluded, often *self-taught*, self-deluded dice controllers, think they should be giving detailed advice because they conceive of themselves as brilliant experts. That's nice; it's fine to have confidence...but anyone who follows such advice might be in for rough sledding in the casinos.

There is one sure and fast rule you can use when reading posts by the same self-styled "gurus," and it is this: note how often they discover new sets, new grips, new throws (overhand, underhand, much spin, little spin, no spin, stacked dice, helicopter shots, sideway throws, over-the-head throws, tabletop throws, and on and on). It seems that after their initial recommendations, these experts discover that what they were recommending doesn't work anymore, so they must switch to something else. Often they will abandon good dice-control techniques because they haven't practiced enough, blaming the technique—as opposed to their lack of work—for the decline in their skill levels.

Some of the ploppy experts' posts are so long they could be novels—and in some ways they are, pushing truly fictitious or foolish ways to shoot and even worse ways to bet, ways that don't work for the average human being and certainly won't work for skilled dice controllers. Often, the more details, the less true content.

Now what about the poor sops who follow such advice? They have sevened-out permanently.

Question: *What is wrong with a tabletop throw? Aren't the dice perfectly aligned then?*

Answer: You are correct that the dice can be perfectly aligned on the table, wall to wall, layout to ceiling at the start of a tabletop throw. Now you grip those dice—and let's speculate that the grip is perfect. It is in the throwing stage that a problem creeps into the tabletop throw. Instead of letting nature take over, as it does with a pendulum swing, the tabletop thrower must use more muscle power and more muscles to get those dice into the air. This usually causes small inconsistencies at the start that get truly magnified at the conclusion of the roll. Having to exert that muscle power on the dice makes the tabletop throw questionable as a premier throw. Golden Touch prefers the pendulum swing, with few muscles adding to the energy of the dice, rather than the tabletop swing. That easy motion allows the dice to be released softy. The tabletop throw is perfect only when the dice are on the table, but it quickly loses its perfection when those muscles awkwardly hurl the dice into the air.

Question: *What does it mean to be a George?*

Answer: A George is a good tipper, someone who takes care of the crew. Dice controllers need friendly, professional, nonintrusive crews so that we have the best environment in which to shoot. We have found that regularly tipping the dealers gets them on your side, and you'll often find that the stick person will move back to give you an unobstructed throw. So, be a George.

Question: *What about mysticism at the tables? Isn't it possible to feel the subtle vibrations at craps that make some tables better to play at and other tables not as good to play at?*

Answer: We know some dice aficionados believe that a mystical approach to craps actually works, and we do not dismiss the need for relaxation while shooting. We are advocates of meditation in this respect, and in our advanced class we teach a powerful meditation technique that can be used at the tables to allow your skills to shine through. However, going to mystical extremes is foolish. You aren't going to walk by a table, get a mystical feel for that table's future, and then dive in to make a fortune. The craps mystics without dice-control skills are every bit the losing gamblers as those staggering around the casinos drunk on hops and hope. Leave the mysticism for the new-age glassy-eyed worshippers.

Question: *Can dice control be below random? With an SRR over 1:6, you say you are controlling the dice. But what about someone whose SRR is steadily under 1:6? Aren't those shooters below random?*

Answer: We have heard that some people are pushing the "below random" idea. It is a stupid concept. The shooter is either a random roller or a controlled shooter. There is no in-between. If his SRR is below 1:6 and this is consistent over a long period of time, then he is controlling the dice. There is no such thing as below random.

Question: *Why can't trend-betting systems overcome the house edge?*

Answer: There is no trend if you are playing a random game. The human brain is always trying to make sense out of what it perceives, and it tries to put events into a neat order or pattern. This cannot be done, as random dictates that numbers will bunch together or be absent from time to time. Although this may appear to be a trend, it can be discerned only after the fact. You cannot use past rolls of the dice to predict the next roll, as each roll is an independent event that previous rolls cannot influence. In a random game the roll probabilities remain the same no matter what has happened on the previous roll or rolls. In the end you will lose the house edge for the bets wagered on the total amount of money you put into action regardless of any perceived trends. All of this is analogous to the voodoo you'll hear from time to time about slot or video poker machines being due, or hot or cold. Random is random, and there are no predictable trends. If there were such things as recognizable real trends, then every casino gambler would be a winner. Controlled shooters are a somewhat different story. See next answer.

Question: *I have seen cold tables. I have seen hot tables. How can you tell me there is no such thing when I have experienced them?*

Answer: There is no such thing, even though you have experienced them. Like looking for trends in randomness, the belief that what happened in the recent past will continue into the immediate future is a wrong-headed idea, and players who think this can't grasp the nature of randomness. One random player could have won at a table that you think is cold; to him it is hot. You might be winning, and he might be losing. Is the table cold or hot? A table is just a table. The events of the past do not herald events of the future. It's hard to see this because we want to find winning and losing patterns that are predictable in randomness. There aren't. However, and this is the big *however*, with controlled shooters there is a much better chance that such shooters will have better throws than random in the immediate future. This has nothing to do with random trends but with skill. With skill, the future has some semblance of structure based on the shooter's skill statistics that change the random nature of the game.

Question: *I am a low roller and I don't have much money. But I love playing craps and I have practiced my controlled throw and now have a small edge. How should I structure my betting so I don't really run the risk of a couple of bad nights wiping me out?*

Answer: First, avoid betting on random rollers if you can. If not, use the 5-Count and look for reasons to turn your bets off. All "off" bets look as if you are a player who has merely weakened in your resolve—a very, very good thing with random rollers. Go to the tables when they are empty and make only one bet—a minimum Pass Line bet with single odds. It will take you time to make money betting this way, but you must not allow your bankroll to get devastated by a bad run and, believe me, you can have horrendous runs even when you have a decent edge. Slow is smart.

Question: *What are the benefits of playing alone at a table?*

Answer: You continually get the dice right back so that you can warm up. You don't have to worry about chips being placed in your landing zone. You can quickly correct a mistake you made with your grip or toss without waiting for the dice to get back to you by going around the table. You can get in your zone easier, with no distractions from other players.

The game gets into a rhythm, your rhythm, because there are no other players making late bets, throwing money on the layout, or making the game go slower by making Crazy Crapper bets.

Question: *What are some of the negatives about playing alone at a table?*

Answer: Fatigue can set in sooner because you are the only one shooting. If your throw is off, there are no controlled shooters around to help evaluate what you are doing wrong. Your success is totally in your own hands. If your game is off that day, you won't be able to have a winning session since no other controlled shooters are there to help you out. There is also the tendency to speed up your throws because you figure the dealers and box person are getting antsy. That will also hurt you.

Question: *What are the benefits of playing with a few others (even chicken feeders) at a table?*

Answer: You have a chance to relax and rest your "pitching arm" after a long roll. It gives you time to evaluate your performance between rolls. If you sevened-out quickly, you have time to think about what you did wrong so that you can correct it. When the dice come back around, you'll be mentally and emotionally ready and make the necessary correction. It gives you time to go to the restroom, wash your hands and face, and return to the table somewhat refreshed. Camaraderie at the table is a good thing as well, having others cheer for you and rooting for them when they get the dice. It becomes an enjoyable, communal effort to beat the house.

Question: *What are the benefits of playing with other controlled shooters at the table?*

Answer: Camaraderie among players and a team effort to beat the casino and win at the craps table are two very important benefits of being with other controlled shooters at the table. The other controlled shooters can evaluate your throw and make it possible for you to make the correction by the time the dice come back around—such corrections should be discussed in the bathroom or lounge, not at the table. Another controlled shooter can guard the landing zone (target) to make sure random players don't put their chips in the way. You can improve your chances of having a winning session by having other controlled shooters at the table. The best scenario is that everyone's toss is looking great and everybody wins.

If one of the controlled shooter's throw is off, chances are that others will be on, and therefore you increase your chances of a winning session. You can tell if the dice are landing on axis or not. You can see if the controlled shooter is throwing strikes or having an off day.

Question: *What are the dangers of playing with other controlled shooters at the table? How about partnerships?*

Answer: Staying at the table too long expecting a big roll every time and betting too aggressively. That is an amateur mistake—and we all have made it. There are distinct advantages and disadvantages of partner play, and before you try playing with a partner or partners, you should know what the pitfalls could be so that you can avoid them.

Most successful shooters are familiar with solo play and the good things about playing alone. When you are alone you can move to other tables or casinos whenever you choose without getting approval from a partner or partners. The ability to move freely within a casino jurisdiction seeking out the best conditions can be the best situation for most shooters.

While playing solo it is very easy to stay in a groove when the dice keep coming back to you to shoot again. Conversely, if you are having problems with your shot or the table, there is no time in between hands to collect your thoughts and decide what adjustments you should make. Playing alone at the table is perfect for an experienced shooter who knows how to make good decisions and adjustments.

If you want to try partner or group play there are five things that you must consider:

1. You will be risking more money. Instead of avoiding the other shooters at the table, you will be wagering on your partners. It is difficult, if not impossible, to know how these partners feel when they are shooting. Unlike playing solo, you have no idea how the partners might be affected by their surroundings.
2. You may be stuck playing where the others want to play. You might not feel as though you have your best game available where others want to play, and this can affect your attitude while you play.
3. You will not always get your favorite shooting position. When playing with partners, the shooting spots must be shared.
4. More shooters means more time in between hands for you. The longer you have to wait for the dice, the less chance you have of being on

your best game. Time in between hands can kill your rhythm and keep you from staying hot and in a groove.

5. The more shooters that are at the table, the more attention you will get from the pit. It looks odd when every shooter at the table throws the dice alike. Are you willing and able to withstand the extra scrutiny?

Solo or partner play? What is best for you? Consider these and other factors that will affect you before you play so that you will know what to expect and have a plan to put into action. Try different situations and keep notes on your play so that you can decide what the best situation is for you.

Question: *What is the average learning curve of someone trying to learn how to control the dice?*

Answer: Although there are always people on a faster learning/performance curve, six months to one year should be good enough to consistently win. That would be about average. And this means practicing almost every day for at least 15 minutes. We can equate dice control to the game of golf. If a golfer wants to learn the game and master it, he needs a good teacher and hours of time on the practice range. Dice control requires a meticulous practice regimen and someone to help you with your technique. If a new student of the technique has the discipline to follow the instruction given, then that student will eventually develop the skill needed to gain the advantage. For some, the advantage may be gained in only six months, and others may take several years to master the technique. Patience is the key to any challenging endeavor.

Question: *How dangerous are random rollers to your bankroll?*

Answer: If you bet the same unit size on the "chicken feeders" as you use when you're shooting, trouble is ahead of you. There are always more chicken feeders to wade though than there are controlled shooters at the table. You may have to wade through up to 13 shooters per every turn you have with the dice. This alone highlights the importance of playing at nearly empty tables. Yes, anyone can get lucky and have a hot hand, and random rollers are no exception. That being said, never hope a random roller gets past the 5-Count. In fact, when a random roller is shooting, you should hope for a quick seven-out. You want the dice back in your hand or in the hand of another controlled shooter.

Random rollers take away what we work too hard to achieve. Don't play at a crowded game where you are the only dice controller. It is just not worth it.

Question: *I saw a controlled shooter hit four 5s in a row. Isn't the 5 now a hot number?*

Answer: The bottom line is a question to ask yourself whenever you see such a "trend" and answer it honestly. Is the shooter's skill good enough from *this moment forward* to overcome a 4 percent house edge, which is the house edge on the 5 (and 9)? If you say, "No, he isn't good enough to overcome the 4 percent house edge from this point forward," then don't bet the 5 on him. Or, if you can't resist betting, go up on the Come and if it goes to the 5, take the Odds. You might have to reduce or take down one of your other bets if you feel you are risking too much money. Many winning controlled shooters just don't have the on-axis skills to go after numbers with edges above 2 or 3 percent.

Question: *How good do I have to be to make the Crazy Crapper bets?*

Answer: Better than most controlled shooters will ever become. Put your money on the low-house-edge bets and maximize your potential return.

Question: *Shouldn't controlled shooters laugh at most of the superstitions of craps?*

Answer: No. Actually, play as if you do believe in all the superstitions. Look like a regular player. Pretend, act, be one with the superstitions...just don't actually believe in them.

Question: *I was winning a lot of money, and I increased my bets quite a bit. When I asked the pit what he rated me as betting, he said a very low figure. I said that I was betting five times that amount for the last hour, and he said, "That's our money you were betting with because you had won it." Is this true? Is this how casinos think?*

Answer: That floor person or pit boss is a ploppy of the first order. You should have asked him at what point does that money become yours? What if you came back tomorrow? Is the money now yours when you bet it? How many hours, days, weeks, months, or years does it take for your win to belong to you? What if you went to a slot machine, put your card in, put the money in—would the casino reject those bets for comps? Of course not! What if you went to a blackjack table? The casino has an edge on every bet a random player makes—that's the fact of the situation. If you win $6 and press it to $12, the casino had an edge on the $6 (win or lose), and now the casino has an edge on the $12—even though you won $6 of it on the last roll. The ploppy who made these statements to you should be fired or should be demoted to the parking-garage sweeper.

Question: *I am a wannabe dice-control shooter, and I consider my biggest fault on the craps table is overtipping. As a rule, I always tip $5 on a losing session and tip throughout a winning session. I was intrigued by your article "Sharing the Wealth" in a magazine.*

A few days after reading the article, I went on a bus trip to Laughlin. I asked a dealer, "Who is the box man?" The dealer asked me why I wanted to know. I told him I had read an article where I could control a tip. The dealer looked at me like I was from outer space and told me they do not play that way there. That was the end of that.

I enjoy watching other players who have a greater interest than just flinging the dice, and after a person learns discipline and skill, it is easy to spot those that take the art of tossing dice to a higher level. Although I do not have anywhere near the skill level you do, I think the highlight for me would be playing at the same table with you someday. The only problem is that I would not know who you were.

Answer: Your Laughlin experience surprised me because I have never run into an occasion where a box person or dealer said I couldn't control a tip—you'd think these people would love tips being given to their dealers or themselves. Okay, so if it is true and this casino in Laughlin doesn't allow "controlling dealer bets" then we'll do it in another way, achieving the same exact thing. Throw your $6 on the table and say, "Place the 6 for $6." Then when it wins, make a big loud fuss and say, "Dealers, you can keep the winnings from *my* bet," and throw the winning chips on the table for the dealers to scoop up. But you still can keep the bet up there because it is *your* bet! So you have stated emphatically that the bet is yours and you can do what you want with the winnings. I would think that would be that. You have accomplished the exact same thing.

You can also put a bet on top of your Pass Line bet, and when it wins, give a loud hoot and throw the bet to the dealers saying, "That dollar is for the crew!" They can't take the bet off your Pass Line bet because, once again, it is your bet.

Question: *What is "muscle memory"?*

Answer: If you learned to ride a bicycle as a child, I'm certain you could get on a bike today and pedal away even if you haven't been on a bike in 10 years or more. Your butt would get sore, and so would your legs, but you would be able to ride. This is because you developed the muscle memory associated with the task.

Developing muscle memory begins with seeing, thinking, doing. This is what happens when you are first learning dice control. You start your throw by looking at the dice and thinking about your grip as you pick them up. Then you think about the movement of your arm as you get ready to toss them, followed by thinking about the correct moment to release them. But after a while, with a lot of practice, the "seeing, thinking, doing" gradually becomes "seeing, doing" because your muscles seem to know and "remember" just what to do. During the practice, your muscles aren't really memorizing anything (memories can be stored only in your brain). Instead, what you see with your eyes is interpreted by your brain in the form of nerve signals to your muscles to make that perfect toss of the dice. When you develop muscle memory, it becomes an unconscious effort to grip and throw the dice with a controlled throw.

There is a saying that "practice makes perfect." This statement is *false*. The correctly worded statement should be, *"Perfect* practice makes perfect."

If you are not gripping the dice and throwing them correctly when you practice, your muscle memory will not learn the correct throw. Instead, it will train you to make the same mistakes when you go to the craps table. Computer programmers use the term "GIGO," a "Garbage In Garbage Out," which simply means you can't expect good results when you input bad information into the computer. Since your brain is the most sophisticated computer in the world you have to make sure you are inputting the correct information (practicing the perfect throw) to get the desired results at the tables.

Muscle memory is the ability to perform a physical task without consciously instructing your various muscles during the activity. We have to practice the mechanics of a perfect throw many times until we can perform that throw without thinking of the various steps involved. The amount of repetitions necessary for an act to be in your muscle memory can vary from person to person based on coordination and ability. It is necessary to be able to shoot without "thinking" about it to be a good controlled shooter. There are so many distractions and variables that we must learn to control those things that we are able to (i.e., the elements of a perfect throw) in order to have the opportunity to overcome the many disadvantages we face at a casino craps table.

Question: *How long does it take for muscle memory to kick in?*

Answer: Developing muscle memory varies from person to person, but most experts feel that you can develop it in 21 to 30 days with daily practice. You don't have to have a marathon practice session each day to train your muscle memory. In fact, several short sessions are much better than one long session. The reason for this is because when you are not practicing, your brain can take the time to assimilate the information you input during your practice sessions. A short practice session right before bedtime is ideal. When you sleep at night your mind replays the day's events while your body is relaxed, and your brain can take the information from your practice session and learn from it. If you can't practice before sleeping, the next-best time for a practice session is first thing in the morning while your mind and body are refreshed.

It doesn't matter when or how long you practice, but it is important that you practice every day for the first 21 to 30 days. This is the only way you will start to develop muscle memory. After the initial time, you will still need to practice to fine-tune your throw and to keep in form. You can't just practice for 21 days, put the dice down, and then expect a good roll when you visit the casino in a month or so. The best advice to follow is this: If you get up and feel like practicing, then *practice*. If you get up and don't feel like practicing, then practice anyway.

Question: *How single-minded do you have to be to become a good controlled shooter?*

Answer: To succeed you need to be focused on achieving success. Successful people start with a goal, and then they make a game plan to achieve that goal. When they are not physically working toward their goal, they are working toward it using one of the most powerful tools available—visualization.

Visualization has been used by top athletes, successful businesspeople, and other winners to achieve their goals. They use mental rehearsal to practice each sequence of events leading to the fulfillment of their goals. By playing and replaying an event in your mind, it can actually help develop your muscle memory to lock in the correct input needed to help your body respond during the actual event. One Olympic skating champion told how she would practice her routine in her mind every night before going to sleep. She would picture every last detail, re-creating her every move. When she was asked about her use of visualization, she said that one thing that helped her most was, "In my mind I never fail."

You can practice your dice throw in your mind when you are away from the tables or not able to practice on your rig. Create a mental movie in your mind of the perfect dice roll. Visualize every detail of the experience as if you were actually walking into the casino to play. See yourself walking up to the table and buying in. As the stickman pushes you the dice, put your money on the Pass Line. Feel the dice in your fingers as you gently pick them up. Go through each motion of the throw. Aim at your target and watch the dice travel in a perfect arc. See them gently touch the back wall and settle on 4 and 2 to establish your Point number. Take the chips from your rack and make your Place bets. Pick up the dice again and picture each move as you watch your dice make your Point. The more details you put in your mental movie, the better your mind will accept them as real. Like the Olympic skater who never fails in her mental practice, you never want to seven-out in your mind.

Practicing through visualization will help you improve your game, and it is something you should incorporate into your daily routine.

Question: *What are the mental traps you have fallen into when you've played?*

Answer: Dominator and I have fallen into every one at the early stages of our gambling careers, and a few still continue to hound us. First, thinking about the money you are betting; if you do that you are betting too much. You should be able to shoot without a second thought on whatever bets you have made. If you think to yourself, *Gee, that's my heart operation on the table,* then reduce the size of your bets.

Never play when you are tired. Never play on the first or last day of your casino trip (if you'll be there for a few days). Not having a prepared plan of attack when you begin your session will hurt you. Changing from your plan of attack because of a comment by a player or crewmember is another no-no.

Never hesitate to quit playing and take a break. Failure to follow your plan of attack in the hope that things are going to change for the better. Shooting out of position. Thinking that your skill makes you unbeatable. Letting other players influence your types of bets and their amounts. There are actually more bad things you can do at a table than good things, and many dice controllers do those to excess. It's a losing formula.

Question: *How should you prepare yourself for play?*

Answer: Careful dice throwing is like pitching a baseball, hitting a golf ball, making a free throw in basketball. Controlled shooting is a physical activity. You need to prepare your body for action. Some bending and stretching will help you get ready. After that, and while still in your room or at home, use your practice rig (or hotel bed) to throw many times until you have a nice smooth, soft, and consistent delivery. Remember that during this warm-up the numbers don't really matter. All you are trying to do is get the dice moving together through the air to land softly and consistently. Visualize the dice in the middle of the table, then see them being slid to you. See yourself setting the dice, gripping the dice, taking your stance, breathing, and softly sending the dice on their way. Watch them as they travel with them looking as if they are glued together, land together just before the back wall, bounce together, and softly come to rest near the wall. See the perfect result of your perfect throw. Meditate. Relax yourself. Focus on the task you have in front of you. As you approach the table and while at the table getting ready for your turn with the dice, continue your meditation. Center yourself. Continue to breathe from your center. Become a warrior at the table. It is yours for the taking.

Question: *Why not ask players whose chips are in your landing zone to move them?*

Answer: Such requests bring too much attention to you, and they also get you out of the zone. The chips really don't interfere with you. There is plenty of room next to, in front of, or behind the chips to land those dice. You see the chips and worry, making them a bigger problem than they really are. Practice shooting with chips at home, and you will see that you can avoid them most of the time without any dire consequences. We prefer not to play at tables with other controlled shooters who don't have enough confidence to shoot around chips.

Question: *What should you do after you play a session?*

Answer: Keep a journal of your playing sessions. In this journal list day and time you played, who you played with, how long you played, the table size, how the dice reacted to the table, how the crew was (and note names if they were very good or very bad), and how you did at this table and session.

Question: *How often do you change your dice?*

Answer: Change your practice dice every two weeks or 2,000 rolls; you want them to be as sharp as the dice in a casino. Also have different sizes of dice and dice with different surfaces on them (frosted or polished for example). You must get used to different dice.

Question: *How do you handle the emotional downs of losses?*

Answer: One must *accept* any loss; it is part of the game. Most rolls will not be winners. We are .300 to .400 hitters; we make the money, but we also strike out a lot. That fact is hard to assimilate, because many players think that with a decent controlled throw they will win every time they get the dice. This is why at GTC we teach having a separate bankroll for gaming (the 401G). This is money we have set aside from our everyday living expenses; this is money we can afford to lose. We all hate to lose, and when we do we must figure out what and why it happened. But we can't change the past; we can only go forward.

Many things can cause you to lose. Sometimes betting too much on others causes losses. Sometimes staying too long at the table causes them. Other times chasing an initial loss causes them. One of the most devastating things that can happen is throwing what appears to be perfect throws and having disastrous Point-7 cycles. One thing is for sure—losses do *not* feel good. How do you deal with the losses? Take a break. Document what happened at the table. Sometimes you did everything right and still lost. That will happen. No one has a 100 percent guarantee of winning in any given session.

Although no one likes losing, dealing with losses is made easier if a couple of things are true. If you are practicing regularly as well as betting and keeping track of your practice-session wins and losses, you will see that losing sessions happen there, also. You will also see that you will overcome those losing sessions with more frequent and greater winning sessions. Having this knowledge is immeasurably helpful in dealing with a live casino loss. The other thing that is a must in dealing with losses is having a large enough bankroll to sustain you.

Question: *I hate playing the Lightside of a craps game. I am a confirmed Darkside Don't player. Give me a game plan to execute after I have a controlled throw.*

Answer: Sometimes you may want to bet on the Don't Pass or Don't Come when you have the dice—or you are a committed Darkside player who hates the Right way of doing things. A group of us were in Atlantic City and we were all betting the Don't because the table was a $100 minimum and we were trying to grind out steady $100 wins. So we were setting for the 7 after our Point was established. Every time one of us sevened-out, a loud cheer came from the table! People were watching behind us because of all the yelling, and some were trying to squeeze onto the table. Then someone said, "What the heck are they yelling for? Every shooter is sevening-out!" It was great fun. There are certain sets that you should use to throw a 7 for certain point numbers. These 7 sets will be different than the Come-Out 7 set used by Rightsiders. So if you want to try shooting from the Darkside, here is what you should do. First use the 2-V Set as your set during the Come-Out roll. This is because you want to try to establish the 4 or 10 as your Point—these are the most difficult Point numbers to hit. If you don't establish either of these numbers as your Point, don't worry, here are the sets that you can use with the other numbers to increase the likelihood of a 7 showing with just a single pitch of the dice.

If your Point is a 6 or 8, use the 6 Half 8 Set. This set has a 6-spot on the top left die with a 3-spot facing you and the 1-spot on the top right die with 4-spot facing you. Hence the name 6 Half 8.

The 6 Half 8 Set.

If your point is a 5 or 9, use the 5 Upside Down 9 set. This set has a 5-spot on the top left die with a 1-spot facing you and the 2-spot on the top right die with 6-spot facing you. Hence the name 5 Upside Down 9.

The 5 Upside Down 9 Set.

If your point is a 4 or 10, use the 4 Half 10 Set. This set has a 4-spot on the top left die with a 2-spot facing you and the 3-spot on the top right die with the 5-spot facing you. Hence the name 4 Half 10.

The 4 Half 10 Set.

We do have to caution you about these sets. We make the assumption that you do have some decent degree of axis control when you are deliberately going after certain numbers. If not, you might find that you aren't having the wins you were hoping for.

Question: *At times my dice flip to the side, and I get the 7. At other times they double pitch, and I get the 7. Maybe I should set for the 7 so that when my dice flip or pitch they will result in a non-7?*

Answer: If you are a competent shooter and you find that your dice are pitching or flipping or flopping to those 7s, you might need to find a dice set that is just right for you. SmartCraps software would have the exact answer based on what faces your dice are showing when your roll is completed. However, just jumping to an All-Seven Set is not the right thing to do. If you are not pitching, flipping, or flopping during most of your rolls, you'll start hitting those 7s more than you are now when your roll is just a little off. The question is this: is your roll more *on* or more *off?*

The objective of dice control is to have the ability to change the nature of your throw, making it more influential over the dice. If you start to think that you will always be somewhat off, then certainly look to increase your edge by coming up with a dice set that enhances your ability, rather than diminishes your ability. But this advice is for seasoned shooters, not novices.

In the first year of play in the casinos, you are going to experience all manner of dice landings and results—and you are going to come up with all manner of theories as to why your dice aren't always behaving as you want them to. The dice are like children—they are sometimes not going to be perfect. The fact is, your control is only marginal—maybe in the 5 percent range when the roll is completed, if you are a good shooter. There's a lot of room for error here. The biggest error is to jump to conclusions based on insufficient evidence. Give yourself a good year with the Hardway Set and/or the 3-V and see if you are winning at the end of that time. We are very leery of looking for the quick "dice-set fix" because many players will think that the set is the key to their winning. The real key is your ability *with* the set. If a shooter has no ability, it doesn't matter what set he uses—he'll be a loser.

Question: *You say to go backward to frontward when analyzing our controlled shot. Explain that more fully.*

Answer: The dice land and are almost always on the Hardway numbers. In the air they look like hell; leaving your hand, they look like hell; they land and split like mad—and for the last 10,000 rolls you have been killing the casinos because the dice land on those Hardways. What do you do? Nothing! If you start to find that your end results are changing for the worse, then by all means begin to work on the earlier elements of your throw, because now you are doing something wrong. That's what we mean by saying you work from the back in. The results come first; if those are consistently good, you don't muck around with anything else. If the results are not good, then you work on fixing what is causing the problem. Interestingly enough, a competent dice controller goes back (results) to front, but a new dice controller goes from front to back. The new dice controller has to try to get those early steps in the process just right before worrying about the end result. Two seemingly contradictory ideas, both equally true.

Question: *What about the bets the stickman calls out for you to make? Are any of these any good?*

Answer: What do *you* think? These are the worst bets on the table. Some dealers are so conscious of how bad these bets are that they merely mumble them.

Question: *How much luck happens even for a controlled shooter?*

Answer: Plenty. Not every throw is controlled. Sometimes the dice miss the back wall—a random roll (probably). Sometimes they go a little crazy in the air—a random roll (probably). Sometimes one die bounces high and one bounces low and they go off in different directions—a random throw (probably). Now, the 7 comes up 16.67 percent of the time, so you are hoping for some luck, or as Dominator yells, "Give me some luck!" Your real control is never 100 percent, even when your throw gives you an edge; and not every throw will be controlled due to various things. Sometimes pitchers have wild pitches—no control there! The longer the roll, the more occasions for some of those rolls to be random. But just yell (to yourself), "Give me some luck!" But overall, controlled shooters win the money from the casinos; even the occasional random rolls can't stop that!

Question: *I've heard of a bet called the "Oddsman's Bet," but I have never seen it in a book or article. Is there such a bet?*

Answer: Yes, it appeared in my book *The Captain's Craps Revolution*, which was published in 1993. If you notice someone who is not taking Odds on his Pass Line bet, you ask him if you can place the Odds behind his Pass Line bet. Go gently with this one. Many craps players will look at you as if you are crazy because they might not understand what you are asking. But it is a way to play a game that is dead even with the house on random rollers and gives you a bet you can overcome with just a teeny-weeny bit of dice-control skill.

Question: *Can setting for the 7 create a non-7 shooter? Can controlled shooters, knowing they can't be 100 percent perfect in their throws, set for a 7 and expect that their imperfect throws will result in a non-7? Can controlled shooters deliberately create a shot that is "off" by just enough that with a sevens-set it will result in a non-7?*

Answer: These are, to be sure, theoretical questions that are not definitively answerable using any kind of valid research, because someone can say that he has done thousands of shots of this sort and "it works." And this someone might not be lying; he just might be using his results and his particular throw as a standard upon which to judge others' potential results. (He could also be deluded—a highly more likely situation.) Much like a pitcher in baseball who throws a split-fingered fastball might have certain results with hand placement, a controlled shooter (assuming an *extraordinary* degree of control) might be able to be so good that he can make the dice react *improperly* enough to result in a non-7 when he sets for the 7.

But I wouldn't bet on it.

To do a variation of something you have to be good at that particular something. In this case, if you were that good at controlled shooting, why would you monkey around with your throw? You're making money on it. For example, if you set the Hardway Set and you have demonstrably shown that you can avoid the 7 using that set, why in heaven's name would you change? You are already avoiding the 7! But if you can't avoid the 7 with the Hardway Set, you don't have any (or enough) control to be predictable when you set the sevens-set either. In short, if you aren't already really good at controlled shooting, you aren't going to be "off" consistently and predictably enough to make any money. You'll be just another random roller who sets the dice and has conned himself into thinking he's an advantage player. Unfortunately, I have seen plenty of these shooters—too many.

The other trouble with the first proposition is the fact that you have to be "off" a predictable number of dice faces to attempt to capitalize on the seven-set coming up on a non-7 number. If the idea is to deliberately throw the dice at an angle so they hit the back wall skewed, you've only succeeded in creating a random game. You can't control skewed angles on a craps table.

Here's the problem as I see it with the second proposition. Keeping the dice on axis when you throw is difficult enough, but trying to deliberately be "off" just enough to consign the 7 to oblivion would take such *extraordinary* control that it would be better and far more profitable for that same extraordinary shooter to just use his control to hit particular numbers, such as the 4 and 10, which are usually the most difficult to hit but return the most. I exclude the Crazy Crapper bets from this discussion, as overcoming house edges in the near-double and double digits requires a degree of skill not found in most controlled shooters.

So can setting for a 7 create the conditions for a non-7? I don't think so. The concept is superficially logical, but upon examination it is fraught with danger, as are many seemingly logical betting systems and wacky-type throws that fail miserably in the long run. Setting for the 7 and then attempting to be "off" or at an angle can, however, create the conditions for randomness, and that's exactly what the casinos would want. Thankfully, no reputable dice control teachers are pushing such an idea. It's merely in the area of speculation—where it should remain.

Question: *If you have 11 other players at the table, how long on average will it take the dice to get back to you?*

Answer: The average number of rolls for a shooter is about eight per hand. So maybe two rolls per minute would equal four minutes. Say there are 11 people at the table; the total amount of time is about 44 minutes (give or take maybe 15 minutes) before the dice get back to you. That's just a guess, but those dice are not in a rush to be in your hands. Obviously, there will be cases of hot rolls where the dice stay with one or several shooters for a long, long time. There will also be more cases of short rolls where the dice get back to you sooner.

Question: *Do you have to have long hands to make money? Can someone with a 1:6 SRR ever be controlling the dice?*

Answer: Although it is fun to talk about and dream about monster rolls, a smart player can make money on rather short rolls of repeating numbers. Someone who is a sharp 6 and 8 shooter can hit those numbers once each (or one of them twice) and then seven-out and show a profit.

Indeed, you could have an SRR of 1:6, which is generally considered random, and be a winning controlled shooter.

Question: *What about negative progressions?*

Answer: You are winning and you lower your bet. If you are playing a controlled shooter or betting on yourself, taking your bet lower is probably a mistake. You need to bet into an edge, not try to skirt an edge. In a random game, going lower is good—you are giving the casino less money to grind out of your bankroll—but lowering bets when you have an edge is not the same. The only exception would be if the controlled shooter's or your technique started to look poor. In such a case, you are lowering your bet (or taking your bet down) because the shot is looking bad, not because you are winning.

Question: *To stop the pit from knowing how much you make, should you "rat-hole" chips?*

Answer: It is the responsibility of the pit to know how many black and higher-denomination chips they have at or leaving a table. Successfully hiding chips will cause them trouble doing this. In addition, they usually know that you are hiding chips, and that makes you look bad. Take your wins and your losses and play just the way every other craps player plays.

Question: *I am a controlled shooter and have had good success after a tough first year. But there are a couple of casinos I go to where the dealers and especially the box man keep telling me that what I am doing just doesn't work. They are the only two casinos that are near me.*

Answer: It is funny that the dealers and box people who tell you controlled shooting doesn't work never tell shooters who fling the dice or shake the dice or throw the dice 90 miles an hour down the table—where they bounce like crazy all over the layout—that what they are doing doesn't work. We know without a doubt that such throws are merely random and are losers in the long run. So how come no annoying comments from these dealers and box people? Oh, wait, maybe because controlled shooting does work and they are trying to get under your skin. If you can ignore them and continue to win, great; if they are getting to you, then save up money to go to Vegas or Atlantic City, where there are plenty of tables that you'll like and plenty of casino personnel who don't get into a huff when they see what you are trying to do.

Question: *If I am a controlled shooter with an SRR of 1:7, what about making the Field bet? I am in action on every roll. If I bet $10 per roll, I will be able to win or lose on each decision.*

Answer: Yes, you will be on every roll, giving the house an edge of 5.56 percent—a loss of $5.56 per $100 bet. So that is the edge your throw must overcome. Better to just Place the 6 and 8 for the same total amount as you would have put out on the Field. Then the monetary edge you have to overcome is just 1.52 percent, which is easier to do and will make you more money. The fact that something is decided a lot is irrelevant if the same total amount of money is being discussed.

CHAPTER 26

Five Days with the Five Horsemen

I met Skinny at 10:40 AM on Monday at McCarran Airport in Las Vegas. We had seen each other a couple of weeks before in Atlantic City, where the Five Horsemen (Dominator, Stickman, Nick-at-Night, Skinny, and me) along with our good friends Marilyn "the Goddess," her husband Charlie "Sandtrap," and Jack "the Raging Baritone" had played for five days. It was a good five days, except for the fact that the casino where we played most of our sessions had a casino manager who should have been quarantined for acute imbecility.

This wild-eyed ploppy came down to the table when we were playing and screamed at us about hitting the back wall (which none of us had missed or would miss for the entire week), and he would time how long it took us to throw the dice (we were all faster than the fastest random roller). He couldn't nail us on these things, and that pissed him off even more. So then he'd scream just to scream. The reason we played there is simple—we kept winning.

"He knows who you and Dom are," the Goddess said to me. "For some reason that scares him."

This dreg even told the Goddess that she couldn't sit at the table and then became beet red when she whipped out a letter from her doctor and some official medical certificate about handicap rights. The Goddess had a bad hip and couldn't stand too long at the table.

He couldn't get us on anything, and that made him even crazier. Even Dominator felt sympathy for the guy, the Dominator kind of sympathy. "What a fucking asshole he is!" Dom stage-whispered, and of course the casino manager heard him. The guy's neck pulsed red with coursing blood. He turned to face Dominator, who just stared right back into this dolt's face.

I felt really bad for this casino manager because we did not have one losing day at his casino. He'd watch us have good roll after good roll, and he'd see those chips heading for our racks. It wasn't just the Five Horsemen on fire; the Goddess, Sandtrap, and the Raging Baritone were all hot as well.

If a person could shoot an eye out of his head like shooting a marble out of his hand, then this casino manager seemed quite capable of doing so. He could have been in *Ripley's Believe It or Not*; his eyes would bulge so much. I expected them to shoot out of their sockets. The dealers thought he was a jerk too. They would roll their eyes as he foamed and fumed over this or that. The dealers didn't want this "dickweed" (as one called him) to screw up the game, which, translated, meant, "Man, you guys are tipping like crazy and you're easy to deal to." The floor person told us that he wasn't responsible for the behavior of this casino manager and that we were welcomed as far as he was concerned.

But now I was in Las Vegas for another go-round against the mighty casino kingdom, one casino in particular.

"Hey, hey, Skinny!" I said and shook his hand.

"Hey, how are you?" and he smiled back.

"Dom and Nick are already at the hotel," I said.

"Stickman came in last night," said Skinny.

"The gang's all here," I said.

"I took your advice and just did carry-on this time," said Skinny as we walked to the limo driver holding the sign that said "Skinny."

"Carry-on is the only way to travel," I said. I always use carry-on when I am traveling. Doesn't matter how long I am away from home. Two pairs of pants, some underwear, socks, a few shirts, and I am set. Just as too many people overbet in gambling, too many people overpack for traveling. If I am gone for a while, there is no place I go that doesn't have laundry service.

One thing I have learned about playing in casinos: never dress up; never wear designer clothes. If a thief is scouring around looking for someone to mug, is he going to follow someone dressed plainly, someone perhaps wearing cheap sweats? Or is he going after someone who looks as if he has a lot of money due to the expensive watch he wears, the gold dangling around his neck and his expensive suit? If you've got money, it is always best to look as if you don't have money.

I can't get that idea through Dominator's head, though. Because Dom used to own fashionable men's clothing stores and has a clothes closet in his bedroom bigger than my living room, because every designer shirt Dom wears is monogrammed, and because his damn underwear is monogrammed too, Dom just won't listen to reason and always dresses well. His watch cost as much as some people's cars. Someday when he is mugged, I am going to say, "See I told you. You should have dressed like me!"

Although this was early March, the morning was a wonderful, sunny 70 degrees. But this new Vegas is not the Vegas of the past. Many of the buildings are now skyscrapers. The casinos are not in motel-style hotels. Vegas is big now, really big. And Vegas has become an amazingly crowded place—the roads are Manhattan West, beautiful temperatures in March, yes, but seemingly 10 billion cars.

"This is the time of year to come to Vegas," said Skinny. He took a water bottle from the limo door and handed it to me. "Got to stay hydrated," he said, lifting one for himself.

Skinny's nickname was given to him by, well, by him. At one time Skinny weighed around 400 pounds. Then he decided to lose weight, and in one year he dropped more than 200 pounds. He has kept most of it off too. He is no longer larger than life. "I will never again have some clown ask me if I am flying in the Macy's Thanksgiving Day Parade this year."

Skinny is a very successful man. He was vice president of information technology for a major financial company with about 300 people working for him. Now retired, he can pursue his two favorite activities: craps and bowling. Yes, Skinny is a masterful bowler, averaging in the low 200s in league play. He's an even better dice controller.

At the hotel we check in at the special VIP lounge, go to our suites to drop off our luggage, and then meet the other three Horsemen at the café for a late breakfast/early lunch. The flight from New York to Vegas is about five and a half hours, not counting arriving at the JFK airport an hour and half before flight time and then getting to the hotel after landing at McCarran. I think of my Vegas travel day as a work day. Even though I was sitting for all those hours, I am actually tired.

At the café we meet the other three Horsemen. The waitress brings us to our special garden-view table, and we take our normal seats—it's kind of like elementary school, with assigned seats.

The waitress gives us our menus. Skinny takes out a small tote bag in which are five small bottles of "hot stuff" that he and Stickman pour on their food. I once took a sniff of one of these bottles and my nose burned like hell. I hadn't even touched the stuff, just smelled it, and it hurt. These guys slather this stuff all over their eggs and even on their fruit.

"I like hot stuff," says Dom. "Let me put a dab on my fingertip to try it."

"Dom, they've been eating this crap for years. Now you want a taste?" I asked.

"I'm being adventurous," replies Dom.

"That's not too hot," says Stickman, opening one of the small bottles. "You should be all right with that."

"Don't worry," smiles Dom. "I'm an old Italian. I like red pepper. No problem."

"I don't like hot stuff like this kind. It's just too hot," says Nick, reading his menu.

Dom dabs a bit on his fingertip. He smells it. "Smells fine," he says. Then he puts a pinch on his tongue. "It's hot," he says. "But it's good."

"That's too mild for me," says Skinny, looking at his menu. "Stickman and I prefer SHU of 500,000 to 2 million. SHU measures the hotness of hot sauce; we prefer 200 times or more the hotness of jalapeño peppers."

Skinny and Stickman check out the bottles and select which burning poison they want to pour over their breakfast.

Then comes a roaring "Ohhhhhh!!!! Fuck!!!!! Oh, shit!!!" Dom grabs his glass of water and pours it into his mouth. He swishes it around and then swallows. "Ohhhhh, shit! It hurts more!"

"Oh, yeah," says Stickman. "You put water on it, and it spreads it around more."

The waitress comes over. "You guys ready?"

"Ow! Oh! Christ!" screams Dom.

"I'll have the egg-white omelet," says Skinny. "Diet Coke."

"Diet Pepsi okay?" asks the waitress

"Oh shit! Oh shit!" screams Dom.

"Diet Pepsi is fine. No ice," says Skinny.

"I'll have the Spanish omelet with the turkey sausages," says Stickman. "Decaf for me."

"Fuck!!!!" screams Dom. "Oh, fuck! Shit! Oh, God!"

Now the waitress turns to Dom. "Are you okay, sir?"

"He just had some hot stuff," says Nick. "I'll have a Rueben. Regular coffee."

As the waitress writes Nick's order, she asks, "What kind of hot stuff?"

Skinny shows her the small bottles. "Oh, I love this one. I'm into hot sauces."

"Bacon, lettuce, and tomato on rye toast. No mayo, just plain. Club soda and cranberry juice, easy on the ice," I say.

"Does this ever end?" screams Dom, now with tears coming out of his eyes and going down his cheeks.

"You'll get over it," I say. "You're an old Italian."

"Bring him a tiny amount of beer," says Skinny.

"Alcohol will reduce the hotness," says Stickman.

"Bring it right now," says Dom, wiping his eyes and his nose, which is now also running.

"Do you want anything to eat, sir?" asks the waitress.

"Cinnamon bun and pancakes," squeaks Dom. "Get the beer, please! I'm dying."

Breakfast finished, Skinny puts it on his room. There are five of us, five days, and each one of us will pick up one of the breakfasts. Makes things go faster. Because we are all RFB, the treat is from the casino.

"Okay, what do you say we go swimming?" I ask.

Dom looks at Nick; Nick looks at Dom. Stickman looks at me. I look at Skinny. Skinny looks at Stickman.

"You guys want to play, right?" I ask.

"I'm feeling good," says Dom.

"You were crying before," I say.

"Me too," says Nick. "Ready to go."

Dom and Nick are the two most aggressive players in terms of wanting to spend time at the tables. Skinny is close to them but has a modicum of restraint. Stickman is like me, much more conservative and cautious.

"You know it's not good to play on the first day. We tell our students not to play on the first day," I say. "Maybe we relax; take naps, then maybe we play after dinner. How's that?"

"Today isn't my first day," says Stickman. "I came in last night."

"Let's give it a shot," says Skinny.

"First day," I say. "I don't know, man, we might be kicking ourselves in the ass come dinnertime. Are we really ready to shoot?"

"We play a little, see how it goes," says Dom. "How's that?"

"Come on," says Skinny. "No big deal."

"It's four to one, Frank," says Nick.

I shake my head, "After all these years we still can't get enough."

So we head to the tables.

"The Five Horsemen ride again," says Nick, laughing.

This casino is a high-end property. The Five Horsemen are all RFB. Our betting averages range from $250 per decision to about $1,000 per decision. It's enough to get us the royal treatment. How long this will last is beyond me. Dominator and I wore out our welcome in Mississippi because we were just too greedy. The Five Horsemen have been pounding this Vegas property for a year and a half. So far we haven't had a losing week, as of this trip.

The dealers know us, and the pit crews know us. Some of them have read my books and seen our DVD. Still, no hassles. Maybe they realize that when we tell people which are the good casinos to play at, we highly recommend this one. The overwhelming majority of players who read my books and articles are not advantage players; they are just looking for a good place to play. So this place treats us well, and I then recommend this place as a top-notch place to play. I guess the management knows this.

Or, being a prime property, even our biggest wins really don't hurt their bottom line. Random players who happen to make fortunes on our hot hands will give it all back and then some when we leave the tables. In Tunica, the Horseshoe Casino, before it was ruined by Harrah's, took a beating one night when Dominator and I had back-to-back monster rolls after which we retired for the night (you can read about this in *The Virgin Kiss*). The next morning I went back to the table we had hammered. The pit boss told me that evening they had made 4 percent more money than they had the year before because all the other players had stayed all night trying to recapture last night's lightning, losing what they had won and then some.

"Hey, hey, look who's back," says one of the floor men.

"Hey, guys!" says one of the dealers.

The other dealers say hello. There are three tables open. The one we are standing at has five people at it, but they are playing the end positions. Stick Left One, Two, and Three are open, as are Stick Right One and Two. Stickman slides into SL1; Skinny slides into SL2; I stand at SL3, at the curve (the mixing bowl). Dom and Nick take SR1 and SR2. Nick is a lefty. Dom is gifted that he can shoot from either side of the table with equal finesse. Dom is the only one whose Stick Left and Stick Right SmartCraps results are just about equal.

"Guys," says the floor person, "you want me to change this to a $25 game?"

"Thanks," I say.

"Now, don't you guys take too much money from us," he says. This floor person has read my books, and when he plays he attempts a controlled throw.

He didn't have to worry that first hour. We all played the 5-Count on the five random rollers who, being pains in the ass, all made it through and then sevened-out on the 6-Count or 7-Count. Even though my bets on them were low—a Come bet ($25) with full 3X, 4X, and 5X Odds, five defeats in a row put me in an immediate hole. Then Dom got the dice, made it through the 5-Count and went down in flames. The numbers he hit between the 1-Count and the 5-Count were garbage numbers, and none of us won money. We just lost what we bet. When Dom sevened-out, he turned his back to the table, lit a cigarette, and ignored the game for a few moments. Dom is okay when he sevens-out quickly. He just smokes a cigarette, relaxes, and prepares for his next turn with the dice. It's when he has monster rolls that there's trouble—which I'll describe shortly.

Nick got the dice. Nick mimicked the Titanic, hitting the iceberg right after establishing his Point.

Now, Nick is a very aggressive bettor and tends to go right up on us when we are shooting. And he really goes up on himself big time when he is shooting. Sadly, he was a ship heading to the bottom of the Atlantic Ocean on that Point/seven-out.

"Come on, Skinny!" I clapped my hands. He went down on the 6-Count, also having hit nothing but garbage numbers between counts one and five.

"All right, Stick, you do it, kid!" Dom said.

Nick was clapping his hands.

When the Five Horsemen play, we cheer and clap and act just like regular gamblers—even when random rollers are shooting. We don't pretend to be professionals with calm demeanors. We throw ourselves into the game. We cheer and moan and pray and do all the things gamblers do. For some reason some dice controllers attempt a professional demeanor, which is nonsense. The dealers are the professionals; we are the players.

Stick got the dice. Now, Stickman is hard of hearing and has two hearing aids. When he shoots he takes them out of his ears and puts them in his shirt pocket. "I hear no noise," he says. "It's just me and the dice."

If you want to see the perfect controlled throw, then go no further than Stickman. At 6'4", he leans far out over the table. His throw is relaxed, and he can do that throw over and over again without any change in form. Those dice go into the air together as if in slow motion. They softly land, and then they die at the back wall. Oh, that form! If there is beauty in controlled throwing, then Stickman's throw is beautiful. And his results are usually just as beautiful.

The weekend before Dominator and I were banned in Mississippi, Stickman had this roll in a Tunica casino where we were playing: 4, 6, 6, 6, 6, 6, 6, 4, 6, 6, 9, 6, 6, 6, 10, 6, 6, 8, 6, 6, 6, 6, 8, 6, 6, 6, 6, 6, 7-out. That was amazing, certainly. Just as amazing—and a lesson to be learned about ploppy gamblers—is the fact that one player at the table kept saying through his black teeth, "I don't bet the 6; it's bad luck." This poor soul had placed the 5 and 9 and was making all sorts of Crazy Crapper bets. He lost money on this phenomenal roll.

So our expectations were high as Stickman set then aimed the dice. Oh, those dice looked so beautiful in the air. They landed so beautifully. His point was a 6. *Here we go again!* I thought. And he went down in flames, throwing an immediate seven-out.

Skinny and Stickman both turned and faced the stick person now so that their backs were to me and they were taking very little space up at the table. I was able to move into Stick Left Two. I sevened-out on my third roll.

Then the random rollers did their dirty deeds against us, as one after another after another after another after another made the 5-Count, we put out bets, the seven-out was called, and we lost our bets.

Then Nick got the dice; he bombed. Then Dom got the dice; he bombed, then put his back to the table and smoked a cigarette. Then Skinny got the dice, and he bombed. Then Stickman came tumbling down. And then me...ba-bomb!

We went another turn around the table. We stunk. Did I say this already? We stunk.

"I think we should quit," I said to Stickman.

"Yeah," said Stickman.

"Skinny? Over," I said.

"Yes," he said.

I walked behind the stick person's back.

"Dom, let's call it a session," I said.

"I want one more turn with the dice. Let's go around the table one more time," he said.

"I want another turn," said Nick.

"Okay," I said. "We each get one more turn, and if we don't get hot we quit."

I told Stickman and Skinny. "One more turn."

This next turn would be our fourth turn with the dice. Usually we would quit after three or four turns if nothing was happening, so staying for that fourth turn was not a big deal...but it was the first day, and we shouldn't have been playing after just arriving. I was beginning the process of kicking myself in my ass.

"I'm kicking myself in my ass," I said into Stickman's ear.

"I beat you to it; my ass is already sore," said Stickman.

"Not as sore as mine," said Skinny.

So we went around the table one more time. Thankfully four of the random rollers sevened-out before the 5-Count and one of them actually hit some numbers after the 5-Count, one of which was my lone number. Hooray! Finally a win!

Dom got the dice. He made his Point, hit some numbers, and sevened-out. I made a little money on him. Nick took the dice and went Point/seven-out. I didn't lose anything because he hadn't made it past the 5-Count. Skinny went Point/seven-out. Same thing, no loss. Stickman hit a few numbers and sevened-out. I made a little on him. We were not getting killed on this turn. I was actually up a little...on this turn.

Then I took the dice. Ba-boom! I put together a 40-roll hand. Before I could say anything, Dom whispered behind the stick person's back, "Another turn. We're getting hot."

Dom knew I wanted to pull the plug, and he beat me to it—no plug-pulling for him. I nodded. Okay, another turn. Two of the random rollers left the table. But one of them was replaced by a young guy who had been watching my roll and who now fumbled with his chips, dropping the load on the layout after he cashed in. The game stopped dead. The New Kid (as I thought of him) was hurriedly picking up the chips in fistfuls, but they wouldn't all fit in his hand. Some would squirt out like watermelon seeds.

The two random rollers did not make it through the 5-Count, and the stick person passed the dice to the New Kid. He shook his head. "I'm not shooting the dice when these guys are here!" he said so loud you probably could hear him in Lake Tahoe.

Dom took the dice and rolled a 19 hand. Good hand, no garbage numbers. When he sevened-out he said the single-most-used word at a craps table, "Shit!" He turned his back to the table, lit up a cigarette, and said again, "Shit."

Nick rolled a 16. A good roll too. Dom had quickly forgotten his anger and was starting to get a gleam in his eye, which meant he was preparing to make a lot of money. If you ever watch Dominator play, look into his eyes. If he gets this gleam—or starts to look insane—then you know he is heading for his rolling zone. He headed there now. When Dom is in this zone, he does remarkable things—like calling out the numbers he's going to hit. Not just the number, but the actual dice faces.

Skinny got the dice and rolled a monster 40 hand. Stickman got the dice—a 32 hand. The dice went to me. I passed them. I was tired. The two random rollers each made it past the 5-Count and sevened-out. I lost a bet on each. The New Kid got the dice and again passed them.

Now Dominator got the dice. His eyes were ablaze. He either looked like a psychic, a monk, or a crazed killer—depending on how you wanted to see it. To me he looked wonderful. Dominator is the best dice controller in the world. And now he ripped out a 52-roll hand, number after number after number. When Dominator gets hot, he gets theatrical. His throws are great, but when the dice leave his hand, he does a swoosh and curl with his throwing hand, then a fist pump as he slams into the person to his right. Of course, the theatricality has nothing to do with the throw. Those dice are flying when he does his swoosh and curl and fist pump and then collides with the person next to him. If you get to a table with us, never stand to Dom's immediate right if you value your life.

As Dom's long rolls progress, you might say he becomes "opposite man." Most shooters start to feel a warm glow as they get into that rolling zone. Not Dom. He gets pissed! As he rolls number after number, you can see the rising anger on his face. It's almost scary if you didn't know he was deep down such a teddy bear—*very* deep down. His face gives the impression that those dice must have said something against his mother. He almost snarls at them.

When Dom finally sevened-out, he slammed his fist on the chip rail, the chips bouncing up and down in the rails, and then he stormed off toward the nearest slot machines. "Where'd he go?" asked the stick person, a new dealer at this casino who didn't know Dom's habits.

"He went to kick a slot machine," I said.

"Isn't he happy?" asked the stick person.

"Yes," I said. "He just shows it differently."

"He'll be back," said the floor person, a fan.

"We'll cash in now," I said.

Stickman put his hearing aids back in his ears. Skinny put his huge stack of purple and orange chips on the table. So did Nick. Those two are our biggest players. Dom came back, smoking, and he cashed in too. We had a great first session on the very first day, violating everything we tell our students not to do and what we rarely do. This time it turned out okay.

The dealers thanked us for the tips—they had made a lot of money during our rolls, because we all bet for them. They were on every number during Dom's roll.

As we stood at the cage to cash in our chips, the New Kid from the table ran up to us. "Hey, I know who you guys are, oh, man, you are the Five Horses!" Then he dropped a bunch of chips on the floor.

"Horsemen," said Nick.

"Sorry, yeah, right, the Five Horsemen. Wow! Boy! I can't believe I played with you guys. I made a lot of money." He was scrambling around on the floor picking up his chips.

"Good, good," said Skinny.

"Can't wait to tell my friends."

I finally got to my suite, put the money in the room safe, fell into the bed, and slept for two hours. When I woke up it was 5:00 AM.

Skinny is in charge of making our dinner reservations. He is our social director unless Marilyn the Goddess is with us. Then she is the social director. Skinny makes our show reservations as well. There are a select number of restaurants where we like to eat, and we tend to make the same reservations during each trip. It's nice to have the waiters know us when we come to their restaurants. We like that personal, friendly attention. We might add a restaurant here or there to see if there are any new ones we'd enjoy. We like to eat early too, 5:30 or 6:00. This way we can be at the tables while most of the other players are at dinner.

At 5:30 PM we met outside the restaurant. It was a good dinner. None of us are big drinkers. Stickman and I will have two chilled Belvederes; Dom will usually order wine or something that he only half finishes. Rarely does Skinny drink. Nick will have a Belvedere and some club soda or some other mixer. We don't want to get tipsy if we are going to play after dinner.

Monday night's session was a replay of the afternoon. We had the $25 table to ourselves for the first half hour, which wasn't a good first half hour, and then the New Kid from the afternoon session showed up with two of his friends. "There they are," he shouted, and they rushed to the table. He threw his money on the table.

"Man, this is $25," said the Tall Friend.

"Look who's gonna be shooting. Get your money out there," said the New Kid.

The Third Guy hesitated, "You know I think that guy is shooting. We should wait." Indeed Skinny was shooting when they came to the table. But the New Kid threw his money down anyway, and the dice stayed in the middle of the table while the three of them bought in. It seemed to take an eternity.

Luckily it was Skinny who was shooting, because nothing bothers him. He has a cool, happy demeanor. He could be Gandhi. Had it been Nick shooting, you'd have seen frustration. Had it been Dominator… well, those kids would have gotten a severe tongue-lashing about proper manners at the craps table.

When the three new players were ready, the stick person passed the dice to Skinny, who proceeded to roll 20 more times before sevening-out. Stickman went next. He rolled 12 times, with seven 6s and three 8s. His point was a 5, which he never made before sevening-out. Damn good roll as we all bet the 6 and 8. I had a 17, a decent hand, and made us some money. Now the dice were passed to the Tall Friend, who picked them up to shoot.

"Are you nuts?" said the New Kid. "Pass the damn dice. Let them shoot." He swept his arm at us. The Tall Friend passed the dice.

By now Dom's face was red. He was really angry at these kids because they were bringing too much attention to us. The New Kid was really loud. Yes, the casino's dealers and floor person knew who we were, but we always played in a way that allowed us to just be regular players in our demeanor. We didn't go around saying, "Look at us, we are the Five Horsemen!" But now we had these kids making a big deal about playing with us.

Dom took the dice. He exploded for a 38, getting angrier and angrier as his hand got longer and longer. When he sevened-out, he stormed off the table, lit a cigarette, and went and kicked a slot machine. Nick followed with a 20. Dom had not yet come back by the time Nick had finished. He must have been really pissed at those kids or the dice…or something.

Then Skinny said, "Let's get some gelato." He was strongly indicating that we leave the table and call it a session. Nick said, "Let's keep going."

Then Stickman jumped in, "Let's get gelato. It's been a long day." Dom came back, saw that we were cashing in, and put his chips down. "Gelato," I said to him.

"Where you guys going?" asked the New Kid.

"We're done for the day," said Nick. The dealers all thanked us for the tips.

And we went for gelato.

Back in my suite I put all the money in the room safe. Day one had been wonderful. I slept the sleep of a winner.

Our normal day of play goes like this: We get down to the tables early, maybe 6:30 AM. We play until we shoot three or four times or until we start to have some bad rolls in an otherwise great session. The great sessions could see us take the dice five or six times, sometimes more. Usually I am the one to say the session is over. Usually Stickman and Skinny will agree. Usually Dom and Nick want to go another round. Generally we compromise. Sometimes we play one more round; sometimes we call it a session.

Then we go to breakfast.

We take our time at breakfast, discussing this and that. The Five Horsemen are a great group of guys. I wish everyone could be a part of a team like this. Sometimes we meet some of our advanced students or fellow Golden Touch instructors and interns, and they join us for breakfast.

After breakfast—always a big breakfast because we rarely eat lunch—we go back for another session. When that session is over, we head for the pool for an hour or so of sun and swimming. For me it is an hour of swimming, for Dom it is an hour of sun. For the others, it is an hour of both.

Then we go back to our suites, shower, perhaps take a nap (I *always* take a nap), and then we hit the tables for a late-afternoon session, then dinner and either a show or another session after dinner; then gelato and then bedtime.

That Tuesday was a spectacular day. We arrived at the tables at 6:30 AM. There were five people standing near the empty table: the New Kid, the Tall Friend, the Third Guy, and two others in their late fifties, it seemed to me, one a Sourpuss and one a Weasel.

We went to the table that was empty; the box man immediately made the table a $25 minimum.

"Wait a minute," shouted the Sourpuss, "this was $10. You just changed it."

We took our spots and asked for markers.

"These guys like $25. The tables over there are all $10," said the box man.

"Oh, no. No, no, no. I know what you are doing," said the Sourpuss. "You don't want us at this table with them!" He pointed to us. Then he bought in anyway, and so did the Weasel friend.

We got our chips, signed our markers, and Dom took the dice.

"You guys better be as good as everyone says," said Sourpuss. "This is a $25 table."

"Let's see what you got," snipped the Weasel.

Dom put the dice down. "Fuck!" he said. "Just play the game, okay?" he said to the Sour Puss. "Just play the fucking game." He set the dice.

Now, when Dom gets angry, he can be scary. He scared Sourpuss, who blanched and shut up. The Weasel looked the other way. Then Dom rolled 15 numbers. Good start. Then Nick banged out a 13. Then Skinny went bananas and blasted a 47. Skinny's dice looked perfect. Stickman was next. He took his hearing aids out. Bang!—a 20 for Stickman.

I passed the dice. My best time for shooting is in the afternoon after my swim and nap. Then I am refreshed and relaxed. More important, my left eye, one that has become the weak link in my body, seems to see better in the afternoon. I have a kind of macular degeneration in that eye. Straight lines look wavy; thus the back wall looks wavy too. It seems to get a little better after workouts. I also seem to dig into my muscle memory better after a workout as well. I have Marilyn the Goddess to thank for that. When I was really depressed about my eye and not taking the dice at all, she said to me, "Frank, you have played for a couple of decades. You could shoot blindfolded. Let your body just do it." And from then on I just did what she said.

"You're the great Frank Scope-bleed-dee, and you don't shoot?" asked the Weasel, getting the pronunciation of my name wrong. Geez, his voice was actually weasely too.

I ignored him. Dom stared at him. So did Nick. Skinny rolled his eyes. Stickman whispered, "Idiot."

The dice went around the table. Good rolls from everyone, again with Skinny popping out a really nice one of 37. The dice went around the table again. All winning rolls, again with Skinny banging out a 32.

That session was marvelous. Not every turn was great, but every round was. We ended the session when our four shooters started to get tired and each in turn sevened-out without a winning hand.

"That's it," I said. No one argued.

"I'm starving," said Stickman.

"When are you guys coming back?" asked the New Kid.

"I don't know," I said. "We want to eat and relax."

The dealers thanked us for the tips.

"Can we have a $10 table now?" asked Sourpuss of the box man.

That whole Tuesday was dreamlike. After breakfast we hammered them again. Luckily we had five of our students at the table, and they knew not to make a big deal of anything—just clap, cheer, and have some fun. They all knew how the bets were paid off, and the game went smoothly. One dealer said, "This is the best group of players I've ever dealt to." We all played just like good craps players should play. It was a refreshing change from the morning.

And we were blasting them, especially Skinny, who had been the star of the morning.

We were 10 players at the table when the New Kid and his friends showed up. They squeezed in. We then had six players on one side of the table and seven players on the other side. Then Sourpuss and the Weasel came over.

"Hey, can we get in there?" asked the Weasel, starting to shove his way next to Dominator, who did not move an inch.

"No," said the box man, who had obviously developed a hatred for these two during the course of the morning. "Table's full; that's it."

"There's seven on that side and only six on this side," said the Sourpuss, pointing.

All of us, including the dealers and the box man, ignored them. Finally they got the message and left for another table.

We finished that session. Everyone clapped. The dealers thanked us for the tips, and we cashed out.

Time to swim. Time to sun. Time to shower. Time to nap. Time for our afternoon session.

That afternoon session saw a small crowd around the table...waiting for us. But we got our spots, and the new players were all nice people. It was a fun session.

Skinny was again the star, with two rolls in the low 40s. Dominator was his usual winning self. He put on a show with several rolls in the high 20s and one of 40. Nick was off; so was Stickman. I took the dice and was damn good, consistently rolling in the teens and low 20s and one big 44. We each took the dice maybe six times. Then it was time for dinner.

That night, with another small crowd waiting for us to return to the tables, we decided to go to a show. We didn't play. We had played enough that day. We called our host, and he got us tickets to a great show. I am sure we all went to our rooms that night, put our stacks of $100s into our overflowing room safes, and slept beautiful sleeps.

And then Wednesday came—the horror show. Dominator stunk. Stickman stunk. Skinny stunk. Nick stunk. I stunk. Both morning sessions. The afternoon session. The evening session. Stunk!

Roll after roll after roll; seven-outs before the 5-Count, which didn't hurt Stickman, Skinny, or me but clobbered Dominator and Nick, who were going right up. Seven-outs just after the 5-Count destroyed Stickman, Skinny, and me but occasionally made Dominator and Nick a little money.

The tables were full that day too. Full of people expecting the Five Horsemen to destroy the casino and make them fortunes. It didn't happen. It was embarrassing.

We couldn't do anything right—although our rolls looked just fine, the results of those rolls were mind-bogglingly awful. Although the aggressive-betting Dominator had been up twice as much as me for the trip, his fall was like Lucifer's—the angel of light flung from the heavenly heights. He wound up right where I was, almost behind at the end of Wednesday evening. The 5-Count protected me on the down climb, while Dom's aggression helped him more on the up climb. We had gone from being way ahead to almost facing economic oblivion during this horrifying day.

Oh, yes, we took breaks, many breaks; we walked, we napped, we'd get some gelato, we'd swim, and then we'd come back to the tables totally refreshed—and get destroyed!

We left our Wednesday-night session stunned. We were like zombies in a George Romero movie. How could the glorious Five Horsemen get butchered like this? How could five Golden Touch dice-control instructors be brought down to earth in one stupefying and miserable day? Our room safes went from overflowing with packs of $100s to small piles of $20s.

But that is the nature of the advantage play. You have wide swings of fortune. I was just praying before I went to bed that the next day would widely swing the other way.

Thursday morning came. I was still in shock after Wednesday. I took a long, hot shower. Then the phone rang. I put on the hotel's bathrobe as I answered the phone.

"Hello," I said. I thought it was Dom. "You didn't kill yourself last night?"

"Frank? Is this Frank?" said the voice. Obviously it wasn't Dom.

"Who is this?"

"You don't know me, but I know you are staying here," said the voice.

"Yes?"

"Just wondering when you guys get to the tables. Heard you get down to the tables early, that's why I called," said the voice. "I got in last night, and I heard you guys were staying here."

"We don't make arrangements to meet people," I said, drying off.

"I'm here. What the hell? I want to hang with you guys," said the voice.

"That's flattering, but we don't really make appointments to play," I said.

"Come on," said the voice.

"If you're at the table when we play, you're at the table, but we just don't make appointments to play with anybody."

"I'll treat you guys to lunch," said the voice.

"You seem like a nice person," I said. "But we just don't make appointments to play with people."

"So when are you coming down to play?" asked the voice.

"In a little while," I said. "I'm just drying off from a shower."

"What's Dominator's room? I don't remember his last name, so I couldn't reach him," said the voice.

"I wouldn't call him," I said. "You'll see him at the tables. Got to go, I'm dripping wet."

I've had calls like that before. One guy once called me and asked if he could come over to my house for dinner because he wanted to "rap about craps." Maybe today's would be the good call though. Maybe this guy had psychically seen what would happen this Thursday. Maybe we were in for a hell of a day in the good sense, unlike yesterday's hellish day.

The five of us met at the slot machines near the craps tables at 6:30 AM. None of us had a good sleep. Dom was the last to join us, as was usual, holding a Starbucks coffee and smoking a cigarette.

"Yesterday is gone," he said. "It's done. We start new today." He took a long drag of his cigarette. "We kick their asses today."

And the day sessions were okay. We won a little at our first session, where we met the caller, who turned out to be a very nice guy. The Sour Puss and the Weasel were nowhere to be seen. The New Kid and his crew were also gone. There was a new group, some of them friends of the morning caller, some of them just people who came to play and didn't know us from holes in the wall.

We won a little before breakfast. We won a little after breakfast. We won some in the afternoon session. None of us were on fire, but none of us were cold either. It was a decent day, certainly far better than Wednesday had been. The only one who just couldn't get it together was Nick. He had carried over Wednesday's horror to Thursday as well.

There were two fun parts to Thursday. Our after-breakfast session was at a $100 minimum table. The $10 and $25 tables were packed with players. Standing around the $100 table was a mob scene—maybe a half-dozen people deep around the whole table. Evidently someone very special must be playing at this table.

The five of us squeezed through the crowd, and what we saw was jaw-dropping. On one end of the table was this Japanese guy, maybe 25 to 30 years old, with one incredibly beautiful and sexy woman hanging all over him, licking his ear—rubbing his face, rubbing herself against him, kissing him, tongue-kissing him, rubbing her breast against his hand when he wasn't shooting—while he played between $25,000 and $50,000 per roll.

But it was the other end of the table where the real action took place. Two "working girls," themselves quite beautiful and as undressed as one could be without being completely undressed, were engaging in intense foreplay. Some of the men in the mob around that table were cheering on these two. And when I say intense, it was *intense*. These girls were betting single $10 bets on the Pass Line. None of the gaggling men cared what these two were betting.

The Japanese guy was swigging champagne and chain-smoking cigarettes and applauding the girls. He was obviously loaded, in money and liquor. While the dealers were scooping up his chips after a fast seven-out, I asked him, "Is this a private table, or can we play too?"

He motioned. "Play, play."

We all bought in. Now, our normal buy-ins will be between $2,000 and $8,000. Playing with this guy and his lascivious girls made us look like paupers.

As the dealers were laying out our chips, Dom asked the stick person, "Who is that guy?"

"He's the Johnny Holmes of Japan," said the stick person.

Dom told me who he was. "Johnny Holmes? He's a ballplayer?" I asked.

"No," said Skinny. "Holmes is a porn star in America. So this guy must be a porn star in Japan."

That's probably why these girls were going nuts—to make Japan's Johnny Holmes feel right at home.

I wish I could say we devastated the casino and made Japan's Johnny Holmes a fortune. Unfortunately, based on how he was betting, which was just about every number on the table, as well as massive Come bets with full Odds, Mr. Holmes actually took a beating when we rolled and an even bigger beating when he rolled. We played the 5-Count on him, and he never made it past the count once.

Japan's Johnny Holmes had the habit of making his Crazy Crapper bets after the dice were passed to the shooter by throwing them into the air and calling them out—and this annoyed Dominator, who said to one of the dealers, "Tell him to make his bets at the right time or we will relive World War II."

Our rolls were pretty good too, with repeating numbers on rolls in the low to middle teens. The Five Horsemen won some money this late morning. Mr. Holmes did not.

When we left the table he was down more than $700,000. We saw him about a half hour later, drunk and staggering back to his room with his three girls, certainly a tough morning for the Japanese porn star. I hope he had a better session in his room.

Thursday afternoon was okay too. We won a little, very little. None of us were really hot, and we certainly were nowhere near making up for Wednesday's awful beating. And still Nick was not having good rolls at all.

During the afternoon session, as Dom was rolling and looking his intense self, a woman at the table whispered, "What's his name?"

"The Dominator," I whispered back.

"Oh, uh, ah, ee, the Dominator," she gasped. "Oh, I love that. The Dominator." She seemed to be in ecstasy.

I don't know what the hell that is. When we say he is called "the Dominator" to women, some of these women melt. "Oh, ah, ee, ah, the Dominator!" I just don't get it.

Then Thursday evening saw a great session by the Five Horsemen. At first, we fell into a hole. In addition, the chicken feeders were getting past the 5-Count and killing us with seven-outs on the sixth and seventh counts.

Thankfully, those chicken feeders left the table because, as one put it, "This table is ice cold," and a bunch of players who were standing behind them, players who knew us, streamed onto the tables to take these chicken feeders' places. These Five Horsemen fans just passed the dice; not one of them shot.

The stage was set.

A young millionaire, an injury lawyer, asked Skinny what Nick's name was as Nick took the dice.

"His name is Nick," said Skinny.

"Hey! Hey!" shouted the somewhat buzzed injury lawyer. "You're Nick-at-Night, so light it up tonight baby!" The injury lawyer took a swig of his top-shelf bourbon.

This lawyer was a big bettor, mostly purple and orange chips, and he was anxious to get some of his losses back.

Nick had been having a tough couple of days. His throw was not off really—it was just a bad streak. As with anyone, he was concerned. We had a talk, and I told him, "Don't worry about it, you're a great shooter, you'll snap out of it."

Nick, a lefty, has an interesting shot from Stick Right. Often his dice will wobble in the air, both wobbling the exact same way. When they hit the table they seemingly decide to do the exact same thing too—that is, they hit numbers. At other times, his dice are glued together. His roll is unique. Because he is so good, there is no need to try to change him into an orthodox shooter.

Thursday evening, Nick, who was now being called Nick-at-Night, *rocked* the house. He got the dice and slammed them for a 40-roll hand— *all Box numbers*. We were all the way back and then some. The next shooter was Jerry from SL1—he hit seven numbers after the 5-Count and made us some dough; then Skinny at SL2 hit for 19 numbers. Then the "ah, oh, ee, ah, oh" Dominator banged them for a 23-roll hand, and Nick-at-Night took the dice once again.

He rolled a 43—a spectacular roll, coming right after his first spectac-ular roll. The injury lawyer had four chip racks filled with black, purple, and orange chips—I'm figuring a $100,000 win. The Five Horsemen were also overflowing with chips. Two spectacular rolls by the man now known as Nick-at-Night had us sailing into outer space. Wow!

The fans were going nuts too! They were seeing what a great dice team could do, seeing the chips piling up, seeing a masterpiece painted by the newly dubbed Nick-at-Night. We were good representatives of controlled shooting that night—that's for sure.

The dice came around the table again, and everyone had more winning rolls in the teens, again with Nick banging out a 29. By the fourth go-round, we called it a night. The gelato tasted damn good that night. The room safes started filling up again. We all slept well.

Friday came with us vowing to beat the casino bloody on our last day. We met at the slot machines at 6:30. This time there were more than 25 players lingering around the craps tables. These were players who had been at the table the previous night to witness Nick-at-Night's spectacular rolls. (I always wonder how they know when we are coming down to play. During one trip, at one Strip casino, dozens were waiting for us in the slot aisles early every morning and even followed us from casino to casino.)

"Our legionnaires," said Skinny, laughing, nodding to the other players.

The players rushed to the craps table we were heading for. They took up every spot at the table. So much for shooting at that table. We headed to a different table, where the box man had immediately put up five "reserved" signs in our spots and then changed the minimum bet to $25.

A mad rush ensued of players trying to get onto our new table. Some of the clever players pooled their money so one could play at the table and the others could also get the benefits...that is, if we won. Sometimes players think we always win. We obviously don't always win, as Wednesday's debacle clearly showed. We've had our losing sessions, losing days, and even losing weeks. This week, overall, had been great...so far.

At the table we took our markers, Stickman took his hearing aids out of his ears, and then Dom took the dice. He sevened-out before the 5-Count. So did Nick, so did Skinny, so did Stickman. We were 0-for-4.

The other players passed the dice around the table. Dom sevened-out before the 5-Count; so did Nick; so did Skinny, so did Stickman. I hadn't lost a penny, nor had Stickman, nor had Skinny, although Dom and Nick, who were going right up, did not fare well.

The dice were not passed around this time, as several of the other players decided to shoot. Two of them made it past the 5-Count and went down on the 9-Count and 10-Count. Neither hit my one bet on them. Skinny and Stickman also had one bet on them, neither of which won. Nick and Dom had two bets on them, losing both. The other two players who shot went down before the 5-Count.

I guess they were shooting because they saw how badly we had shot. They figured they couldn't do any worse.

Then Dom got the dice and put on one of his classic shows—a 58-roll hand! Oh, he was singing and playing an air guitar, and then as the roll got longer and longer he started to get angrier and angrier. When he sevened-out, I yelled over to him, "Kick the slot machines in the high-limit area. You deserve it!" Even Dominator laughed at that one.

We went to breakfast. I was feeling pretty good, and I took over Skinny's spot when we came back to the table and our legionnaires. I rolled a 51 right off. Not bad at all. "Do you want to go kick a slot machine?" whispered Stickman in my ear. The next rounds of rolls were mediocre. We won some, lost slightly more. But the morning had been a spectacular win with monster rolls and winning shorter rolls too.

Our last session (or so I thought) would be Friday in the late afternoon after our pool sojourn. The great Stickman exploded with two 40-roll hands that afternoon. Skinny also had a 40-roll hand that afternoon as well. Dom, Nick, and I rolled 25s. We had good short rolls too.

It was a hell of an afternoon. Our legionnaires were in heaven, and so were we. As always, the dealers were happy, as those tips piled up for them as well.

We went to dinner a little later than we normally would because our session lasted so long. At dinner we discussed a new advanced betting system that we have been flirting with for a couple of years. It was decided that Stickman, a computer expert, and Skinny, a math expert, would do an intensive study of this betting system to see if it actually worked or was merely a craps dream. The betting system will appear in my next craps book, a book for advanced players.

After dinner, Dom said, "We are playing another session. We're hot. That's it." No one disagreed. We had been hot. Even I figured, "What the hell?"

We had a slow start at the $100 minimum table that evening. None of us shot well in our first two turns with the dice. I told Dom behind the stick person's back, "Two more turns, and if nothing good happens, we stop." He reluctantly nodded. Whether he would stop or not was another question entirely.

When Dom got the dice, he rolled a respectable 17. Nick hit 11. Skinny rolled an 11 too. Then Stickman blasted a 40.

Okay, we were winning big now.

The next turn saw Dom, Nick, and Skinny go down before the 5-Count. No harm done.

And Stickman took the dice. He established his point of 4 and never made a 7 until the end of this amazing, epic, roll. No 7s in 77 rolls! Yes, you read that right—a 77-roll hand and no 7s. No 7s on the Come-Out, no 7s at all. It was as if Stickman had magically made the dice lose their ability to make a 7.

And he hit Box number after Box number with almost no garbage numbers in the mix, just Box numbers, Box numbers, and more Box numbers, except for that pesky 4, which was his Point. He was already at 37 before that 4 finally showed. By then our bets were through the roof, and he just kept rolling. We were clapping and cheering, cheering and clapping. So were the dealers, who were on every number and with each roll were locking up green and black chips in their tip box.

A big crowd had gathered around the table, peering in to see the mounds of chips on the layout. Some of these people recognized us, and you could hear whispers, "That's *those* guys!" The table was full of people too.

A few even asked me for my autograph. One was tapping Dominator on his shoulder, trying to find out where he was playing next. We told them all to wait until the roll was over—which we were hoping would be after Armageddon.

We did have high-rolling chicken feeders at the table—whose chips were right where Stickman had to land his dice. Nothing upset him. He isn't one of those neurotic shooters who lets a little thing like chips bother him. Those dice just sailed gently over the chips to land plunk on the table and touch the back wall, dying a placid death on the layout.

About two-thirds through the roll, the chicken feeders realized they should move their bets out of the way (they were slow learners), and then Stickman started streaks of the same number over and over. I remember in one streak he hit a successive series of 9s. We were up on all the numbers; in fact, we were all essentially betting Come bets along with Place bets.

At one point, the casino had to stop the game to buy back our black chips—there were none left in the casino's chip piles, just a vacant area of dust.

I was hoping that Stickman could get to 80, but his dice double-pitched on 5:2, and there was silence.

Then the explosion—a gigantic cheer went up, resounding throughout the casino, and there was thunderous applause similar to the applause that greeted the Captain's roll of 147 in 2005.

Seventy-seven for the Stickman. There are very few players who have made it into the 70s, Dom being one of them with a 79.

We quit after Stickman's monster roll.

This trip was one of the best—one bad day, four good to great days. Although epic rolls are fun and highly profitable—and we had many of those on this trip—our shorter rolls were nice money-makers too, and over time these rolls actually dictate whether you become a long-term winner at dice control. It is fun to write about those monsters—they are like 600-foot home runs—but it is those pesky, regular singles that probably make you more money over time.

Yes, the Five Horsemen ultimately destroyed Vegas once again. I always look forward to the next trip with the great Dominator, Stickman, Skinny, and Nick-at-Night. And yes, the Five Horsemen will ride into battle again—you can bet on that!

CHAPTER 27

A Final Word
from the Captain

Read this book carefully and linger over the pictures, because becoming a rhythmic roller is a difficult task and takes training and discipline. You must know the proper form to use, and you must get your body used to the method for you to become good at it.

Frank has mentioned that "the Arm" was the greatest shooter he has ever seen, and she was the greatest shooter I have ever seen too. What made her good were concentration, relaxation, and a very soft delivery. Nothing bothered her. When she focused on shooting the dice, a hurricane could blow through the casino and she'd be unaware. Her whole being was on delivering those dice to the back wall, which they touched and then died at.

This book shows you the controlled throw that I have used in the casinos since the late 1970s. It works. I was lucky that I got to play a lot in the 1980s and 1990s, so my casino time was extensive.

My old crew are now playing craps in heaven. From my understanding God offers a very fair game!

A rhythmic roll must be used to win in the casino, but you must also limit your exposure to random rollers and keep your betting on them low. You also must make the best bets on yourself.

Beating craps is not easy. But it can be done.

Some shooters have more natural talent than other shooters, but all shooters, except maybe for a very few, with hard work can alter the nature of craps to favor them. Effort is the key.

My final word to you is this: Make the effort. It's worth it!

All the best,

The Captain

Glossary

401G Account: A bank account or money-market fund where a player keeps his gambling bankroll. The *G* stands for *Gambling*. See Chapter 20.

5-Count: The Captain's method for eliminating 57 percent of the random rolls. Players who use the 5-Count will bet only on 43 percent of random rolls. In terms of comping, most 5-Counters have found they get the same comps for less risk because their body time is counted, not their risk time. See Chapter 6.

Action: The amount of money being bet at a table or the amount of money an individual bets.

Adda from Decatur: The 8.

Any Craps: A one-roll bet on the numbers 2, 3, and 12.

Any Seven: A one-roll bet on the 7. Also known as Big Red.

Arm, the: The woman considered by Frank and the Captain to be the greatest dice controller of all time.

Axis: Think of the dice glued next to each other with a stick going through the middle of both of them. The stick represents the axis around which the dice spin. Whenever we set the dice, there is an invisible axis going through the middle of them.

Axis Control: The ability to keep the dice on axis more than probability indicates.

Backline: Old term for Don't Pass.

Back Wall: Sides of the table covered with foam rubber Pyramids that should be hit with each shot. These are there to randomize dice rolls.

Bar: Refers to a tie bet on the Come-Out roll for Darksider players. The 12 will not win or lose for the Don't player. Some casinos will bar the 2 instead of the 12.

Barber Pole: Bets made with various colored chips, often not arranged in denomination order, high on bottom, low on top.

Below Random: The mistaken idea that something can be less than random. A dice throw is either random or controlled. There is no such thing as less than random or more than random.

Bet-All Players: Players who bet on every roll of the dice or on all shooters from the beginning of their rolls.

Beveled Dice: Fixed dice.

Biased Dice: Dice that are fixed to favor certain dice faces over others. Also called Fixed Dice or Capped Dice.

Big 6: Even-money bet in the bottom corners of some craps tables.

Big 8: Even-money bet in the bottom corners of some craps tables.

Big Dick: The number 10.

Big Red: A one-roll bet on the 7. Also known as Any Seven.

Blacks: Chips usually worth $100.

Blues: Chips usually worth $1.

Body Time: How long a player stays at a table. Bets are not necessarily always at risk during the player's body time at the table.

Bones: Another name for dice. Original dice were probably made from the bones of animals and perhaps people.

Bowl: Where the dice are kept in front of the stickman.

Boxcars: A 6:6 combination of the dice equaling the number 12.

Box Numbers: The 4, 5, 6, 8, 9, and 10, which appear in boxes at the top of the layout. Also known as Point Numbers.

Box Person: Individual who sits between the dealers. He is responsible for cashing in players' money, counting out chips, and making sure payouts are correct. He also settles most of the disputes at the table.

Boys, the: Synonym for dealers.

Browns: Chips usually worth $5,000.

Buffalo: A bet on all the Hardways and on the Any Seven.

Buy Bet: Paying a commission to get true odds, as opposed to house odds, on certain Place Bets.

Buying a Player's Don't Bet: Paying a small fee to take over a Don't bet when the Darkside player wishes to take that bet down. This can give the "buyer" an edge over the game.

Call Bet: Making a bet without any money or chips showing in one's hand. Usually not accepted.

Capped Dice: Biased or Fixed Dice.

Captain, the: The world's greatest craps player and thinker. He is the developer of the 5-Count and of Controlled Shooting, also known as Rhythmic Rolling and Dice Influence.

Card-Counting: Keeping track of the relationship of high cards to low cards. Speed Count is an example of card-counting that is extremely easy to learn.

Casino Cage or Cage: The "bank" of the casino where players can cash in their chips, receive markers for slot play, and cash in some coupons or checks.

Charting and Charting Tables: Checking to see what trends are happening at a given table or with a given shooter. If the game is random, all charting is a waste of time.

Checks: Another name for chips.

Chicken Feeders: Another name for Random Rollers. Created because some shooters throw the dice in a way that looks as if they are feeding chickens.

Chips: Tokens used as money at casino table games.

Chip Tray: Holds chips. Often called the Rail in craps.

Cocked Dice: Dice that land against a chip or against the wall in a slanted manner. The stickman will make the call based on what number would come up if the chip had continued the way it was going.

Color Up or Color: Player hands in chips at the table when finished with play to get higher-denomination chips.

Come Bet: After a shooter's Point is established, a bet that can be made during the Point Cycle of the game. The first placement of a Come Bet will win on the 7 or 11 and lose on the 2, 3, or 12. Once up on a Box number, the bet wins if the number is hit and loses if a 7 is thrown.

Come-Out Roll: The shooter's first roll(s) before establishing a Point. Wins on the 7 or 11; loses on the 2, 3, or 12. If shooter makes his Point, the Come-Out Roll occurs again. If shooter sevens-out, shooter gives the dice up and the next shooter gets them.

Comps or Complimentary: Casino gifts to the players such as food, drink, free or discounted hotel rooms, parties, presents, and sporting or special events tickets. Comps are based on the casino's analysis of what types of losses the player is expected to have. These are known as Theoretical Losses.

Contract Bets: Pass Line, Point, and Come bets that cannot be taken down or called off once on a number. These are two-part bets where part one (Come-Out or first Come placement) favors the players and part two (the Point or Box number) favors the casinos. For the casino to make money, it must be able to have part two favor it in order to overcome the players' edge in part one.

Controlled Shooters: Someone who can change the probabilities of the game by his throw of the dice. Also known as Rhythmic Rolling and Dice Influencing, among other names.

Crapless Craps: The 2, 3, 11, and 12 can be Points. There are no Don't bets.

Crapping Out: Rolling a 2, 3, or 12 on the Come-Out Roll. It is *not* a term for sevening-out.

Craps Numbers: The 2, 3, and 12.

Crazy Crapper Bets: High-house-edge bets. Most of these are in the center of the layout.

Crossroader: A cheat or thief. See also Railbird

Darkside or Darksider: The Don't bets. A Darksider is a person who makes Don't bets.

Dead Table: A table where no one is playing, or a table where shooters have had a series of early seven-outs.

Dependent Trial Game: A game where what happened before has an impact on what happens next. An example is blackjack. If all aces have come out, no one can get a blackjack.

Devil, the: A term for the 7.

Dice Influencing: Someone changing the probabilities of the game by controlling the throw of the dice. Also known as Rhythmic Rolling and Controlled Shooting, among other names.

Dice Set: A specific arrangement of the dice before a shooter throws them.

Do and Do Players: Betting with the number (or Point) and against the 7. A player who bets the Pass Line, Come Bet, Place Bets, and Crazy Crapper bets where he is rooting for the number to appear. Also known as Lightside or Rightside and as Right betting.

Doey-Don't: Betting both the Pass Line and Don't Pass simultaneously. Betting both the Come and Don't Come simultaneously.

Don't Come: Bet placed after shooter's Point is established. First placement wins on the 2 or 3, loses on the 7 or 11, and pushes on the 12 (sometimes the 2 and 12 are substituted for each other). When up on a number, the bet wins if shooter rolls a 7, and the bet loses if the shooter rolls the number.

Don't Pass: Opposite of the Pass Line. On the Come-Out Roll, a player wins if a 2 or 3 is rolled; he loses if a 7 or 11 is rolled; he ties if a 12 is rolled (sometimes the 2 and 12 are substituted for each other). After the Point is established, a 7 wins for the Don't Pass, and the appearance of the Point loses for the Don't Pass.

Don't Place: A Place Bet against a number, where a 7 wins and the number loses.

Double Odds: A game that offers 2X Odds behind the Pass Line, Don't Pass, Come, and Don't Come.

Down: Bet is taken off the number and is given back to the player. Can be done with all Place Bets but not with the contract bets of the Pass Line or Come.

Down Behind: A dealer announces that a Darksider's Don't bet has lost.

Down with Odds: A player's Place number hits and his Come Bet goes to the number. This means the Odds are put on the Come and the rest of the Place Bet is given back.

Drop Box: Where the player's money is put when he cashes into a game to get his chips.

Easy Way: Numbers not made with doubles. Also known as the Soft Way.

Even Money: A bet that is paid off 1-to-1, such as the Pass Line, Come, Don't Pass, and Don't Come. Also known as Flat Bet.

Expected Win Rate or Expected Win or Expectation: What the math shows you will either win or lose in the long run based upon how you bet.

Eye in the Sky: Video surveillance area above the casino floor.

Fever: The 5.

Field Bet: Betting on the numbers 2, 3, 4, 9, 10, 11, and 12 at once. If any of these are hit, the bet wins. If the 5, 6, 7, or 8 appear, the bet loses. On layout, the Field is just above the Pass Line.

Fig Vig: Buy bets that collect the commission (also called the "Vig" or "Vigorish") only on winning bets.

Fire Bet: A bet that the shooter will establish and make each number as his Point during his turn with the dice.

Fixed Dice: Dice that are biased either by design or by accident.

Fixing the Dice: Antiquated term for Setting the Dice.

Flags: Red, white, and blue chips worth $5,000.

Flat Bet: Bet paid off at Even Money.

Floor Person: Individual who stands behind one or several box persons in a pit and who is in charge of making sure everything is run smoothly. Can also be the person who gives out some Comps.

Gaff or Gaffed Game: A rigged gaming device, such as dice.

Gambler's Fallacy: The belief that if deviations from expected behaviors are observed in some *random process* that these deviations are likely to be evened out by opposite deviations in the future.

George: A player who tips. A player who is easy to deal with.

Giving Odds: The same as Laying Odds. Taking the long end of a bet.

Gold: Chips usually worth $5,000.

Golden Touch Craps: The premier school for learning dice control.

Greens: Chips usually worth $25.

Grays: Chips usually worth $5,000.

Grind Joint: A low-level casino that shuns high-roller action.

Hardways: A number that comes up in doubles: 1:1, 2:2, 3:3, 4:4, 5:5, and 6:6.

Hardway Set: A set with Hardway Box Numbers all around it: 2:2, 3:3, 4:4, and 5:5, with the 6-spot and the 1-spot on the axis. These doubles are called Hard numbers.

Hedging Bets: Using one or more bets to offset the impact of one or more other bets.

High-Low: Betting the 12 and the 2 at the same time.

High Roller: Big bettor.

Holding Pattern: During the 5-Count process, after the 4-Count if no Box number is rolled, the 5-Count can't be completed yet and is said to be at "4-Count and holding."

Hook or Corner: Where the craps table turns. Area of pyramids under the hook is considered the Mixing Bowl, where the dice tend to be randomized even for controlled shooters.

Hop Bet or Hopping Bet: One-roll bet that a certain number will come up, usually in a certain way such as an 8 with 5:3.

Horn Bet and Horn High Bet: Multi-number bet in units of $4 that the 2, 3, 11, or 12 will be rolled. $5 variation allows a $2 bet on any of the four numbers. This is called a Horn High bet.

House Edge: The percentage of each bet that the house keeps. The house does this by winning more bets than the player or by taxing the players' wins by not paying off at correct odds.

In and In For: How much the player has cashed in for.

In Control of Tip: The player puts down a tip for the dealers and says, "I control it." This means when the bet wins the dealers can take down only the winning portion, not the original bet.

Independent Trial Game: All the previous decisions at the game have no influence or bearing on what is coming up next.

Inside Numbers: The 5, 6, 8, and 9.

Jimmy "Hicks": The number 6.

Juice: Another term for casino edge. Also a term for a high-rolling player who gets what he wants.

Juice Joint: A casino that cheats.

Lay or Lay Bet: To bet against a number at craps and for the 7. The player pays the long end of the odds on such bets.

Laying Odds: When the Darkside bet is up on the number, the player may put Odds on the bet. The player puts the long end of the Odds because he is betting that the 7 will show. The 7 has an edge against every number and is the favorite to show.

Lightside and Lightsiders: The overwhelming majority of craps players bet with the Pass Line at the game. The Pass Line is a Lightside bet. Lightside players bet with the numbers and against the 7 during the Point Cycle of the game. Also called Rightside players.

Little Joe or Little Joe from Kokomo: The number 4.

Live One: A player who tips.

Lock the Chips: Bets or extraneous chips that no one claims are taken by the casino.

Low Roller: Small bettor.

Markers: Casino credit. Is essentially a check to the casinos for borrowed money and has a specific time frame in which to be paid back.

Martingale: Betting increasingly more money when you are losing to make up for previous losses. Also known as a Negative Progression. Most players will double their bets after losses, thinking, *I have to win at least one bet.*

Maximum Bets or Table Maximum: The most a player can wager on one bet at a given table.

Midnight: The 12.

Minimum Bets or Table Minimum: The least a player can wager on one bet at a given table.

Mixing Bowl: Where the craps table turns and where the dice tend to be randomized even for controlled shooters.

Monetary Edge: The players' expectation in the game coupled with comps gives the player more money than he loses.

Money Plays: Playing with real money instead of chips.

Monster Roll: A long roll.

Nailing a Player: Catching a player cheating.

Natural: A 7 or 11 on the Come-Out roll or on the initial placement of a Come bet.

Negative Progression: Betting increasingly more money when you are losing to make up for previous losses. Also called Martingale.

Nickel: A $5 bet.

Nina Ross and the Bucking Horse: The number 9.

Ninety Days: The number 9.

No Bet: Late bet that is not accepted by the dealers.

No Roll: A roll that does not count.

Odds: The likelihood of something happening against the likelihood of that something not happening. The 7 will come up six times for every three times the 4 will come up. The odds are 6-to-3 or 2-to-1. The Odds bet in craps can be placed on Pass Line, Don't Pass, Come, and Don't Come bets and is paid off at its true value. For example, a 4 would pay 2-to-1 on the Pass Line, and on the Don't Pass it would pay 1-to-2.

Odds Working: On the Come-Out roll the Odds can work on all Come and Don't Come bets if the player desires.

Off: Odds and Place Bets can be turned off, which means the bet is not working and can neither be won nor lost.

Opposition Stance: Right-handed shooters standing at Stick Right; left-handed shooters standing at Stick Left.

Outside Numbers: The 4, 5, 9, and 10.

Over Seven or Under Seven: The player can bet that the next roll will either go over 7 or under 7. If a 7 is hit, the bet loses.

Parley: Letting the win and the initial bet ride on the next decision.

Pass and Passers: The shooter is making his Pass Line Points. The term for a shooter who makes his Pass Line Points.

Passing the Dice: Player prefers not to shoot the dice and passes them to the next player.

Pass Line: Player is betting that the 7 or 11 will win on the Come-Out roll and that the shooter's Point will be made before the 7 is rolled.

Past Posting: Making a bet after the decision has been called. This is the most common form of cheating.

Pay Behind: Dealer call to pay off Don't bets.

PC: Abbreviation for percentage.

Pendulum Swing: With right-handers standing at Stick Left and left-handers standing at Stick Right, the swing looks like a pendulum as it takes place.

Phoebe or Little Phoebe: The number 3.

Pinks: Chips usually worth $2.50.

Pig Vig: Buy bets where the commission (Vig) must be paid on all wagers, whether they win or lose. House edge is much higher on these than on Fig-Vig Buy bets, where commission is taken out only of winning bets.

Pips: White dots or spots on the sides of the dice.

Pit: A group of table games looked over by a Pit Boss.

Pit Boss: The executive in charge of supervising table games in a given pit.

Place Bets or Placing Numbers: Going right up on a number without using the Pass Line, Come, Don't Pass, or Don't Come. The casino takes a higher percentage of money from the players for such bets.

Place Odds: Payment of Place Bets at "house odds," which means they do not pay off at the true odds of the bet.

Ploppy: Multifaceted term that describes foolish, stupid, idiotic, and pathetic dopes and dingbats and also those who look these parts. Not a compliment. Ploppy can be used to describe players, gambling writers, casino personnel, and even people who never go near a casino.

Point: The number the shooter establishes that he must hit before the appearance of the 7 for the Pass Line bet to win.

Point Cycle: The part of the craps game where the shooter is looking to make his Point on the Pass Line and avoid the 7.

Point Numbers: Also known as Box numbers. The 4, 5, 6, 8, 9, and 10.

Positive Progression: Increasing your bets when you are winning.

Power of the Pen: Casino employee who can write Comps for the players.

P.O.W.E.R. Plan: How to focus the mind and relax the body to get the most out of a physical skill such as dice control. See Chapter 21.

Post Holes: The Hard 8.

Press: Increasing one's bet. Usually means doubling it, but the increase can be in any amount.

Pressure: Increasing one's bet.

Primary Hit: Hitting the numbers that your dice are set for. On the Hardway Set these would be the Hard 4, Hard 6, Hard 8, and Hard 10. On the 3-V, these would be 6s and 8s.

Probability: The likelihood that an event or decision will occur.

Progressive Betting: Increasing or decreasing one's bet based on past decisions.

Proposition Bets: High-house-edge bets. Also known as Crazy Crapper bets.

Puck: Black (Off)/white (On) disk that shows whether game is on Come-Out Roll or which Point number has been established by the shooter.

Pumpkins: Orange chips usually worth $1,000.

Puppy Paws: Another name for a Hard 10.

Purples: Chips usually worth $500.

Push: A tie.

Put Bets: Placing of a Pass Line or Come Bet with Odds without going through the Come-Out or initial bet on the Come.

Pyramids: Foam-rubber pyramids at the back of the table (also known as the Back Wall) that players' dice should hit with each throw. These are used to help randomize dice throws.

Rail: Term in craps for where a player's chips are held.

Railbird: A criminal who steals players' chips from their rails, usually when they are shooting or watching the game and not paying attention to their chips.

Random Rollers: Shooters who have no dice-control skills and shoot the dice with results being determined by randomness. One type of these shooters is called a Chicken Feeder.

Random Rolls: Dice rolls that are determined by randomness and exhibit no control whatsoever.

Rat-Hole Chips: Putting chips in your pocket, usually to prevent the casino from knowing how much was won.

Reds: Chips usually worth $5.

RFB: Stands for Room, Food, and Beverage and is a term used for high rollers in the casinos. These players get most or all of their expenses comped.

Rhythmic Rollers: Shooters who take care with the dice and with their throw. Early term for Dice Control, Dice Influence, and Controlled Shooting.

Rightside and Right Player: Betting with the Point and against the 7 during the Point Cycle of the game on Pass Line, Come, and Place Bets. Also known as Lightside.

Risk Time: The amount of time a player's money is at risk.

RLFB: Stands for Room, Limited Food (usually non-gourmet), and Beverages. Comp step that is just under RFB.

Same Dice: Many shooters will ask for the same dice when one or both of their dice go off the table. The superstition is that when dice go off the table and the shooter is given new dice, he will seven-out.

Save the Odds: When a 7 is rolled on the Come-Out and the Come Bet Odds are not working, these will be returned to the player.

Savvy Players: Smart players who make the best bets at the table.

Secondary Hit: The dice hit a number you are not specifically setting for but that contains one or two of the numbers whose faces are a part of the initial set.

Session: Amount of time a player spends at a table from cashing in to finishing playing.

Seven-Out: Call made by the stickman indicating that the Pass Line bet lost and that the dice go to the next shooter. Expression that your roll ended.

Shill: A casino worker who plays games with casino money to entice others to play that game.

Skinny Dugan: The number 7.

Sleeper: Money left on the table that the player has forgotten about.

SmartCraps: Software program composed of three tests to gauge the axis control of a shooter.

Snake Eyes: A 1:1 combination of the dice equaling the number 2.

Soft Way or Soft Bets: Dice combinations not made with doubles.

Split House: Casino where dealers pool their tips.

SRR: Seven-to-Rolls Ratio. A random dice roll averages six 7s for every 36 rolls in the long run. The SRR is therefore 1:6. An SRR above 1:6 or below 1:6 over an extended period of time would probably mean the shooter is influencing the dice.

Stick Left (SL): On the left-hand side of the stickman.

Stick or Stickman: Individual who uses the stick to move the dice to and from the shooter. Individual who calls the numbers when rolled and indicates which Proposition bets have won. Sometimes called the Stick Person.

Stick Right (SR): On the right-hand side of the stickman.

Stiff: A player who doesn't tip.

Suits: Those working the pits who wear suits. Generally a negative connotation.

Supersystem: Betting the Do and Don't at the same time. Also called Doey-Don't.

Sweat: Casino personnel who get upset when they lose money or have to deal with savvy players.

Table Dumping: A table losing money.

Tabletop Throw: Shooting the dice from the tabletop before lifting them. Requires more muscle action than a pendulum throw.

Taking Odds: On the Pass or Come, putting extra money in play when the number is established. This extra money is called Odds or Free Odds.

Testes Tanking: When a male who is shooting for the first time sevens-out quickly.

Texas Sunflowers: The Hard 10, 5:5.

Theoretical Loss: How much a player can expect to lose in the long run betting as he does. This "loss" is the baseline used for Comps.

Tip: A gratuity.

Toke: A tip specifically given to a dealer.

Too Tall to Call: A die or both dice land on the chip rail. Also, "In the wood, no good!"

Trend(s): Dice were hitting certain numbers or were missing certain numbers in the recent decisions. In a random game, these decisions are meaningless for future decisions.

True Bounce: Bounce that comes from a 45-degree angle on a traditional table.

True Odds: The correct payout based upon the real Odds of a bet.

Tub Table: Small, one-dealer craps table that resembles a tub. Players sit to play the game.

Two Ways: Same bet for both the player and the dealer.

Unit or Units: Minimum bet a player makes. If a player's minimum bet is $5, a bet of $10 for him would be a two-unit bet.

Vigaigh: Another name for the casino edge. See also Fig Vig.

Vigorish: Another name for casino edge.

Virgin Principle: The superstition that a woman who has never rolled the dice before will have a good roll.

Watermelon: Chips worth $25,000.

Whirl or World Bet: A wager that the 2, 3, 7, 11, or 12 will be rolled.

Whites: Chips usually worth $1.

Working Bets: Bets that can be won or lost.

Wrong Side and Wrong Bettor: The Wrong Side of a craps game is rooting for the 7 instead of the Point during the Point Cycle of the game. During the Come-Out roll, the Wrong bettor is rooting for the 2 or 3 for a win but does not want a losing 7 or 11 to be rolled. Also called Darkside or Darksider. Compare with Rightside.

Yo: Another term for the 11.

ABOUT THE AUTHORS

Frank Scoblete

Frank Scoblete is the No. 1 best-selling gaming writer in America. He has written over 20 books and has also created audiotapes, videotapes, CDs, and DVDs.

Frank writes about all the casino games and has developed methods for getting real mathematical edges at craps, blackjack, Pai Gow poker, and even certain slot machines.

Frank has written for over 50 magazines, newspapers, and websites in America, Europe, Canada, and the Islands, including *Jackpot, Fun & Games, Midwest Gaming and Travel, Casino Player, Strictly Slots, CasinoCityTimes. com, Southern Gaming and Destinations, GoldenTouchCraps.com,* and *Gaming South*. He has also written several television shows.

He has appeared on many television shows on various networks, including the History Channel, the Travel Channel, TBS, the Discovery Channel, CNN, the Learning Channel, A&E, and the National Geographic Channel.

Frank has beaten the casinos for over 20 years and he has shared his knowledge and insights gained from such winning experience with millions of readers.

Dominator

The Dominator is an expert dice controller in craps, an advantage card counter in blackjack, and an excellent poker player. He runs his own sports service, Dominator's Golden Touch Sports Service. He is believed to be the best dice controller in the world!

Dominator writes for many magazines and websites, including *Southern Gaming and Destinations, Casino City Times, The Craps Club,* and *Golden TouchCraps.com*. He also appeared in the DVD *Beat Craps by Controlling the Dice!*, where he demonstrated his amazing controlled dice throw.

His winning story *The Dice Dominator* was a hit feature on the History Channel. In addition, he and Frank took on three casinos on A&E in an unedited show—and won! Dominator has appeared on the History Channel, the Travel Channel, the National Geographic Channel, and A&E.

Collectively, Frank Scoblete and the Dominator are two of the most devastating players to ever hit the casinos.

SmartCraps: Training Software for Dice Controllers

SmartCraps is a fundamentally new way for dice controllers to win at the casino game of craps. With SmartCraps, you will learn:

- How to prove that you are influencing the dice outcomes, using our powerful and new Pro Test® method, or the standard SRR.
- The optimal dice sets and best bets given your unique dice-control skill.
- Your edge over the casino (i.e., how much money you can make playing craps).

Features in SmartCraps

SmartCraps is crammed with features designed to help dice-control experts maximize their potential wins in the game of craps. Nothing ever developed comes close to the advanced simulators and tools in SmartCraps:

Pro Test® dice control metric: Learn about the Pro Test® dice-control test, the most accurate and powerful statistical test for dice control in the game of craps. Instead of needing many thousands of rolls for statistical certainty with tests like the SRR, Pro Test® can tell you in a few hundred rolls whether you are influencing the dice.

Dice set optimizer: Use our mathematical calculators to immediately determine the optimal dice set for any craps bets, including Pass and Don't Pass. You'll be amazed to discover what the best dice sets are for you at different points in the game. Prove exactly how much money you can make with your Pro Test® dice-control skill!

Professional craps simulation: You can model every possible aspect of the game, including rare but important aspects such as Odds, payouts rounding, commission bets (buy bets), multiple shooters, your own betting systems, known and *blind* betting on shooters, Lay bets, random table walkups/shooters, and much more. You can simulate games with SRR shooters, Pro Test© dice controllers, or even random shooters.

SRR Support (Seven-to-Rolls Ratio): Run craps simulations with different minimum and/or maximum SRR values. Find out what edge you have based on your SRR values.

Risk-of-Ruin (ROR) calculators and simulation: Find out how much bankroll you need to survive in any given game with your unique dice-control skill. You can use our ROR simulator to empirically derive your bankroll requirements through multiple simulation sessions. Or you can easily use our ROR calculators that immediately estimate your ROR from well-known mathematical formulas.

Plus more than 100 pages of online help and documentation: A wealth of detailed help is available at the press of a button in every dialog and at any time. Learn about Pro Test®, proof that it works, and even how to take a dice-control test the correct way.

Available for Windows only. **Just $129.95**

www.SmartCraps.com/GTC

Learn the Golden Touch™ from the World's Greatest Dice Controllers

Are you a winner in business, in your chosen job, career, or profession but a long-term loser at craps? If your answer is yes, it doesn't have to be, because you can learn how to win at craps. Craps *can* be beaten! It isn't easy and not everyone can do it, but then again, not everyone can be successful in business and life. If you are interested in how to win at craps, read on.

There is only one way to beat the game of craps in the long run, and that is through precision dice shooting and perfecting your dice control at the table.

Dice control is a *physical skill* that can be learned by disciplined players who are willing to practice and perfect the techniques we teach them in our exclusive Golden Touch™ Craps dice-control craps seminars. Our teachers are the greatest dice-control specialists in the world, many with books and major publications to their credit, *all with years of winning casino experience behind them!*

That's why prominent sports figures, enlightened professionals, and successful businessmen and women take the Golden Touch™ dice-control seminars. You get what you pay for with Golden Touch™:

- Intense one- and two-day craps seminars in the physical elements of precision shooting: stance and scanning, set, angle, grab, grip, delivery, spin control, and bounce control!
- Hands-on small-group workshops with great coaches who show you how it's done and work side-by-side and step-by-step with you to master the physical elements of dice control.
- Strong tutoring in maintaining mental discipline, focus, centering, and stamina for making your Golden Touch™ last at the craps table no matter what the distractions!
- Betting strategies based on applying sound mathematical principles rather than superstitions so that your Golden Touch™ is not tarnished by poor gambling practices!
- How to maintain your edge while random rollers shoot at the table, based on recent mathematical research.
- How to win the game within the game of casino craps!
- How to assess your edge and optimize your betting strategies to exploit it!

Classes forming now!

Call us TOLL FREE at 1-866-SET-DICE or 1-800-944-0406